THE SHOOTING SALVATIONIST

THE SHOOTING SALVATIONIST

J. FRANK NORRIS AND THE MURDER
TRIAL THAT CAPTIVATED AMERICA

David R. Stokes

STEERFORTH PRESS
HANOVER, NEW HAMPSHIRE

Steerforth Press L.L.C.
45 Lyme Road, Suite 208, Hanover, NH 03755

Library of Congress Cataloging-in-Publication Data:

Stokes, David R.
 The shooting salvationist : J. Frank Norris and the murder trial that captivated America /
David R. Stokes.
    p. cm.
 Includes index.
 ISBN 978-1-58642-186-1 (alk. paper)
1. Norris, J. Frank (John Frank), 1877-1952. 2. Baptists--United States--Clergy--Biography.
3. Trials (Murder)--Texas--Fort Worth. 4. First Baptist Church (Fort Worth, Tex.)--History.
5. Fort Worth (Tex.)--Church history. 6. Fundamentalism--United States--History. I. Title.
BX6495.N59S69 2011
286'.1092--dc22
 [B]
                         2011015168

ISBN 978-1-58642-186-1

1 3 5 7 9 10 8 6 4 2

FIRST EDITION

For Karen, my wife and best friend,
who has always believed in me.
We don't always read the same books,
but we are forever on the same page.

CONTENTS

AUTHOR'S NOTE

THIS BOOK CHRONICLES what is probably the most famous story you've *never* heard. But at the time it happened, it was page-one news across America.

The Shooting Salvationist is not merely *based* on a true story — it *is* a true story. Everything appearing in quotes in this book comes from a newspaper, magazine, court record, archived collection of personal papers, or other published work. The words of the characters have not been imagined or contrived, but are presented verbatim — as they appeared in other private or published documents. In "A Note on Sources" at the end of the book, I discuss the various works and records from which I have drawn detail and dialogue.

One word for the reader — for whatever reason, it was a very common thing several decades ago for men to use their initials in the place of full names. Whenever possible I've tried to locate the full names of people appearing on the pages of this book, though many records from back then only use initials. Also, dialogue obtained from trial transcripts is reproduced here verbatim. Some of the language is colloquial, crude, and grammatically awkward, but it was the language of that moment.

J. Frank Norris was in many ways a gifted and unique man. But his personal values and code of conduct ultimately ensured that whatever gifts he had would be overshadowed by outrageous and egregious behavior and its consequences. This story is a sobering reminder that any cult of personality — whether in the religious, entertainment, business, or political realm — is fraught with peril.

— David R. Stokes
Fairfax, Virginia
November 2010

CAST OF CHARACTERS

John Franklyn "J. Frank" Norris. A fiery fundamentalist pastor during the Roaring Twenties, Norris had a penchant for controversy and sensationalism that brought him fame and fortune, not to mention several criminal indictments along the way. His abilities as an orator and organizer drew thousands into his orbit, but his intemperate and often violent tendencies ensured that he would never be accepted as a mainstream religious leader in America — a role he craved. He built his church, First Baptist in Fort Worth, Texas, into what was for a time one of the largest in the world. It was America's first megachurch.

Henry Clay "H.C." Meacham. The first mayor of Fort Worth, Texas, under a new city charter approved in 1924, Meacham had already made a name for himself as the owner of one of the city's most successful department stores. His tenure as mayor would be marked by conflict with J. Frank Norris, who never heeded the adage "You can't fight city hall."

Ossian E. "O.E." Carr. Hired as the first city manager for Fort Worth under the new charter, he brought to the city on the Trinity River vast managerial experience. One of his specialties was to find ways to collect new revenue for municipalities, even if it meant raising taxes or looking for those who, in his opinion, had not paid a fair share. He wasn't on the job very long before he started examining J. Frank Norris's enterprises.

Amon G. Carter. The wealthy and powerful owner of the *Fort Worth Star-Telegram,* as well as radio station WBAP, was Fort Worth's chief booster in the 1920s. He and a tight-knit band of unofficial oligarchs virtually ran Fort Worth in those days from the elegant confines of the Fort Worth Club. One of the few newspaper owners to beat William Randolph Hearst at his own game, Carter was the city's first media baron.

Dexter Elliott "D.E." Chipps. A wealthy lumberman who ran a successful wholesale business from his offices in Fort Worth's Wheat Building, Chipps was a proud member of the Fort Worth Club. He and Mayor Meacham became close friends.

Mae Chipps. The estranged wife of D.E. Chipps had long hoped she could be reconciled with her husband for the sake of their fourteen-year-old son, Dexter Elliott Jr. She had never stopped loving Mr. Chipps.

Lillian Gaddie Norris. A pastor's wife, strong, and passionate, Mrs. Norris was a full partner in life and work with her lightning rod of a husband.

Jane "Miss Jane" Hartwell. The devout daughter of Baptist missionaries, Miss Jane, as she was known, was Norris's secretary, office manager, and gal Friday. She carried herself with a slightly aristocratic air and was referred to at times as "the generalissimo." Hartwell was, above all, a fierce defender and guardian of her pastor, someone who would do just about anything for him.

Marcet Haldeman-Julius. One of the most famous journalists of the era, Marcet was the co-publisher of a highly popular monthly journal, the *Haldeman-Julius Monthly* — better known as *The Little Blue Books* — which sold millions of copies in the 1920s.

Jack Gordon. As popular writer for the *Fort Worth Press,* Gordon provided readers color and detail about Norris and his antics. This was possible because the preacher seemed to be willing to talk to him. Gordon never figured out why, but he was just glad to have access.

W.P. "Wild Bill" McLean. One of the best-known lawyers in the American Southwest in the 1920s, he was known for his "colorful" and highly effective courtroom methods. He also hated J. Frank Norris.

Dayton Moses. A highly popular Texas lawyer, he put his reputation on the line to defend J. Frank Norris. The standoff between Moses and McLean became a story itself.

Lloyd P. Bloodworth. J. Frank Norris persuaded Bloodworth, a longtime Methodist minister, to become a Baptist. Norris ultimately ordained him and placed him on the First Baptist Church payroll. He also happened to be the Grand Dragon of the local chapter of the Ku Klux Klan.

William Jennings Bryan. The Great Commoner, as he was known, was in the twilight of his career when he visited J. Frank Norris and First Baptist Church. He was clearly impressed with the ministry — and the minister. Norris cultivated, some might say exploited, a relationship with Bryan. And when Bryan died, J. Frank Norris sought his mantle as America's premier fundamentalist leader.

FOREWORD

WHEN I WAS growing up in Fort Worth, they used to tell us, "Fort Worth is where the West begins," and for years that motto was emblazoned across the top of our hometown newspaper, the *Fort Worth Star-Telegram.*

What they didn't put on the front page was the other part, "and Dallas is where the East peters out," which is what everyone who lived in Fort Worth sincerely believed because we thought Fort Worth was where the fun stuff happened and Dallas was just like a lot of other big cities.

Fort Worth got its motto early. If you were coming from the East in a covered wagon, everything beyond Fort Worth was Indian Country — hence the title "Where the West Begins." From those wild days on, Fort Worth has always been a town that was as Texas as Texas could get — the "Texasmost" city, author Leonard Sanders once called it. My buddy Dan Jenkins the sportswriter once quipped, "If you want to see Atlanta, go to Dallas, if you want to see Texas come to Fort Worth."

Big Dallas with its trendy department stores and skyscrapers always looked down on the smaller Fort Worth as an unsophisticated cowtown, but it never bothered Fort Worth, which just stared right back. Because most people know that when Dallas people wanted to have fun, they did what Butch Cassidy and the Sundance Kid did in the old days — they headed to Fort Worth. Fort Worth folks also took quiet pride in noting that when the Dallas Chamber of Commerce tried to entice new businesses to relocate there, they listed Fort Worth's world-class art museums as one of the area's major attractions.

The two cities have always been rivals, but they would agree on one thing: When it comes to characters and a colorful past, Fort Worth wins hands down. From Butch and Sundance during the early shoot-'em-up days when Fort Worth was the place where cowboys came to spend their money at the end of the trail drives to modern times when legendary oil tycoons like Sid Richardson and media baron Amon Carter ruled, Fort Worth was a place of larger-than-life characters.

For all the colorful characters who became part of Fort Worth's history, surely none surpassed J. Frank Norris, the fiery fundamentalist preacher at Fort Worth's First Baptist Church, in pure outlandishness. His oratory and penchant for publicity brought thousands into his congregation; at one point First Baptist was among the largest churches in the world, a megachurch before the phrase was coined. Unfortunately, for all his oratorical skills, Norris's horizons were limited by several criminal indictments brought on by his tendency for violence.

In this book David Stokes tells the J. Frank Norris story.

If I hadn't grown up in Fort Worth, I would have thought someone made all this up, but no one did.

It really happened.

— Bob Schieffer

THE SHOOTING
SALVATIONIST

PROLOGUE

THE DOOR OPENED at exactly nine o'clock on Friday morning, January 14, 1927, and the bailiff shouted his instruction so everyone in the corridor could hear.

"All witnesses in the courtroom!"

Like an impatient crowd at any major happening, a large group of people immediately converged on the door, and within a few minutes the courtroom was more than full. Many, if not most, brought a lunch along, not wanting to risk losing a prized place during a break. The largest courtroom in the old courthouse, in the entire county for that matter, would simply not be sufficient to accommodate all those who wanted to be there that day or for many days to come. Nearly 150 folding chairs had been put down, increasing the seating capacity to a little over 300, something unheard of for this particular venue. Beyond that, a couple hundred more onlookers could stand if they really wanted to, and they did.

Those entering the room for the first time were immediately struck by the unusually high ceiling. This feature of the room had the tendency to seduce words up and away from those who wanted to hear. "Speak a little louder" was the most commonly used phrase in the room when court was in session, usually uttered by the presiding judge. In fact, he regularly moved his embarrassingly battered and worn swivel chair toward the end of the bench nearer the witness stand in order to better hear given testimony.

The courtroom walls were of green plaster and scuffed appearance. A large, glittering chandelier hung down from the center of the ceiling almost directly above an old, rusty stove. The kiln could serve a dual purpose: giving off heat and receiving tobacco remnants.

Several high-arched windows lined the courtroom, and the judge's walnut bench very much resembled a large pulpit in an ornate church. The linoleum floor had seen better days.

Despite the chamber's well-worn condition, it was a special room for the city and county — in fact for the entire state of Texas. Important judgments had been handed down here, some involving monumental amounts of money, others impacting politics, some decisions becoming famous, if not infamous.

Among the throng squeezing into the celebrated courtroom that morning was the largest representation of the local, state, and national press ever to assemble up to that time in a Texas court. The big dailies from New York, Chicago, Washington, St. Louis, and Kansas City had sent their journalistic stars. Five wire services were represented. One of them even brought along the newest, most state-of-the-art printing machine in the country, something that would itself become a tourist attraction during trial recesses. They all prepared to cover this trial even more thoroughly than they had the sensational Scopes trial in Tennessee a year and a half earlier.

At 9:25 AM the door near the judge's bench opened and a rather short, robed man entered. The bailiff snapped to attention and excitedly called all those not already standing to their feet. The jurist making his way to the bench was a man in his mid-sixties with gray hair, soft blue eyes, barely the whisper of a mustache, and a receding hairline. He wore a stiff white collar and little black bow tie. His eyeglasses were attached to a gold chain that was, in turn, fastened to the lapel of his coat. Like most experienced judges, he exuded self-assurance.

When the crowd was seated, the judge gaveled for order. The murmurs instantly collapsed into silence.

"Gentlemen," he said, "proceed with the case."

The prosecuting attorney stood, turned, and faced the famous defendant. People throughout the room shifted, leaned, and otherwise contorted their bodies to be able to see the man, a radio pioneer, tabloid editor, and pastor of the nation's largest Protestant church, sitting at a table with one of his many high-powered, high-priced attorneys. His dark blue suit looked almost black in contrast with his silver-streaked hair.

"J. Frank Norris, stand up, please."

Norris's attorney instinctively stood quickly. The defendant himself, however, took his time, rising slowly and deliberately, then turning and folding his arms. He glared at the prosecutor while barely chewing a very small piece of gum. He listened as the indictment was read. Once during the reading the defendant put his right hand to his lips in one of his characteristic gestures, but — as if catching himself — he quickly pulled it back and crossed his arms again.

Accused of first-degree murder, the prominent minister was on trial for his life.

When the prosecutor was finished, he looked up from the paper he was reading. The judge then addressed the defendant: "J. Frank Norris, how do you plead?"

Norris, still glaring at the prosecutor, then pivoted and nearly shouted in his firm pulpit voice, "I am not guilty!" If found guilty as charged, he would face death by the electric chair.

CHAPTER ONE

"The Outstanding Fundamentalist of This Country"

HIS HAND FIRMLY fixed on the throttle, veteran engineer Henry L. Miller eased the special Southern Railway train away from the gravel platform surrounding the tiny red-brick rail station at Dayton, Tennessee. It was shortly after nine o'clock in the morning on Wednesday, July 29, 1925.

The train would snake through the hills and towns of a section of rural America on its five-hundred-mile trek. The trip would be interrupted again and again as the train made frequent stops, some scheduled, others by popular demand, en route to its final destination: Washington, DC.

Miller approached his duties that day with a mixture of sadness and pride. He shed tears along the way. His was a tough business, not something for the tenderhearted, but he could not help having to go back again and again to his large handkerchief as he wept. Just as he got his emotions under control the train would slowly pass yet another group of grieving witnesses, and the tears would flow anew.

The famous passenger making his final journey in the last car of the train was the cause of this overwhelming sadness. He was also for Miller an immense source of pride.

Engineer Miller had accompanied the same passenger over these familiar Tennessee rails twenty-nine years earlier, in 1896. Back then his charge was a youthful and charismatic political phenomenon who, at the just barely constitutionally qualifying age of thirty-six, had eloquently and rousingly talked his way to the presidential nomination of the Democratic Party. He had a way with words.

The young candidate narrowly lost the election that November. In fact, he would go on to lose two other national elections to Republican rivals: William McKinley and William Howard Taft. But in doing so he would make quite a name for himself, earning the lasting loyalty and deep affection of a vast throng of everyday people across the country. They are the people President Abraham Lincoln was surely referring to when he talked about how "God must love the common man, because he made so many of them." These common people felt that the man with the silver tongue was one of them. And somewhere along the way, the unofficial title of "the Great Commoner" permanently attached itself to populist politician, Christian statesman, and hero of the little guy William Jennings Bryan.

He had been in tiny Dayton to participate in what became a celebrated courtroom drama. It was already being referred to as the trial of the decade; some said, the century. All the fuss was about evolution, specifically the fact that a schoolteacher in the Tennessee town had violated a recently enacted state law forbidding the teaching of "Darwinism." But the trial's scope became much bigger than a handful of pupils in one small classroom. It amounted to a war of ideas and ideals.

On one side, armed with religion and righteousness, were the forces of traditionalism and a young but rising movement sweeping the country, fundamentalism. On the other were the forces of modernity and skepticism. Mr. Bryan was the hero of the fundamentalists. Famed barrister Clarence Darrow represented modernism. It was an epic battle. The two went toe-to-toe for several weeks, captivating the nation. Bryan won the battle on points, gaining a conviction of the schoolteacher, one John T. Scopes, swelling the coffers of the commonwealth by one hundred dollars when the fine was paid. But in the judgment of many, Darrow had all but knocked out Bryan, and the verdict of history was a win for those who preferred to believe that, if there was a God, his actions weren't literally those described in Bryan's Bible.

Now William Jennings Bryan was dead, having passed away in his sleep the previous Sunday afternoon. He fell sick after the trial had suddenly ended, and when he did finally leave town, it was in a coffin in the back of a train.

One man who had watched the trial with great interest, but from afar, was the Reverend Doctor J. Frank Norris, nationally known revivalist preacher and pastor of America's original megachurch, First Baptist in Fort Worth, Texas. He, in fact, had played a crucial role before the Scopes trial by urging and ultimately persuading Bryan to take the case in the first place. He had planned to be there himself but decided against it at the last minute, sending his own stenographer, L.V. Evridge, to take down every word of the trial instead. Now Norris was among the millions of Americans mourning the passing of the nation's premier fundamentalist.

Norris's sadness, however, was tempered by ambition. As Bryan's train meandered through the hills of Tennessee, Norris sat at his cluttered oak rolltop desk in his book-lined church office, directly under the Great Commoner's portrait. Pen in hand, the preacher was putting the final touches on the latest edition of the tabloid newspaper he published every Friday. It was called the *Searchlight,* and he knew that its more than fifty thousand paid subscribers would be impressed by what they'd see on the front page: a photograph of "Bryan's last letter."

A couple of days earlier, on Monday morning, the day after Bryan's death made national news, Pastor Norris went through his mail and noticed an envelope postmarked "Dayton, Tenn." It had been addressed by hand, and in the upper left corner he instantly recognized the initials: "W.J.B." He quickly grabbed his letter opener and opened the envelope. It was indeed a personal note from the Great Commoner to J. Frank Norris. As he read it, then reread it, he smiled and instantly knew he was holding a journalistic nugget, and a golden opportunity for himself. He showed it around the office, impressing the secretaries. The note said:

> My Dear Mr. Norris, Well, we won our case. It woke up the country if I can judge from the letters and telegrams. Am just having my speech (prepared but not delivered) put into pamphlet form. Will send you a copy, I think it is the strongest indictment of evolution I have made. Much obliged to you for your part in getting me in the case. Much obliged to you too for Evridge. He is delightful and very efficient. I wish you would let me correct my part in the trial before you publish it. Sorry you were not there. Yours, Bryan

The note was an undeniable link between a late, great leader and a man who knew he wanted to take up the fallen icon's mantle. Norris had been singing the praises of the Great Commoner for many years. When he'd invited Bryan to speak at his church the year before, that event had drawn a crowd of more than six thousand.

John Franklyn Norris embodied the combative and charismatic elements of fundamentalism. He was strong-willed, aggressive, and fiercely ambitious, and the news of Bryan's death set him on a mission to seize the moment. There were, of course, other men mentioned in the papers in the days following Bryan's death as potential heirs apparent, but no one caught up with Norris once he began to make his move. Within a year nationally known journalists were writing things such as: "Since the death of William Jennings Bryan, the Rev. J. Frank Norris has been the outstanding Fundamentalist of this country."

His church was reputed to be the largest local Protestant congregation in America, a fact even his critics had difficulty discounting. During his sixteen-year pastorate, the First Baptist Church in Fort Worth had grown from a few hundred members (after an initial mass exodus protesting Norris's methods and motives) to more than seven thousand active and aggressive congregants, an unheard-of number for a Baptist church in those days. During his visit to the church, Bryan himself had referred to Norris as a "genius" and was clearly impressed with the facilities and work of First Baptist.

J. Frank Norris was a new kind of clergyman well suited to the Jazz Age. He was at once conservative in his approach to Christian doctrine and culture, yet pioneering in his use of state-of-the-art methods to promote his message and himself. Norris was not to be limited to preaching serene sermons and being on call during times of need and bereavement. He was just as comfortable around boards of trade and in political back rooms as he was in the church pulpit or sanctuary.

Described as a "go-getting, up and coming, fire-eating parson," the Texan boasted regularly about the influence he wielded through his church, radio station, and newspaper. The periodical, in keeping with the rise of tabloid journalism in the 1920s, was largely a vehicle for unbridled self-promotion, as well as a weapon for Norris's celebrated and calculated fights. The circulation of the *Searchlight* would more than double over the next couple of years.

At forty-seven years of age, J. Frank Norris had a hunger for notoriety and a knack for getting close to important people. He had succeeded in developing a personal and working relationship with Bryan, which he sought to leverage in any way that might help him make a name for himself. Having been for a few years involved in battles against the teaching of evolution in Texas and with the Baptist denomination, Norris told Bryan that the Scopes trial represented "the greatest opportunity ever presented to educate the public, and will accomplish more than ten years campaigning."

J. Frank Norris stood just over six feet tall and was described at the time as "lean, clean shaven, and clear skinned with graying, rather closely cut hair." His forehead was said to be "narrow," and one observer curiously described his nose as "aggressive." But it was his eyes that got to people. They were, according to one interviewer, "the gray blue of an uncut lake." Another observer described them as "messianic," suggesting that he shifted them quickly in a manner that was "penetrating and veiled." He used them to look into others and to conceal part of himself. He moved about with "lithe ease," and he had the presence of someone with a reserve of nervous energy.

There was a sort of eleventh commandment in Fort Worth: "Thou Shalt Not Mess with J. Frank Norris." Known throughout his city, the state of Texas, and increasingly the nation itself as someone difficult to ignore or manage, he was the spiritual ancestor of all culturally crusading clergymen to come thereafter. He perfected sensationalism as an art form, controversy as part of his showmanship.

Norris was the biggest show in town in Fort Worth during the Jazz Age, drawing thousands to his church week after week. There those in the pews would hear him rail against bootleggers in his sermons, "busting fruit jars of illegal moonshine against the side of a galvanized tub." He was even known to fill a washtub with rattlesnakes — anything to make sure crowds would show up. And they came in ever-increasing numbers to witness the latest extravaganza by the clergyman known as the Texas Tornado and Texas Cyclone.

People around the country were hearing and reading about "the largest fundamentalist flock in America, the ten thousand strong congregation of Reverend J. Frank Norris' First Baptist Church in Fort Worth, Texas." One popular periodical in the early 1920s called him "the shrewdest, strongest and most romantically adventurous figure in the movement." His personal tabloid's masthead depicted him shining a large searchlight on the Devil. His national influence had grown exponentially via what was described as his "publicity-rich sideline of revivifying big-city churches with high pressure revival sermons followed by intensive fund raising."

One writer, observing Norris at the time, said the preacher was "high-chinned, hard of face and eye, he seemed to me more like a foreman of a wildcatting crew than a minister of the Gospel."

When Pulitzer Prize–winning novelist Sinclair Lewis was researching and writing *Elmer Gantry,* his book about a disreputable preacher who was a master of manipulation, he made it a point to visit Fort Worth and catch a glimpse of Norris in full glory. He had a file filled with newspaper clippings about Norris's "fame for his flamboyant anti-vice crusades."

J. Frank Norris was a "gaunt and haunted man" who was seen by some as "a hero, a populist prophet of God fighting against corruption." To many others, however, he was merely a hatemonger, not to mention "a blight on Fort Worth and its citizens." If not the most famous, he was certainly the most notorious clergyman in the country, having been in his early days in Fort Worth indicted for the crimes of arson (he was accused of torching his own church) and perjury. Juries found him not guilty, but the court of public opinion was not so sure.

From provocative sermon titles such as "Should a Prominent Fort Worth Banker Buy Expensive Silk Stockings for Another Man's Wife?" to spectacles such as letting a cowboy who was getting baptized bring his horse into the baptismal pool with him and having a monkey dressed in a suit and tie on the platform with him as he railed against evolution, Norris was quite the showman. Years later one historian would describe him as "one of the most controversial figures in the history of Christianity in America."

Many felt the Reverend Norris to be "ambitious, aggressive," and completely void of "scruples as to methods." His numerous critics were sure "he loved money, craved power, and was a glutton for notoriety." But his loyal followers believed him above reproach.

Norris was a dogmatic man, comfortable in his own extremism. One writer would later say: "An account of ultraconservative religion, and perhaps right-wing politics, in this country would be incomplete without a knowledge of his career."

At the midpoint of the Roaring Twenties, the fundamentalist movement, part dogma, part culture, part reaction to culture — and in large measure driven by several key and dynamic personalities — was at its high-water mark as a social phenomenon. Though certainly no fan, in fact a persistent critic of the movement, H.L. Mencken, the caustic journalistic sage of Baltimore, observed its clear influence, writing at the time: "Heave an egg out of a Pullman window, and you will hit a fundamentalist almost anywhere in the United States today."

The decade known as the Roaring Twenties was a time of prosperity and optimism in America; it was also described as an era of "cultural integration (some said degeneration) produced by the Model T Ford, A&P Grocery Stores, Twentieth Century Fox, and WXYZ's weekly Lone Ranger." And the prevalent cultural zeitgeist made a lot of people uncomfortable. They longed for quieter, simpler times. As a reaction to a swift-paced race toward modernity, many retreated into movements promising the kind of postwar "normalcy" Warren Harding had talked about during the presidential campaign of 1920.

The decade of the 1920s was known for "a mélange of new fads and mores, uncontrolled consumption, and political conservatism." It will be forever associated in historical writing with "flappers, prohibition, bathtub gin, rum running, radio, movies, all manner of crazes (flagpole sitting remains inexplicable), petting, and fundamentalists."

Fundamentalism was a religious and political phenomenon fueled by fierce passion to protect long-held dogmas from erosion. But it was also very much a social reaction to seismic cultural change. Two issues best represented the hopes and fears of fundamentalists: They were hopeful about the success of Prohibition and quite fearful about the teaching of evolution. These were the hot-button social issues of the day.

The Eighteenth Amendment to the US Constitution, prohibiting the manufacturing, sale, and transportation of intoxicating beverages, having been ratified by thirty-six states in 1919, became the functional law of the land in January 1920. This sweeping legal and social mandate was the culmination of decades of temperance movement efforts. It would also create tension and become the backdrop for many of the great political and cultural challenges of the era (the law would be repealed in 1933).

Fundamentalists were unapologetic and aggressive in their support of Prohibition.

The issue of evolution was also destined to be the topic of a great national debate in the 1920s. As communities, denominations, colleges, and the population in general wrestled with the implications and applications of what Darwin had articulated decades before, fundamentalists fought on the side of the anti-evolution forces. J. Frank Norris was one of their four-star generals.

The Scopes trial in the summer of 1925 promised to be a decisive battle in the long war. Although the trial is now — decades later — seen as the moment when fundamentalism began its drift into decline, and its adherents retreated to their homes and churches to become more of a subculture, these conclusions were by no means clear at the time. In fact, the energy level of fundamentalists in the wake of the trial was higher than ever. Many actually thought they were winning a great social war.

The death of William Jennings Bryan left the movement without a singular and well-known leader. And the short list of names most commonly mentioned as likely candidates to become the voice and face of fundamentalism in America was led by J. Frank Norris. He was sagacious, extravagant, and, most important, unparalleled as an opportunist. He set his sights on leading a national movement and channeled his boundless energy into a determined personal campaign. Like the tornado to which he was compared, he garnered his strength and plotted his strategy. It seemed as if nothing could stop the preacher's ascent.

But it was all to come crashing down slightly less than a year later due to one of the most breathtaking scandals ever to involve a famous member of the clergy, or any prominent figure for that matter.

CHAPTER TWO

"Charisma and the Capacity to Connect"

AT THE PEAK of his career in the mid-1920s, J. Frank Norris was living out one of his childhood dreams. He was a traveling man, riding the nation's rails — here, there, everywhere.

In June 1925, a little more than a month before the death of William Jennings Bryan, Norris left Fort Worth on one of his long trips. He seemed to delight in telling everyone how many miles he was perpetually covering. He wrote to his congregation via his tabloid, the *Searchlight:* "I'll cover a total distance of over 7,000 miles. Be in Seattle only three days and strike straight across to Dayton, Tennessee, and by invitation of counsel for the state, assist with fight for the Bible against the onslaught of the infidelity of Clarence Darrow."

Norris used the pages of the *Searchlight* for fights, sermons, and causes, but also as a personal diary of sorts. He would, almost in a cathartic way, write about his life in great, often tedious, detail. On this West Coast trip he wrote about California, calling it "the greatest country in the world for millionaires." He told his readers that "moving picture shows, show people, and real estate agents run the country. They can show anything and sell for any price." He added, "If I had a million dollars and wanted to retire, I'd move to Los Angeles — better make it five million."

From Los Angeles he headed north toward Seattle for a Baptist denominational meeting, changing trains in San Francisco. While he waited for the northbound Oregonian, he walked over to the Palace Hotel, where President Warren G. Harding had died nearly two years earlier. Norris compared that previous scene, the death of a national leader, with what he saw on his visit: "The hotel was draped in mourning; the whole city was hushed in grief. But last night, while I sat in the magnificent high-arched, chandeliered dining room of this same hotel they were dancing to sensuous jazz."

The preacher's attention to detail, and his self-absorption, led him to describe the process of looking for a new hat in San Francisco — telling his readers that his old one was stolen along the way, noting, "I came all the way from El Paso bare-headed." Not finding anything other than what he referred to as "a cheap Jew-store" open that night, he "had to settle for a cap, instead of a hat." The ethnic epithet would scarcely bother his loyal readers. Many of them were members of the Ku Klux Klan, and a lot of people assumed the preacher was as well. Many of the high-ranking Fort Worth members of the Invisible Empire also belonged to First Baptist Church.

Though he had written about the invitation to go to Dayton, Tennessee, to be part of the celebrated trial, the truth is that Norris never made it there. Matters in Seattle kept him occupied longer than he had anticipated, and he was scheduled to begin a large tent-revival campaign in Arlington, Texas, on July 5. For a man who had ambitions to be famous, this scheduling snafu turned out to be quite an oversight. In Dayton, Bryan found himself inexplicably abandoned by most of the prominent fundamentalist leaders in the country. Norris could have featured himself prominently at his side.

It is puzzling that most of the big-name movement leaders did not try harder to travel to Dayton that hot summer for the showdown between Bryan and Darrow, the Bible versus evolution. Perhaps they failed to discern just how historically momentous the trial would be. Such a failure of insight would have been unusual for Norris, who had a knack for reading popular culture.

Or maybe Clarence Darrow scared them off. The famous attorney acknowledged that Bryan and what he described as "several young men who were to be his field marshals" saw the Tennessee trial as a potential "Waterloo of science." He, however, characterized Bryan's team as being akin to "Crusaders under Richard the Lion-Hearted." Darrow was no run-of-the-mill opponent, and he did ultimately make Bryan look bad. Possibly the famous fundamentalist pastors feared the same fate.

With no time, he insisted, for even a quick trip to Dayton, Tennessee, Norris was back in Fort Worth to speak to his Bible class at First Baptist on July 5. Immediately following the ten o'clock class, he raced over to nearby Arlington to launch a massive summer tent revival at eleven o'clock.

It was left to Dr. Lloyd P. Bloodworth, a Methodist minister who would very soon become a Baptist ordained by Norris, to speak to the home crowd that day. Bloodworth was also the Grand Dragon of the Fort Worth chapter of the Ku Klux Klan. He ruled the roost at their North Main Street headquarters. Though the Klan's popularity had peaked a few years before and was now on the wane, it was still a formidable force in the town's civic life.

People came from great distances to the Arlington tent meeting. Just a year earlier, Norris had concluded very successful and protracted engagements in Houston and San Antonio, capturing a lot of coverage in the papers and adding thousands of new members to the local churches that hosted him.

His meetings were always great public spectacles and could be used as vehicles for drawing attention to any cause. The Northern Texas Traction Company ran ads that read: "Dr. Norris' meeting in Arlington all the month of July can best be attended through the use of the Electric Interurban — it's the best way to go. We appreciate your patronage."

Late on Sunday, July 26, after a long day of Texas tent revivalism, J. Frank Norris learned of Bryan's sudden death. A reporter from the *Fort Worth Record* called him for comment. "How wonderful and how glorious that a soldier should die on the field of battle, fall with his face to the enemy and die as he lived, and awake in the presence of the Lord," the paper quoted Norris as saying.

The next morning he discovered Bryan's letter to him in the mail. Norris was ecstatic. He published the letter in the *Searchlight* and within weeks he would opportunistically offer copies of the brief Bryan epistle to subscribers of his paper, complete with a photograph of him shaking hands with the Great Commoner.

Though the trial was the biggest media event of the decade, by sending L.V. Evridge to record every word of it, Norris had scored another coup. He quickly rushed to print Evridge's unabridged account in book form, claiming that the press had largely "garbled" Bryan's testimony on the stand.

From what he said in his note to Norris — "I will you would let me correct my part of the trial before you publish it" — it seems that Bryan himself wondered if he had garbled his delivery.

As J. Frank Norris raced to exploit the death of Bryan, the Great

Commoner traveled toward Washington, DC. People came from miles around to stations in Tennessee towns like Graysville, Coulterville, Melville, Hixson, and Boyce, en route to Chattanooga, Cleveland, Athens, Sweetwater, and beyond — all just to catch a glimpse of the flag-draped bronze coffin. They took off their hats and bowed their heads. Bryan's widow, Mary Baird Bryan, who was largely confined to a wheelchair due to chronic illness, was deeply moved by the crowds she saw at each stop.

As night fell the train crossed into Virginia, stopping first at Bristol and then Lynchburg at 2:15 AM. Bryan's daughter, Ruth Owen, was amazed to see that a great crowd had gathered. She ordered the doors of the funeral car opened to accommodate those who wanted to view the casket. A few hundred made it through, but the train began to move on after ten brief minutes, disappointing hundreds in a town that would be connected with another famous American fundamentalist, Jerry Falwell, whose career decades later would link back to the empire and activities of J. Frank Norris.

The journey ended with the train's arrival in Washington, DC, shortly before 8 AM on Thursday, July 30. Hundreds of railroad employees met the train and removed their hats in respect. That same day, more than twenty thousand mourners filed by the casket as Bryan lay in state at the church of the presidents, New York Avenue Presbyterian, in Washington. The next day Dr. Joseph R. Sizoo told those gathered in the church that "the supreme glory of the Christian faith is in the new meaning it gives to life and the new hope it gives to death." These words were carried across the country. The Bryan funeral was broadcast live on radio for millions of his fellow citizens to hear.

Following the service, the bronze coffin was carried through the capital city and across the Potomac toward Arlington Cemetery. One reporter noted the irony of laying "the great pacifist to rest among the bodies of soldiers." Flags flew at half-mast across the country. And in Dayton and Toledo, Ohio, fiery crosses blazed, lit by members of the Ku Klux Klan, insisting this was appropriate "in memory of William Jennings Bryan, the greatest Klansman of our time." They were honoring the man who had led the fight against an anti-Klan platform plank at the Democratic Party Convention just a year before.

Along with the eulogistic tributes published in the *Searchlight,* J. Frank Norris, never one to miss a sensational moment, conducted a mammoth memorial service for Bryan in the auditorium of First Baptist Church on Sunday, August 2, 1925, two days after the DC funeral. The *Fort Worth Record* described the scene as a crowd of six thousand gathered to hear the preacher's tribute to "W.J. Bryan, The Fundamentalist."

The three-hundred-voice church choir sang "Faith of Our Fathers," and Norris drew parallels between Bryan and spiritual leaders from the past such as John Huss, Girolamo Savonarola, Martin Luther, and John Wesley. He particularly commended the Commoner for his stand on Prohibition, suggesting that "if Bryan had done nothing more than bring about Constitutional prohibition, his place would be secure among the immortals."

L.V. Evridge, having completed his assignment at the Scopes trial, was in his usual place prepared to take down Norris's address word for word. Norris tended to build the intensity of his delivery as he moved toward the end of his sermons, and he reserved particular passion for the final point he made that day: "What Bryan Saw in Heaven."

"I want to answer that my friends. There isn't a bit of doubt in the world what he saw. I am as certain as to what he saw as I am that I see this great audience of several thousand this morning. To die is gain. My friends, he didn't go into an unknown world," Norris proclaimed. He then proceeded to describe imagined celestial encounters between Bryan and Abraham, Isaac, Jacob, Moses, and other notable biblical characters, culminating with Jesus.

Putting words into the mouth of the great orator, he envisioned Bryan testifying in heaven about his final battle in that Tennessee courthouse. Norris imagined that he heard William Jennings Bryan saying: "I am glad that I have had the time and the last act of my life was to stand yonder at Dayton, Tennessee, against the infidelity of the world for a gospel that can make a heaven like this."

It was J. Frank Norris doing what he did best, using his gifts of communication to move hearts, and some would say manipulate minds, in a great crowd. Even critics reluctantly acknowledged his skills as a preacher-orator, and admirers marveled at the way he could work an audience. He was at the top of his game, ready to seize the moment. He would rise up and take Bryan's message to the nation. And he would become the undisputed leader of American fundamentalism. He would use his pulpit, charisma, and capacity to connect with a crowd as key elements of a national campaign.

CHAPTER THREE

"The Awful Curse That Wrecked His Father's Life"

AS A YOUNG boy J. Frank Norris developed a passion for books. They provided escape for him, not only from the tedium of rural life but also from the brutality of his own family dysfunction. Young Frank, as he was called back then, read with great personal interest the recently published book by Mark Twain called *The Adventures of Huckleberry Finn*. He lost himself in fantasies of adventure and drama. But the part that resonated with him the most had to do with Huck and his pap, a man who loved his liquor.

James Warner Norris was, like the fictional Finn's father, a hopeless drunkard, and a mean one at that. In dramatic contrast, his wife, Mary, was by all accounts a proper, even tenderhearted woman, despite the obvious severities of her life.

Once, when Frank was ten years old, he mustered the courage to find his father's supply of booze. He broke every bottle. When Warner found out about this, he was livid. He asked his son why he would do such a thing. The boy replied, "It's because I love you, and I love Mother." The elder Norris took a heavy blacksnake whip and began to beat the boy mercilessly. The cruelty was only interrupted when Mary Norris threw herself between her husband and his son.

All this happened on a Christmas Eve.

The next morning, as Warner came to his senses and his son tried to get out of bed, his lacerated body bearing witness to the crime of the night before, the father knelt by the boy's bed in remorse. He said, "Daddy didn't do it! Liquor did it." Years later Norris would claim to his audiences that his remorseful father prayed the following Christmas morning: "O God, liquor has ruined my life, and my home. Take this boy that I have been so cruel to and send him up and down the land to smite the awful curse that wrecked his father's life and broke his mother's heart."

Of course, the story was likely embellished if not outright apocryphal, as with many of the preacher's tales, but it was an effective rhetorical tool whenever he spoke about the evils of booze and the virtues of Prohibition.

John Franklyn Norris was born September 18, 1877, in Dadeville, Alabama. His father's habits ensured that life would be marked by disruption and deprivation. Struggling to find and hold jobs, Warner Norris moved his family from town to town, from Alabama, to Arkansas, then back again to Alabama, all in the hope of finding something better.

Then for some reason, the frustrated father had the idea that if he could somehow move his family to Texas, things would improve. Mary Norris was skeptical but, having run out of options in Alabama, she agreed to a long-distance move. Most of what little money they had went for train tickets for the family of five. Frank was the oldest child, just shy of his eleventh birthday. His sister Mattie was seven, and his brother Dorie was not quite two years old. They embarked on a three-day-and-night journey to a relatively new community called Hubbard City in Hill County, Texas.

Arriving at the tiny rail station early in the evening one August night in 1888, the Norrises encountered a small town built around a railroad and the regional cotton business. A few scattered businesses lined deeply rutted dirt avenues that would hold water like a sponge. There was a grocery, a general store, a seed store, a church, the cotton gin, and other enterprises common to small-town America. In the evening locals would sit around on porches to whittle, chew tobacco, and trade knives. They would always, of course, talk about cotton — the key to the local economy.

Warner Norris would place his hopes and dreams for a better life on the fluffy flower. The family moved into what Norris years later described as a "two-room, old boxed house, two miles from Hubbard City." His determined dad began to work as a sharecropper. He managed to get seed planted every year for a few years, but by harvesttime the family was inevitably out of money. Warner continued to drink, and over time he descended deeper into addiction and financial debt. At times Mary Norris would take steps to try to modify her husband's behavior and save him from himself. She tried to enlist neighbors and friends in this effort, begging people not to give or sell whiskey to Warner. Most people were sympathetic and cooperated with Mrs. Norris, but not everyone.

There was a local drinking establishment, a notorious dive called the

Blind Tiger. Despite all Mary's pleadings, the proprietor would not refuse service to Warner Norris, and there were times when every cent in his pocket would disappear after he'd bought round after round of whiskey. At her wit's end, Mary decided one Saturday afternoon to send young Frank to deliver a note, again pleading with the barkeep to refrain from serving her husband. He walked barefoot to town and entered the saloon. After reading the note from Mrs. Norris, the proprietor laughed at the boy. Everyone in the place joined in. Mocking and cursing him as a drunkard's son, the group threw young Norris out, and he ran the two miles to his home crying and scared.

When his mother heard the story, her generally mild manner transformed into fierce indignation. Sending Frank to the barn for the mule and wagon, she rode with him to town, where they entered the seedy establishment and made their way to the bar, this time being noticed by all in the place.

"Frank, is that the man who cursed you?"

When Frank confirmed that it was, he was sent back out to watch the mules. Mary Norris then drew close to the proprietor, making quick and effective use of a long gray plaited leather horsewhip, repeatedly hitting the man, who soon ran away. Then, in the manner of Carrie Nation, the surprisingly strong woman proceeded to break all the bottles she could find. No one challenged her. Her business at the bar done, she left, to the shocked stares of all in the room, and took her son back home.

The source of Mary Norris's strength was her faith. Deprived of the emotional benefits of a healthy marriage or material abundance, she sought solace in religion. She prayed for her husband's deliverance from demon rum, but those prayers were weighted with doubt. She prayed with greater optimism and fervency for her children, particularly young Frank. She saw in him her hopes for the future, a successful son who would make his mark on the world.

Summertime in Hubbard City meant oppressive heat, backbreaking labor in the cotton fields, and the curiously contagious community-wide event known as the summer revival. It was a time for all God-fearing people to come together for the spiritual betterment of the community at large. For a brief moment local churches of various Christian denominations united to spread the good news to their neighbors. These meetings transcended religion in some ways, though they were fervently devout. They were also about patriotism, morality, and fellowship. In fact, they were as popular in those days as were county fairs.

These meetings were highly anticipated events on the social calendar and would be remembered fondly years later for bringing "bright relief to the gray monotony of village and country life." As the August 1890 Hill County revival approached, Mary Norris wondered if maybe this would be the time when her boy Frank heard the call. It was. Norris would always remember this summer revival as the precise moment of his religious conversion.

About a year later, Frank, then just shy of his fourteenth birthday, was working in the garden near his home one typically hot summer day when suddenly he heard shouting and then the unmistakable sound of gunfire. He raced toward the noise and saw his father falling to the ground.

Apparently, Warner Norris had recently furnished information to the authorities about a gang of horse and cattle thieves. One of the accused, John Shaw, confronted the elder Norris and shot him. Shaw would later claim in court that he acted in self-defense and that Warner intended to kill him.

Whatever the case, young Frank charged at Shaw with a knife, and for his efforts to defend his father, the boy was shot three times. The father's wounds were superficial and his recovery quick. Not so, though, with the son. Young Norris languished between life and death for several days.

Shaw was convicted for shooting Warner Norris and sentenced to three years in prison. The charges against him for shooting young J. Frank Norris were dismissed, presumably over the issue of self-defense. But the wounds the young man received that day in the cotton field put him in critical condition for a lengthy period and led to gangrene and inflammatory rheumatism. His complete recovery would take more than three years.

These would be formative years in the life of J. Frank Norris. The process of physical healing, combined with the energetic focus of his mother, who used the time to mold her son's mind and heart, transformed the boy into a man; a man with an unbridled ambition to be great and famous. He would eventually emerge from his bed of affliction determined not only to live but, more important, to make his mark on the world.

CHAPTER FOUR

"This Fellow Carries a Broad Axe and Not a Pearl Handle Knife"

AS YOUNG FRANK Norris recuperated from his near-death experience, a process requiring painstaking rehabilitation, a new preacher moved to Hubbard City to lead the Baptist flock where Norris's mother attended church. His name was Catlett "Cat" Smith. He paid regular visits to the ailing teenage boy. When Frank had sufficiently healed, the pastor baptized the lad in the nearby creek. Smith became to him, for a while at least, a surrogate father and spiritual mentor rolled into one. They talked often about what the young man was going to do with his life. It was through these conversations that Norris sensed the call on his future. He would be a preacher.

Mary Norris was beside herself with joy.

Soon Preacher Smith was using the young minister-in-prospect as an assistant of sorts, helping with work around the church, even baptisms in the creek. When Norris was twenty years old, he served his first pastorate at nearby Mount Antioch Baptist Church, being recommended there by Cat Smith. That was how it was done in many places in those days; one became a minister, as was the case with so many lines of work back then, via apprenticeship.

J. Frank Norris, however, soon decided to play by a different set of rules: He would go to college. Largely through the influence of the family doctor, W.A. Woods, Norris opted to go to Baylor in Waco, the physician's alma mater. It was also the chief training institution for future Texas Baptist ministers at the time. One of the Hubbard City Baptist Church's previous interim pastors, J.S. Tanner, was a professor of biblical languages at the school. Frank asked Dr. Woods for a loan of $100, and the doctor gave him $150, a tidy sum of seed money in those days. Not long after this, the boy, now nearly twenty-one years of age, boarded the Cotton Belt Railroad for the trip to Waco, Texas.

Arriving in the college town in September 1898, Norris moved in with

Professor Tanner, who ran a little boardinghouse for students. One of the other students living there was Joseph M. Dawson, another future Baptist leader.

Norris excelled as a student at Baylor. He was determined, ambitious, and disciplined. In addition to the benefits derived from his studies, three developments during those years helped shape the man he would become.

First, he met the love of his life, a preacher's daughter named Lillian Gaddie. Her father, J.M. Gaddie, was then serving as general missionary for the Texas Baptist General Convention. They would marry in May 1902.

Also during his Baylor years, Norris was called to pastor the Mount Calm Baptist Church. He served as a part-time pastor there from 1899 to 1903. The significance of this appointment lies in the fact that this Baptist congregation was "dominated by a Southern Baptist splinter group known as the Haydenites." In light of his later battles with his Baptist brethren, conflicts that would pit him against leaders including his old boarding-house roommate Joseph Dawson, Norris's connection with the followers of Samuel Hayden — who had led a revolt in the 1880s against the Baptists of Texas, accusing them of fraud and infidelity — was an early indicator of his propensity for schismatic dogmatism.

Norris's acceptance of the Mount Calm church, with its implicit connection to the splinter group, led to a break between Norris and his early mentor Cat Smith. In fact, Smith rejected the invitation to participate in Norris's ordination.

The third portentous incident from Norris's days in Waco involved Baylor's president at the time, Oscar Henry Cooper. Remembered as "a former Yale professor who was respected in the academic community," and as someone who had also studied years before at the University of Berlin, Cooper was the victim of a student prank. It was in President Cooper's reaction that Frank discovered a particular kind of pleasure, an almost sadistic joy in making someone squirm. During a chapel service in a room on the third floor of the administration building, some mischievous students smuggled a dog into the room — a noisy dog.

Oscar Cooper reportedly "became so enraged when the dog would not stop howling that he seized the animal and threw it out of a window." The college president quickly caught himself and apologized, but Norris, who had not been involved in the prank, led a student uprising, ultimately even informing the local Society for the Prevention of Cruelty to Animals, as well as the college's trustees. Eventually, Dr. Cooper resigned under pressure, though he would go on to a continued and distinguished career. He would even, years later and while president of Simmons College (now known as Hardin-Simmons University) in Abilene, Texas, oversee the granting of an honorary doctor of divinity degree to J. Frank Norris, the preacher's only actual claim to that title in the years to come.

As for Norris, it was the first taste of controversy that would eventually become a kind of bloodlust for him. He, as one historian suggests, "would delight in going one on one with powerful people, especially when it meant his own notoriety would be enhanced."

NORRIS GRADUATED FROM Baylor in 1903 and resigned from the Mount Calm pastorate shortly thereafter, opting for a sabbatical from the pastorate in order to attend the Southern Baptist Seminary in Louisville, Kentucky. He completed the rigorous master of theology program there, which usually required at least three years of full-time effort, in two years, graduating at the top of his class.

He gave the valedictory address at commencement in 1905. And in keeping with his self-styled sense of expertise in global politics, he spoke on the subject "International Justification of Japan in Its War with Russia." Norris pronounced the speech a "humdinger" and had copies of it (his remarks had been printed in *The Louisville Courier-Journal*) sent to his friends and relatives far and wide. Years later he wrote: "Ever since I was a boy on the farm I was a close student of international affairs, in fact I became an 'expert' before I left the farm."

J. Frank Norris, fresh from a successful seminary experience, was now ready to make his mark on the Baptist world. He had several prospects for pastorates, including congregations in Roanoke, Virginia, and Corsicana, Texas, but once he heard about the opportunity at McKinney Avenue Baptist Church, none of the others even garnered his serious consideration. It was not so much the church itself; he actually knew very little about the ministry. It was *where* the church was that interested him.

Dallas, Texas.

He accepted a call from them sight unseen, later reflecting: "Talk about marrying by correspondence, that is nothing. They thought I was some pumpkin, and I thought they were some pumpkins, because they were in Dallas. No young Roman Catholic priest ever looked with stronger devotion towards St. Peter's at Rome than I looked on the denominational headquarters at Dallas."

He and Lillian, their family now including a daughter also named Lillian, moved to Dallas in June 1905. Norris faced his new congregation the first Sunday of that month on an unseasonably hot morning. He wore his best suit for the occasion, a heavy winter garment with a white vest. The ensemble was rounded out with a heavy black silk tie and stovepipe shirt collar. He clearly hoped to at least look the part of a distinguished minister.

Norris had prepared a fine sermon, in keeping with his seminary training in homiletics. But when he got to church that morning, only thirteen people greeted him. He was disappointed, but also determined. The prepared sermon stayed in his coat pocket, and instead he delivered an impromptu message about faith.

From that modest beginning Norris worked hard for the next three years, building the congregation to more than a thousand active members, a feat that received the notice of powerful denominational leaders; men such as George W. Truett, pastor of Dallas's prominent First Baptist Church. His success also led to Norris's being offered the editorship of the *Baptist Standard,* the leading Texas Baptist periodical. Eventually, he bought controlling interest in the paper and began a career as a religious journalist, something he would work at for much of the rest of his life. His boardinghouse companion Joseph Dawson worked for the paper, but the two men had a falling-out, and within a year Dawson resigned.

It was while running the *Baptist Standard* that Norris got his first taste of moral crusading, the kind of activism that would mark his ministry in decades to come. He received a lengthy letter one day from a mother from southeast Texas. Her son had killed himself, she said. He had worked at a bank and embezzled funds because he had a gambling problem; he lost big time on the races. Norris decided to investigate racetrack gambling in Dallas, and he published the results of the inquiry in the *Baptist Standard* under the headline: "Racing at the Dallas Fair Gambling Hell."

His writing became the catalyst for an ultimately successful effort to outlaw such gambling in the state of Texas, a ban that lasted for twenty-five years. He would later refer to the episode as "My First Big Fight." One historian has written, "Significantly, it was Norris' political activity, not his preaching, that put him in the public eye of Texans for the first time." The success of the anti-gambling campaign received notice even outside Texas. An edition of the national periodical *Literary Digest* contained an item about the effort: "Two ministers, Drs. J. Frank Norris and W.D. Bradfield, fought the combined forces of book makers, and what former governor, Charles E. Hughes, did for New York in 1905, these two Texas ministers did for the Lone Star State four years later."

Along the way he made more than a few enemies, not only in the ranks of those who supported gambling, but also among some of the very men who had guided his early career advances. While they supported the idea of banning gambling, they were not comfortable with Norris's methods or what they saw as his aggressive personal ambition.

Because the undertaking had been exhausting, and had apparently hurt, not helped, his standing with Baptist bigwigs, Norris soon extricated himself from the *Baptist Standard,* selling his interest and resigning as the editor.

In fall 1909 Norris traveled to the Texas Panhandle town of Plainview to spend some time with his friend J.H. Wayland, who was organizing a college. Norris briefly considered moving there and working with Wayland in the venture, but while there he received an invitation that would change his life and have a significant impact on the culture and history of a major Texas city.

Norris was called by Mr. G.H. Connell to fill the pulpit at the First Baptist Church in Fort Worth for an honorarium of twenty-five dollars. He accepted, and after preaching that Sunday he was invited back the next week. The church was in the process of looking for a pastor, and the pulpit committee was reportedly close to calling Dr. Samuel J. Porter, an inspiring speaker who would ultimately lead the Roger Williams Church in the nation's capital. Norris was asked to fill in for several weeks, and he liked the idea of having a regular place to preach for a month or so as he tied up the loose ends related to his departure from the *Baptist Standard.*

One Sunday morning, just before Norris preached, the chairman of the pulpit committee stood before the congregation and announced that on the following Wednesday every member should be present when their recommendation for a new pastor was brought to the church for a vote. They all assumed it would be Dr. Porter.

When time for the church meeting came, Judge R.H. Buck, who served as judge of the Forty-eighth District Court in Tarrant County, told the church that Dr. Porter would not be coming. Norris's name was brought up, which led to a thorough discussion, then a church vote. Three hundred and thirty-four people voted, and Norris received all but the votes of banker J.T. Pemberton and his wife. Pemberton, who would become one of Norris's staunchest supporters over the years, explained his opposition to those gathered in the church sanctuary that night: "I am not opposed to J. Frank Norris; I am for him, but this church is not in condition for his type of ministry. If he comes there will be the all-firedest explosion ever witnessed in any church. We are at peace with the world, the flesh, and the devil, and with one another. And this fellow carries a broad axe and not a pearl handle penknife. I just want to warn you. But now since you have called him I am going to stay by him."

Later that night Judge Buck called Norris in Dallas and said, "As chairman of the notification committee I am happy to tell you that you have been called to the pastorate of the First Baptist Church, Fort Worth." But instead of accepting on the spot, or even the next Sunday, Norris took some time to think it over, largely because he was wrestling with personal depression. His experience with the *Baptist Standard* had drained him, and he was even struggling in his faith. He acknowledged that his experiences with Baptist leaders had rattled him. He even talked of quitting the ministry.

But eventually he realized that the pastorate of such a church provided structure and security for his family, and he accepted the call. The Norris family soon moved into the church's parsonage on Fifth Street, near downtown Fort Worth.

By all accounts the Fort Worth church was a premier pulpit in the Texas Baptist world. First Baptist was known as "the church of the cattle kings," and at one time the membership included more than a dozen millionaires.

There were nearly a thousand members on the rolls, though most Sundays fewer than half that many attended services. And the money was pretty good. In fact, Norris soon began to draw what was reportedly one of the largest salaries in the nation for a pastor.

J. Frank Norris settled in and settled down to a benign and boring ministry. He decided to get along and go along, not wanting to make waves or fight. He attended denominational meetings as a rising star, stayed away from controversial issues, and enjoyed a measure of prosperity, the kind that would lead to the *Memphis Commercial Appeal*'s describing him as "the best dressed preacher in the Southern Baptist Convention." All was peace and prosperity at First Baptist Church and in the city by the Trinity River. But this would not last long.

CHAPTER FIVE

"A Deliberate Shift to Sensationalized Sermons"

NOT YET A decade into the twentieth century, Fort Worth was in those days described as "more than ever a blend of Broadway and the range." It was still in so many ways a cowboy's town, but it also had an emerging urban and cosmopolitan feel to it.

As J. Frank Norris took up his new duties as pastor of one of the city's most important and influential churches, the more than nine hundred registered automobiles in town still competed with horse-drawn carriages for hegemony on its streets. Most of the main thoroughfares were by this time paved with brick, while others remained dirt and gravel, which became mud with enough rain.

By 1909 the city's Wild West aspects were waning but by no means gone. As the stockyards grew and increasingly more rail lines were routed through, Fort Worth took on a well-deserved reputation for "colorful" enterprises.

Hell's Half Acre was "a wild 'n' wooly accumulation of bordellos, cribs, dance houses, saloons and gambling parlors." Fort Worth's strategic location along the storied Chisholm Trail, where cattle were moved from south Texas up through Kansas, made it a popular stop for men looking for excitement. The famous and infamous, men such as Bat Masterson, Doc Holliday, and Wyatt Earp, not to mention two guys named Robert Leroy Parker and Harry Longabaugh — aka Butch Cassidy and the Sundance Kid — spent a lot of time in the Acre. And for decades the local citizenry quietly tolerated its establishments and their activities.

Significant opposition to what went on in Hell's Half Acre would flare up only in the wake of violence, such as the shooting of "Longhair" Jim Courtright by Luke Short outside the White Elephant Saloon in 1887. Or the death of a young Tarrant County district attorney named Jefferson Davis McLean, shot to death by the gambler known as "One-Armed" Bill

Thompson in 1907. That killing created enough anti-gaming sentiment to help the cause when then-editor Norris was lobbying for the gambling ban in Austin around the same time.

It is one of the great ironies in the history of the city that its First Baptist Church, which would one day become the headquarters for so many moralistic crusades, had actually been significantly helped along in its early days by gambling interests.

Founded by two Baptist ministers, J.R. Masters and W.M. Gough, in September 1873 with twenty-six charter members, First Baptist grew along with the city through the years. During J. Morgan Wells's twenty-year pastorate before the turn of the century, the church built a new eleven-hundred-seat auditorium at the corner of Third and Taylor Streets.

When Dr. Wells began his campaign to build his new church, "the good reverend, decked out in his finest, made the rounds soliciting money from gamblers, saloon keepers and others of ill repute until he had raised the incredible sum of $65,000." He then used the money to help build a beautiful edifice, "an English Gothic structure uptown completely free and clear of debt."

Fort Worth had a population of around seventy-five thousand when Norris arrived. It had grown by nearly fifty thousand in the previous decade and would continue to grow by nearly a hundred thousand more over the next twenty years. Around the same time, Texas Christian University moved from Waco to Fort Worth, and Southwestern Baptist Theological Seminary was founded. Norris was actually instrumental in bringing the Baptist institution to town.

At the beginning of 1909, the relatively young and struggling *Star* merged with the older *Telegram* to become the *Fort Worth Star-Telegram,* destined eventually to boast the largest circulation of any newspaper in the American South. To make the deal happen, Amon G. Carter put together financing by using four diamond rings and a diamond-and-pearl scarf pin as collateral. He also persuaded some friends, most notably H.C. Meacham, owner of a downtown department store, to invest. So around the time J. Frank Norris hit the brick-paved streets of Fort Worth, most of the factors that would make the city an eventual political and economic powerhouse were in place, from education, to media, to business.

Oil would come later. Big time.

The first two years of Norris's tenure at First Baptist Church were uneventful. He was content to "fit the mold of a big-city preacher who ministered to the establishment without ruffling the feathers of the affluent and influential members of his flock." But he became increasingly restless and frustrated.

He actually contemplated resigning within a year and a half of taking the pastorate at First Baptist but put that notion aside after having a mysterious and transformative experience while conducting a revival meeting at a friend's church in Owensboro, Kentucky. There Norris determined to reinvent himself. He had a vision for success and committed himself to a populist ministry. He also decided to make what he called "a deliberate shift to sensationalized sermons." From Kentucky he wired the *Fort Worth Record* with text for an advertisement (a rarity for a church in those days) of his sermon at First Baptist the next Sunday night: "If Jim Jeffries, the Chicago Cubs, and Theodore Roosevelt Can't Come Back, Who Can?"

The eleven-hundred-seat church was packed that Sunday night, a welcome change from the hundred or so he usually spoke to in the evening services. He raised his voice, shed his coat and tie, and thundered, pleaded, and cajoled. At the end of the message several new converts were added to the church. Norris was hooked.

He said, "The question of sensational preaching was a serious one with me. I knew that with a great many people it was taboo, especially among the so-called conservatives." But he knew that he wasn't making headway with what he called "the present, dull, dead, dry method." And many years later, "Norris recalled that he switched to this extraordinary style of preaching because he had noticed that those preachers who engaged in it were the ones most successful in winning converts."

Norris was attracting more people to First Baptist Church than had ever before attended the church. Soon the crowds were so large that many couldn't find a seat. He reveled in the logistical problems his popularity created. Once, the crowd was so large that he had some of the overflow sit in the choir area. And when the choir tried to come in to take their regular seats, he had them stand elsewhere.

Many choir members were infuriated, and the choirmaster vowed to complain to the church board of deacons. A great number of the long-term members of the church "were growing disgruntled" with what they considered Norris's "unorthodox approach to preaching." One influential church member told Norris that he was, in effect, "ruining" their church, particularly by "bringing in lower class people." He responded, "I would rather have my church filled with the poor, the halt, the lame, the sinning, than to have it filled and run by a high-brow bunch." It was only a matter of time before the church experienced a painful split and, before it was all said and done, more than six hundred members left First Baptist with bitterness.

The catalyst for the fissure, the proverbial last straw, was when J. Frank Norris began to crusade against the moral evils in Fort Worth, particularly what was left of Hell's Half Acre. In 1911 the infamous part of town was still a vice zone. At a meeting of the Tarrant County General Pastors Association, a committee of ten clergymen was appointed to research the issue. Norris, then not yet thirty-four years old, was the youngest man in the group; he was also its most zealous member. They hired a private investigator named George Chapman to help with the details.

When Chapman reported back to the group, he shared information about eighty houses of prostitution. Chapman's sleuthing also revealed to the ministers that several of the most prominent houses of ill repute were owned by high-profile members of the community, not to mention their churches. Some even served on congregational boards.

Before learning of the involvement of their own key church members, the ministers had agreed they were going to go before their congregations and read the names of those Chapman discovered to be financially underwriting Hell's Half Acre. However, once the names were revealed, all except Norris abandoned the plan.

Norris advertised he'd be delivering an address titled "The Ten Biggest Devils in Town and Their Records Given." Once he started to name names, the preacher had crossed the point of no return. Norris created many enemies within the church and without. And he seemed to relish the attention and controversy. At least, he would often claim, people were no longer ignoring him or First Baptist Church. He led the church to vote on a statement for the record that no congregant could continue as a member in good standing "who has any interest, directly or indirectly, in a disorderly house of any kind or class."

One Norris biographer wrote of his development during this period: "He became a saint or a demon, a noble crusader, a vile power-obsessed preacher. Few remained neutral."

As part of his new commitment to showmanship in the pulpit, J. Frank Norris bought a large "worn, faded, gray circus tent, which had been used by Sarah Bernhardt in her national tours." Paying only the cost of storage, he erected the tent on an empty lot on Tenth Avenue between Houston and Throckmorton Streets and announced that he would conduct a three-month-long revival meeting that summer. There was to be a special election that July, and on the ballot was a measure that would make Tarrant County a dry one; in other words, booze could be banned. No moral cause could be more dear to the heart of the preacher who had suffered such cruelty and humiliation at the hands of a drunkard father. Having transcended the moral realm and become a political issue, however, the question of county-wide prohibition was also tailor-made to suit Norris's sensational style and thirst for publicity and power.

National Prohibition, via constitutional amendment, was still nearly a decade away, but en route to this country-wide ban on the sale of intoxicating liquors many places enacted their own strictures. J. Frank Norris made sure that his tent revival, which was drawing thousands every night, would be a forum for him to rail against what he loved to refer to as the liquor interests.

That the preacher was mobilizing prohibition forces in a town like Fort Worth, still not very far removed from its wide-open Wild West days, did not sit well with many of the influential business leaders and politicians. The preacher "would most generally weep and tell about the tragic abuse alcohol had brought in his own early life" through his father's addiction. It was a very effective campaign, and for a time it looked like his soapbox efforts under the big tent might actually make the difference in the vote.

About a week before the election that summer, Fort Worth Mayor W.D. "Bill" Davis told Norris to take the tent down, calling it a fire hazard, though the real reason likely had to do with Norris's political preaching. The preacher told the mayor where to get off, and a feud quickly escalated.

Within a couple of days Mayor Davis sent the police and fire departments out to the site to take down the tent by force. They rendered it unusable in the process. Norris had tried to get an injunction to stop the action, but to no avail.

Six days later the anti-liquor forces narrowly lost the election. Enraged, Norris declared war on local vice interests as well as city hall. Being now forced to move his revival meeting indoors, Norris preached night after night to overflow crowds at the church building at Third and Taylor Streets; people would even gather outside the opened windows and doors to hear the latest diatribe. He later reflected about those days, "I paid my respects to the whole city administration. I attacked them right and left and smote them hip and thigh. I called them by their names and told everything I knew or could hear of what they had done."

Around this time he noticed an item in the newspaper that was ripe for his exploitation. W.P. Lane, the state comptroller, indicated that four hundred thousand dollars of Fort Worth city funds could not be accounted for. This was all Norris needed to present to his ever-swelling crowds to build a case against Mayor Davis, his new nemesis. There was no evidence that the mayor had actually done anything wrong, but Norris was never one for nuance.

Not long before all this, a group of local citizens, including First Baptist Church officer G.H. Connell, started a weekly newspaper to "give publicity to the acts of public officials and to all matters and conditions calculated to encourage the growth of our city along the best lines." The periodical was called the *X-Ray* and was edited by a local citizen named J.T. Franklin. Norris already had significant experience in the newspaper business, with his editorship of the *Baptist Standard*. Since leaving that paper and selling his stake in it, he had not committed to another newspaper venture. The *X-Ray* would suit him perfectly and he encouraged the new initiative, indicating that he would be happy to contribute occasional pieces to it.

Winfield Scott had been a prominent and influential Fort Worth citizen, and one of its wealthiest, when he died in October 1911. He was named for the famous American general; some took to calling him "General Scott" as a sort of honorific. He left a large fortune and was called "Fort Worth's heaviest taxpayer" in his obituary. He owned much of the real estate in the downtown area of Fort Worth in those days, as well as properties in Hell's Half Acre. His most celebrated holding was the famous, or to some infamous, White Elephant Saloon.

While Winfield Scott was being eulogized in the papers and mourned by the citizens of the city, J. Frank Norris wrote an article for the *X-Ray* called "A Happy Contrast." It attacked the prominent citizen for his support of liquor and gambling interests. Written in longhand, Norris made the piece available to editor Franklin, who printed and published it without attribution. There was widespread speculation, however, that Norris had penned the piece. It infuriated Mayor Davis and many others in town, who began to wonder what to do with the troublesome preacher.

Shortly after the new year began in January 1912, word was spread in certain quarters of the city that there was going to be a big meeting at city hall on the topic of what to do about J. Frank Norris. About three thousand men reportedly attended the meeting, where they heard Mayor Davis defend the honor and memory of Winfield Scott. Along the way, Davis justified "the activities of the city administration, with heated, belligerent assertions against the pastor of the First Baptist Church." At the end of his two-hour address, he reportedly shouted, "If there are fifty red-blooded men in this town, a preacher will be hanging from the lamp post before daylight."

Norris, having heard about the meeting, worked with the editor of the *X-Ray* to insert a stenographer into the crowd listening to Mayor Davis. The mayor's remarks were then published in the next edition of the periodical under the headline "Liars." The city administration heard what had happened and got an injunction to suppress the paper. Only a few copies ever saw the light of day. Years later Norris would tell the story over and over: "I sent a court stenographer down and he took down every word of his speech. It was so hot that it was not permitted to go through the mails."

Over the next few days and weeks, a series of mysterious incidents took place.

On Thursday, January 11, 1912, a fire broke out in the First Baptist Church building. It was quickly contained, never spreading beyond a back room, and causing about nine thousand dollars' damage. Though the circumstances were curious, the fire was largely blamed on a wiring issue having to do with the church organ.

The following Sunday the officers of the church presented an annual report to the congregation that was published in full in the *Fort Worth Record*. Presented to the church by banker and passionate Norris supporter J.T. Pemberton, it was called the best report in the church's thirty-eight-year history. The church had received a record 479 new members in 1911, more than twice as many additions as in any previous year. Norris certainly saw this as vindication of his new way. Converts were the bottom line.

Tellingly, the report also contained a section about the church's renewed commitment to the moral life of Fort Worth. It said, "The church is formally separated from state, but should vitally influence every phase of the moral welfare of both state and society."

That night, as J. Frank Norris sat in his study around ten o'clock following another lengthy and highly successful evening service, he heard a loud noise, then another, and realized that someone had fired two shots through the stained-glass windows, barely missing him.

The rest of January passed uneventfully, but as the first Sunday of February approached, a series of strange letters found their way to Norris and Mr. G.H. Connell, one of the church officers and an organizer of the *X-Ray*. The handwriting was distorted and the tone threatening. One passage read:

> Mr. G.H. Connell: I and others have tried to warn that damb [*sic*] preacher of yours. He continues to slander the best men in town. We have the dope on him where he was caught with a woman from Ft. Worth in a St. Louis hotel last year. How can you keep such a man when the above is known all over town? If he remains the proof will be coming.

The letters were unsigned and had been written on stationery from the city's Worth and Westbrook Hotels.

Shortly after 2 AM on Sunday, February 4, 1912, First Baptist Church exploded into flames. A night watchman working a few blocks away excitedly fired three gunshots into the air as an alarm of sorts, and those who heard "were awakened to see the low-hanging sky orange and illuminated with surging flames, and billowing black oily smoke." It became quickly evident that this blaze, unlike the smaller fire that had been discovered in the facility a few weeks prior, would not be contained. The beautiful church building that J. Morgan Wells had built became, within a few hours, a heap of smoldering rubble.

At about the same time the church was being engulfed in flames, a small fire broke out on the back porch of the Norris home, the church parsonage at 810 West Fifth Street. Mrs. Norris discovered a sack saturated with coal oil and bundles of papers on the back porch and put out the flames, kicking the sack out into the cold yard.

Members were stunned but determined. The financial secretary of the church, Mrs. K.K. Taylor, told a reporter, "Of course it is premature to say what we will do, but we will rebuild as soon as possible. Our church is far too strong to be without an adequate place of worship and I am sure that our congregation will take steps as soon as possible to replace the building destroyed this morning with an edifice which will be a credit to Fort Worth."

CHAPTER SIX

"What to Do with Norris"

THE SMOKE FROM the big fire at Third and Taylor Streets had barely dissipated before city leaders seized the moment. Under the leadership of Mayor Davis, many of Fort Worth's prominent citizens held a meeting and decided to put up a thousand-dollar reward for the capture and conviction of the arsonist.

Within hours of the fire, rumors were rampant about who might have started it. To most church members, it was likely a case of arson inspired by hatred of their pastor. To many in town, however, the finger of accusation pointed in the direction of J. Frank Norris.

In an effort to gain sympathy, and deflect suspicion from himself, Norris went public the day after the fire with the story of the threatening notes he had received, adding that they had burned in the fire. G.H. Connell, however, had two or three in his possession.

An editorial in the *Fort Worth Record* seemed to speak for what many in town must have been feeling: "There is some sort of deviltry afoot in this town and every decent citizen will join in seeking it out. The recent apparent attempt to assassinate Rev. J. Frank Norris, the burning of his church and the effort to burn his home and his sleeping family constitute a set of circumstances manifestly connected and devilishly malicious."

It fell to a man who had recently left the membership of First Baptist Church because of disagreements with its pastor, Judge R.H. Buck of the Forty-eighth District Court, to charge a Tarrant County grand jury with investigating the fire. In 1909 Buck had been the one to telephone Norris notifying him of his call to the pastorate.

J. Frank Norris was summoned as a witness, and on February 13 he was questioned about those anonymous threatening notes. He testified that he had no idea who had written them, but other testimony pointed to the possibility that the preacher may have created them himself.

The grand jury was sufficiently convinced of this possibility that on March 1, 1912, they returned a true bill of indictment for J. Frank Norris on the charge of perjury — lying about not knowing the origin of the threatening notes. Within three hours of the indictment, "the minister had been arrested and released on a bond of $1,000 signed by prominent citizens and members of his congregation." The preacher seemed to take the development in stride, telling a reporter, "You can announce for me that I will preach Sunday morning and Sunday night at Byers Opera House, where we have been holding services since the destruction of the church."

As the local papers reported the indictment of Pastor Norris, they also told readers of yet another mysterious incident involving an alleged threat on the preacher's life, one that had taken place just a few days before the indictment. Norris and a man named George E. White told police they had been walking from the Worth Hotel to Mr. White's house on West Second Street when a man who had been following behind attacked them. They fought him off, they claimed, and he ran away into the night down Lexington Street.

The very next day, Saturday, March 2, the Norris family was awakened in the early-morning hours by yet another fire. This time the preacher and his family barely escaped the flames and smoke via a second-story window. Years later Norris would describe the incident this way:

> To the end of eternity, neither the members of my family nor myself can ever forget the night that our house burned. It had an old fashioned form and sharp rook on the gallery. It was a bitter cold night. There was a norther and sleeting. My oldest boy, seven years old had pneumonia. After two o'clock in the morning hours we were awakened to find the building in flames from top to bottom. Our consternation cannot be imagined. The entire family, and the sick boy were in the second story. In front of the one story gallery was a three-foot concrete sidewalk. There was not a ladder or a way to get down. We were tying bed sheets together and trying for Mother to go down first and I was to drop the children to her. Shingles were covered with ice, making it impossible for us to stand on it. We barely escaped in our night clothes.

A day later Norris received another mysterious and threatening note: "Dear Sir, You have escaped thus far, but look out. The end is not yet. There is more to come."

Meanwhile Pastor Norris became aware that he still faced the very real possibility of a second indictment, this time for arson, for setting the church fire himself. His supporters had been briefly encouraged by the arrest of three immigrants who had been suspected in the church fire, but charges against them were quickly dismissed, due in large part to the aggressive and effective legal defense of one of the bright young lawyers in town, W.P. McLean, who was already making a name for himself around the courthouse, with some even starting to call him "Wild Bill" McLean.

By this time Norris was shaken. On Wednesday, March 27, he tendered his resignation as pastor of First Baptist Church, citing bad health, and left town with his family to spend some time back in Hubbard City. He wanted to visit the family physician, Dr. Wood, the man who had fronted young Norris the money to go to Baylor. Wood was now running a sanatorium near Norris's old home. The church rejected their pastor's resignation, and he would eventually withdraw it.

As Norris got off the train in Hubbard City, those greeting him broke the news that he had been indicted for arson back in Fort Worth a few hours earlier. Fort Worth newspapers carried dramatic headlines the next morning, such as, "Mr. Norris Hurrying Back," and "Hurrying Here to Answer Charge."

His trial began in April with a defense motion for a change of venue. Norris argued that he couldn't get a fair trial in Tarrant County, but Judge James W. Swayne, himself an outspoken critic of Hell's Half Acre, denied the motion. Over the next three weeks, witness after witness gave testimony for and against the preacher. Mrs. K.K. Taylor, who had been the church's financial secretary, told about how she had prayed hard to figure out the truth but in the end had too much suspicion that her pastor was not telling the truth. She told the court that Norris had given her several letters with the instruction that she was to mail them at a certain time and that she had refused to do it.

Norris told the financial secretary, according to her testimony, "Mrs. Taylor, the forces of an evil age are against us. We are in a mighty conflict, which I realize. Unless our people awake to responsibility, we will be over-come. Unless some great calamity should come to arouse them, they will not do their duty." The *Fort Worth Record* described K.K. Taylor as torn with a "fight of two spirits within her, one spirit whispering that the minis-ter was guilty of the crime — the other telling that he was not."

Handwriting experts weighed in on the mysterious and threatening letters, matching them with a writing sample from the original longhand version of the article "A Happy Contrast" about the late Winfield Scott that had appeared anonymously in the *X-Ray*. Testimony suggested that Norris had written it in his own hand. Experts indicated that the same man who wrote the article penned the notes. One fireman testified about finding a scrap of paper in Norris's coat pocket as he went through the house follow-ing that property's devastating fire. Supposedly, that scrap of paper fit like a puzzle piece with one of the mysterious and threatening notes, further suggesting Norris's involvement in writing them.

As the trial proceeded, it remained front-page news in papers through-out Texas and the South; not even the sinking of the *Titanic* that month could push it off page one. Some papers published complete stenographic accounts of the testimony. The story of a preacher being accused of burn-ing down his own church and lying to a grand jury was compelling and sold papers.

In the end, though, Norris was acquitted of the charge of perjury. When the court read the verdict, his supporters were ecstatic, even breaking into song right there in the courtroom.

When the arson case was ready for trial a short time later, the judge in the case issued a directed verdict for dismissal. But the story would not go away. Many Fort Worth citizens believed Norris was getting away with a crime. In 1913 another Tarrant County grand jury indicted him again for arson. This time there was a trial, but it didn't take place until January 1914, nearly two years after the church had burned. And from the start it was clear that the judge in the case had no inclination to let things go too far, even being quoted as saying, "There will not be a conviction." Norris was once again acquitted.

We will probably never know who burned First Baptist Church in 1912. Certainly, many maintained for years that J. Frank Norris was, in fact, an arsonist and perjurer. Others saw him as a man who had been persecuted for the fact that he had the courage to take on social and moral causes few clergymen would.

Even before his second trial, and buoyed by acquittal in the perjury matter, J. Frank Norris immersed himself in the work of building up his congregation numerically, as well as the actual rebuilding of a facility for the church. A temporary structure was built on a lot at Seventh and Lamar Streets, while plans were made to build a new permanent edifice, this time on the corner of Fourth and Throckmorton. And around this time, the preacher met with the officers of the church "to tell them in glowing language with a kindled imagination of the vision which now possessed him; a vision to build 'The World's Largest Sunday School.'"

In 1913 regular attendance at the church, decimated by the fire and the exodus of more than six hundred members who rejected Norris's ministry and methods, was likely around five hundred. It swelled here and there on special days, especially during Norris's Sunday-evening spectacles. By 1917 more than twenty-five hundred regularly attended, and that number nearly doubled long before 1920. And in the early part of the Roaring Twenties, between five and six thousand regularly attended First Baptist in Fort Worth on Sunday mornings. It was, by then, indeed widely considered to be "the World's Largest Sunday School."

AS THE WORLD went to war in 1914, with America joining the conflict in 1917, J. Frank Norris focused his energies on making his church the biggest and best in the nation. Along the way he earned the respect and admiration of many ministers, but he also became something of an annoyance when it came to denominational politics. And as the movement that would come to be known as fundamentalism began to coalesce, Norris jumped on the bandwagon, one tailor-made for his skills and ambition.

This often put Norris at odds with the mainstream Southern Baptists, and the tension between J. Frank and his denomination increased as his church and influence grew. He was always on the lookout for signs of any weakening in the area of theology at his alma mater, Baylor, and conducted a series of campaigns against faculty members he perceived to be weak on the faith. Most of the leaders in the denomination, now including Joseph

Dawson, who was pastor of Waco's First Baptist Church in the shadow of Baylor, were perplexed as to what to make of Norris, or what to do with him.

A popular poem among Baptist clergymen of the day ran:

> And what to do with Norris
> was a question broad and deep.
> He was too big to banish,
> and he smelled too bad to keep.

In the years following the fire, J. Frank Norris achieved remarkable success at attracting and sustaining a large crowd, a clear reflection of his ambition and personal charisma. After ten years as pastor of First Baptist Church, a main sanctuary had been built, then renovated again to where it would accommodate five thousand worshippers. Beyond that, the church gobbled up the entire city square block bounded by Taylor, Throckmorton, Third, and Fourth Streets. The church also owned property across the street, including a multistory building, with the upper floors used for church ministries (including its own auditorium large enough to seat nearly twenty-five hundred); the ground floor was available to businesses for lease.

By 1920, given the church's growth, its impact on the downtown area, and the rising national influence of Norris himself, many locals chose to forget the conflicts and trials of a few years before. Building up his church and battling with denominational leaders took up so much of his time and energy that Norris found little to fight about in Fort Worth's civic life. Some old enemies even became somewhat friendly to the preacher.

Certainly this was the case with W.D. Davis, who served again as Fort Worth mayor from 1917 to 1921, after leaving office in 1913 during the Norris church fire controversies. By 1920 he and Norris were warm friends, and when the latest renovations of First Baptist's facilities were dedicated, complete with the expansive auditorium and a three-story educational building, Davis was on hand to congratulate Norris and the church.

How had this reconciliation come to pass?

While out of office, Davis had become very ill with peritonitis due to appendicitis. Because his life was threatened, his doctor told him: "Mr.

Mayor, if you have anything to attend to you better do it at once." Davis decided to call Norris. The preacher visited the sick man. In fact, he spent the night with him at the hospital, praying and getting word to others in the congregation to pray.

The mayor soon recovered and was forever grateful. J. Frank Norris loved to tell the story in years to come, seeing it as one more confirmation that he was some kind of special instrument of God.

CHAPTER SEVEN

"The Southwest Was Ready for the Klan"

BY THE EARLY 1920s Fort Worth had become a boomtown. When the nation went to war in 1917, a training facility called Camp Bowie was opened just outside of town, with more than a hundred thousand men coming through in a short period of time. This had the effect of reviving Hell's Half Acre, which J. Frank Norris had almost put out of business. And for a brief spell, saloons again badly outnumbered churches in the downtown area: 178 to 16. One theater "had the gall to name itself Pershing in honor of the general who had been chosen to lead the US forces against the Kaiser." The entertainment there was described as "a basic show-and-tell, now-you-see-it-now-you-don't, girlie burlesque show."

Norris was not happy, and he joined forces with some of the military brass at Camp Bowie to fight the vice. The camp newspaper joined the cause: "Uncle Sam has rolled up his sleeves and started in to make a genuine cleaning out of 'houses of ill-fame, brothels, or bawdy houses.' These places of the devil and aides to the Kaiser will not be asked to move, they will be made to clear out."

When the war ended, a serious outbreak of influenza threatened the city via soldiers coming back to Camp Bowie from France. Thousands of men were quarantined there, and not long after the camp was closed.

The local economy didn't miss a beat. By this time Texas Tea had ushered in a real and sustained boom. Oil had been discovered in several places in Texas over the years, but it took the Great War to make many realize how important the commodity was and would be in the modern world. As a faraway war raged, there was a new cry for oil, and a generation of ragamuffin men called wildcatters began looking for the stuff in the Texas earth around Fort Worth.

In 1917 "the town of Ranger belched forth black gold." The wells were actually a bit of a fluke, having been discovered by Texas Pacific

Coal Company engineers, who had drilled a hole looking for coal. The Ranger discovery, and others like it around that time, "drew thousands of newcomers into the Texas oil fields." Roughnecks worked on the rigs and laid down "pipelines that began to snake around the state."

Buckley Burton "B.B." Paddock, one of the great city fathers of Fort Worth, a newspaper editor and mayor at one time, wrote: "The discovery of oil in north central Texas came at the end of a year's drought, and the enormous amount of money spent for leases and development relieved a very serious financial depression." And after the war was over, while most of the rest of the nation struggled financially, Fort Worth prospered.

Fort Worth, already a major transportation hub, became a gateway to the rich fields. By 1922 the city would be home to twenty-two refineries. First Baptist Church took advantage of the times and vastly expanded the size of its congregation and facilities.

In downtown Fort Worth, the Westbrook Hotel occupied a full block from Main to Houston at Fourth Street, just one block away from Norris's church. The Westbrook was developed by Benjamin Tillar in 1910 as a luxury hotel on property he had inherited from his father, which included the aging Delaware Hotel.

Tillar and his wife, Genevieve, traveled across Europe looking for ideas and inspiration. They bought marble in Italy and brought a statue back from Greece. It weighed about three hundred pounds, stood about seven feet tall, and was made of plaster and resin. It was dubbed "the Golden Goddess" and took up residence in the middle of the Westbrook's magnificent lobby. And somehow, some way, those in the oil business got into the habit of rubbing the statue for good luck every time they passed it. The seven-story hotel became an instant favorite of local businessmen.

Though myriad petroleum companies occupied much of the downtown office space, inspiring the construction of many tall buildings, the Westbrook was really where deals got done. Speaking to an audience in Washington, DC, around that time, and fresh from a stay at the Westbrook, the famous evangelist Billy Sunday said: "Fort Worth is a good town four ways from the Westbrook Hotel. Fort Worth is full of oil millionaires, but there ought to be more of them here. I don't know anyone I met in Fort Worth who I didn't wish had a million."

At one point during the boom, "All the furniture had to be dragged from the hotel lobby so more oil speculators could crowd their way inside." One colorful and successful oilman seemed to typify the spirit of so many others at the time when he "took a thousand dollar bill, set it afire and calmly lit a cigar," right in the middle of the Westbrook lobby.

To J. Frank Norris, however, the oil boom's attendant excesses seemed more like the roar of the Devil. He saw a time of change coming to the nation, a time when the values important to him would be tested, a time when someone needed to stand for the way things used to be. Somewhere along the way he decided to answer his own call.

To advance his causes, not to mention himself, beyond the walls of First Baptist Church and the boundaries of Fort Worth and Tarrant County, Norris got back into the newspaper business in 1917. He had dabbled in the experiment some of his friends had conducted back in 1912, with the brief and now long-forgotten publication of the *X-Ray,* but he had only been a contributor, and sharing the spotlight or power was not J. Frank's style.

He called his weekly paper the *Fence Rail* for the first few years, changing it to the *Searchlight* in 1921. It became many things to J. Frank Norris. It was a place to publish his sermons and those of some others who agreed with him on one topic or another. It was a tool to promote himself and his enterprises. And it became a weapon to use against his enemies, real or perceived. He conducted an ongoing war with the Southern Baptist denomination on the pages of his paper, directing particular criticism to something called "The Seventy-Five Million Dollar Campaign," a major fund-raising initiative he opposed. He attacked Baylor anytime he suspected someone of being insufficiently zealous for his brand of now-fundamentalist orthodoxy. And he attacked denominational leaders by name, no matter how popular they were. Readers regularly saw the names George Truett, L.R. Scarborough, and Joseph Dawson in Norris's paper, usually as the objects of his criticism and ridicule. As his attacks on the Baptists became more and more vociferous, Norris found himself increasingly and deliberately marginalized by denomination leaders.

The newspaper was also a window into J. Frank Norris's mind, and its pages bore witness to someone who saw the nation itself under attack by sinister forces. The early 1920s was a time when a variety of social, political, and religious movements were emergent. Many times it was hard to distinguish the political from the religious.

Whether it was the cause of Prohibition, a fight against evolution being taught in America's schools, or what he became increasingly obsessed with — a Roman Catholic conspiracy to undermine America — J. Frank Norris aired it all in the pages of his paper. Along the way he welcomed support from enemies of his enemies, and allied himself, to the extent such a lone wolf could, with men and movements he could use en route to making a name for himself as the nation's premier guardian of righteousness.

As the Jazz Age got into full swing, J. Frank Norris's approach meant that he was supported by, and became supportive of, the white-hooded hoodlums of the Invisible Empire, the Ku Klux Klan.

The Ku Klux Klan of the 1920s was actually the second Klan, with the original movement having died off with the end of post–Civil War Reconstruction. In 1915 pioneer motion picture maker D.W. Griffith had made a movie based on a novel written ten years earlier by a minister named Thomas Dixon Jr. The original Klan featured prominently in the book. The film was called *The Birth of a Nation* and is today generally considered Hollywood's first blockbuster. It featured "unprecedented action, huge battle scenes, and blood-stirring Klan charges." It was a big hit across the country. President Woodrow Wilson saw it in a private screening at the White House and loved it. "It is like writing history with lightning. And my only regret is that it is all so terribly true," commented the reputedly "progressive" president.

One man deeply affected by the moving picture was William J. Simmons. Simmons had tried to be a Methodist preacher, never quite making it. Fascinated with fraternal organizations, he decided to form one based on the old Ku Klux Klan. He persuaded thirty-four men, three of whom were actually members of the original group, to start a new KKK with him. During a Stone Mountain, Georgia, ceremony, Simmons thundered: "Under a blazing, fiery torch the Invisible Empire was called from its slumber of half a century to take up a new task and fulfill a new mission for humanity's good and to call back to mortal habitation the good angel of practical fraternity among men."

Early on, Simmons realized that the religious movement of fundamentalism provided a large pool of potential Klan members. He capitalized on the fact that his group and the fundamentalists "shared several important characteristics: an intolerance for ways of life different from their own, a frustration with post-war change, and a passionate commitment to restoring things as they used to be."

By 1922 fundamentalism was being described as "the largest, most written about, and most widespread religious doctrine in America," and the movement had much in common with the Klan. Several thousand fundamentalist ministers would eventually join or endorse the Klan. Fundamentalists were Protestants; so were Klansmen. Fundamentalists were white; so were Klansmen. Fundamentalists opposed the Catholic Church not just over doctrinal distinctions, but because they saw it as a potential conspiratorial threat on the nation itself; so did Klansmen. Fundamentalists believed in what they considered to be old-fashioned traditional values; so did Klansmen.

Though racism played a significant part in the culture of the Ku Klux Klan, it was a nativist movement, and so skin color was neither its main focus nor its primary recruiting tool. Anti-Catholicism, anti-immigration, and anti-Semitism were also major themes and attractions, particularly in the American Southwest.

A case has been made that fundamentalism's "most critical impact on our social and political history was that, without it, the Ku Klux Klan would never have enrolled the fantastic numbers nor have gained the remarkable power it wielded between 1922 and 1925."

William Simmons developed a marketing plan for the growth of the Klan, one that would make him rich and afford many others the chance to make some big bucks along the way. And from town to town went his representatives, using "high-pressure salesmanship, the attraction of mystical fraternalism, and the traditional appeals of Nativism" to recruit thousands, ultimately millions, of Americans.

A key part of the Klan's appeal in those days was that it at once harnessed and assuaged the fears many had about the future. This was particularly true of the bloc referred to as the "white Protestant citizen of the southwest." Men in towns across Texas had fears about their property, the chastity of their daughters, the honor of their wives, and the peace of their communities. They saw danger lurking everywhere via "foreign immigration, the Catholic hierarchy, insolent Negroes, greedy Jews, and Bolsheviks." And when the perceived enemies never actually took over, these same citizens tended to give the credit to the Klan.

In the Lone Star State, many in those days "were ready to adapt the Klan to their own needs and use it as a shortcut to political and moral renovation, to the reestablishment of law and order. The Southwest was ready for the Klan; this truth the order's Kleagles would gleefully discover when they undertook the Kluxing of Texas, the first state of Klan prominence."

CHAPTER EIGHT

"John the Baptist Was into Politics"

THERE IS NO evidence that J. Frank Norris was ever an "official" member of the Ku Klux Klan, though it is nearly impossible to sift through the remains of such a secretive and paranoid organization. But it is clear that he endorsed and promoted the Klan in his ministry from his pulpit, on the radio, and in his newspaper. It is equally clear that the good old boys in the white sheets liked J. Frank Norris a lot. And why not? They were for and against the same things. Beyond that, the membership of First Baptist Church was filled with Klan members, a group that included many of the city's most prominent citizens.

Readers of the *Searchlight* regularly saw advertisements for Klan activities and publications in its pages, such as one featuring a hooded man in the top left pointing over to a glowing cross in the top right corner. In between it said: "The Truth About the Klansmen Every Week in The American Citizen," which readers could subscribe to for one dollar per year.

Another ad encouraged Norris's followers to attend "The Fat Stock Show, Klan Rally and Naturalization In Our New Klavern." It was signed, "Exalted Cyclops, Klan No. 101."

A number of Norris's friends, including powerful attorney and former state senator William A. Hangar, who helped defend Governor Jim Ferguson during his impeachment trial in 1917, were members of the KKK. So was Lloyd P. Bloodworth, who while serving as Fort Worth's Grand Dragon would join First Baptist and ultimately be ordained as a pastor by Norris, all while still serving the Klan.

If Norris in fact did not join the Invisible Empire, it was likely due to the fact that he was a rogue, someone who didn't work well within anyone else's structure. He liked being on the outside, but always near enough to know what was going on, or to throw rocks if he thought it necessary.

Another possible reason for Norris stopping short of joining the Klan might have had to do with his view of the Jewish people. When it came to "Negroes" and "Catholics," the preacher was on the same page as the Klan. But the issue of anti-Semitism was another matter. For all his paranoia and prejudice, J. Frank was among the earliest fundamentalists to sympathize with the Zionist movement, particularly in the post–World War I era. He even hinted that the war itself was allowed by God as part of a movement to bring "His people" back to "the promised land" in literal fulfillment of biblical prophecy, as he understood it. So Norris may have squirmed a little, though not likely too much, when the KKK's anti-Semitic rhetoric flared up.

The local Klan in Fort Worth, number 101, built a large hall for their meetings on North Main Street. Someone bombed the original building in 1924, and it was quietly replaced. The Klan Hall was more than a place for paranoid men to gather and plot how to "save" their city; it was also a venue for entertainment.

The Klan Hall was destroyed in 1924 just days before a minstrel show was to take place there. J. Frank Norris offered the auditorium of First Baptist to the Ku Klux Klan so the show could go on. The local newspapers put the story on page one. When Norris made the offer, though, he somehow forgot that a group called The Euterpean Club, basically an association of musicians and music lovers, had received permission from First Baptist to hold a concert in the church auditorium that same night.

This caused what one newspaper called a "muddle," and the offended club sought relief from the Forty-eighth District Court in Tarrant County. The musicians had been advertising their event for several days and were shocked to hear that Norris had sent a telegram to "Cyclops Julian Hyer of the local Klan" granting them permission to use the buildings by "fiat." But the Minstrel Show went on.

Many Texans were hostile toward the Klan. When the hooded ones tried to exercise political or legal muscle, they were not without opposition. One Saturday night in 1921 the hooded ones had saturated the town with posters and placards, bearing the words:

WARNING!
The vagabond must go.

The idler must go.

The rounder must go.

The pimp must go.

The bootlegger must go.

The gambler must go.

The agitator must go.

The lewd woman must go.

The houses of ill-fame must go.

The innocent law abiding citizen need have no fear.

One hundred percent Americanism must prevail!

THE KU KLUX KLAN.

The following Monday, Judge James R. Hamilton of the Criminal District Court of Travis County (Austin) instructed a grand jury "to make a thorough investigation of this unlawful, clandestine organization and of the peace officers of this city and county." And he made sure that his words were publicized. He received a warning from the KKK: "We have an order here now that will do away with your courts and juries."

Other politicians, however, craved Klan support, seeing it as the difference between winning and losing elections. Mr. Earle B. Mayfield ran to represent Texas in the US Senate with the backing of the Klan, not to mention J. Frank Norris. Mayfield was up against impeached former governor Jim Ferguson, a man Norris described as "anti-Prohibition." During the campaign, Norris "urged all Protestant ministers to endorse Mayfield." Mayfield won that election, but a protracted legal battle followed, challenging the results. Mayfield was represented in the matter by W.P. "Wild Bill" McLean, whose reputation as a courtroom operator continued to grow. It was more than a year before Mayfield actually began serving in the Senate.

In the 1924 national presidential campaign, the issue of the Ku Klux Klan divided the Democratic Party so much that the election was virtually conceded to Republican incumbent Calvin Coolidge. On one side were the anti-Klan forces led by Catholic New York governor Al Smith. The opposition used the aging statesman and three-time party nominee for president, William Jennings Bryan, to make their case. He argued that they "ought not be singled out for censure by the Democratic Party" because many Democrats were members. Klansmen everywhere saw Bryan as one of them.

For Texas governor that same year, J. Frank Norris endorsed Klan-backed Felix D. Robertson. He was opposed by Miriam "Ma" Ferguson, the wife of the impeached former governor, who was running as her husband's virtual surrogate. The issue and influence of the Klan were unavoidable for a time during the first part of the decade as the KKK "was as intensely active in politics on the state level as it was on the local."

Getting involved in electoral politics was a pretty novel thing back then for a Baptist minister, but Norris had no qualms. He told his flock, "The truth of the business is, some of these preachers who are so afraid they will get into politics, it's not because of so much courage on their part — it's just — they aint foolin' nobody but themselves. John the Baptist was into politics. Martin Luther was into politics."

Although Norris spoke on a wide variety of subjects, his obsession in the middle of the 1920s was Roman Catholicism. It was also his primary common ground with the Klan. Norris was viciously anti-Catholic, and his sermons during this period dripped with venom and vitriol. He would prey on the prejudices and fears of his audiences: "Right at this very minute Tammany is moving earth and lower regions to nominate a wet presidential candidate." Wet, as in anti-Prohibition.

Norris's views on what he regularly referred to as the "menace of Catholicism" meshed with those of the Klan. Together they "envisioned a plot whereby the Pope planned on taking over the country and making America Catholic."

During a protracted speaking campaign in San Antonio in May 1924, J. Frank Norris attacked that city's news media for being biased against him and for the Roman Catholic Church:

> Now, ladies and gentlemen — I don't know how many thousand people are here. I am going to tell you that I have the proof of it, and I am saying it, knowing it's being taken down by a short-hand reporter, and knowing that, I am in a position to prove to you tonight, that because a majority of the officials and certain members and pastor of this church are members of the Klan, and

have been active in it, that these two papers have set to damn this church and this meeting — that's what I charge!

Now, I want to tell you something: If there had been a Knights of Columbus convention that would have had anything like the attendance that this meeting here has had, they would have had the picture on the front page of the whole black-bosomed, long-gowned, hind-part-before-collar crowd everyday!

There was prolonged applause.

Norris warned the readers of the *Searchlight* that July about the prospects for an actual religious war in America: "Are we to return to the days of St. Bartholomew, when Catholics and Protestants fought, when the blood of 100,000 Huguenots flowed in the streets of Paris?"

J. Frank Norris's religious, political, and social vision was, by the summer of 1924, fully developed and well known. He was nearing his prime as a public figure as his church gathered at the end of July on a hot summer Sunday night to see and hear him. He had advertised his message for that evening as "The Menace of Roman Catholicism in Politics."

Norris had for years conducted these summer meetings outdoors, enjoying the freedom the forum offered. Also, the crowds were usually too large to actually fit in the five-thousand-seat church auditorium. So the open-air meetings on the lot on Hemphill Street, several blocks from the church, had long been a cultural staple in Fort Worth. Members of other churches would be seen in the crowd, no doubt to the chagrin of their regular pastors.

On the platform with Norris that evening was Felix D. Robertson, candidate for the Democratic nomination for governor of Texas, endorsed by the preacher and backed by the Ku Klux Klan. The son of a Confederate general, Robertson was a lawyer and former corporation court judge. Just the day before, he had received enough votes in a four-way primary election to qualify for a runoff with Mrs. Ferguson. That election was scheduled for August 23. Norris said that he had invited the other Democrat running, Jim Ferguson, ignoring the fact that it was actually Ferguson's wife whose name was on the ballot, but the preacher said the other guy had declined. It would be an evening of old-time religion, J. Frank Norris–style, and politics, Texas-style. And it was by far the hottest ticket in town.

One report indicated that "ten thousand people crowded the benches and automobiles, while hundreds stood." Mr. Robertson sat on the choir platform with Dr. Norris, a choir of several hundred voices behind them.

The Klan in Texas was at or near the peak of its power. One Klan newspaper in Houston predicted that the 1924 campaign would be "the greatest and fiercest political battle ever waged in Texas," and this certainly came true. That same paper said that the "fight is between the KKK's and the JJJ's — Jew, Jug, and Jesuits."

Robertson's opponents regularly referred to "Felix and his Ku Klux preachers," with Norris the most prominent of them all. Norris liked Robertson, not only because he was a staunch defender of Prohibition, but also because the judge, sometimes called a "praying judge," understood the God-speak he thought Americans needed to hear. So when the candidate said things such as: "America and Texas have forgotten God and are drifting toward the same materialism that caused the decay and ruin of Rome and Germany," he was singing J. Frank's song.

Norris introduced Robertson with these words: "If I were talking to you prophetically I would say he will be the next governor of Texas, the honorable Felix D. Robertson."

When the applause died down, the candidate addressed the crowd: "My good friends, I would not of course presume to make you a speech tonight. I came over for the prime purpose of listening to the this golden-voiced soldier of the cross preach here tonight, but I will take the opportunity, my friends, of thanking the Christian people of Tarrant County who so nobly voted for me on last Saturday, and tell you that I appreciate from the bottom of my heart, and ask your continued support in the election which is to follow."

Then it was Norris's turn to speak, and for the next hour and a half he held forth on the issue, as he called it, of "Romanism versus Americanism." He told the crowd, "Roman Catholicism is anti-American and anti-Christian," words that were quite familiar to his followers. Robertson, still on the platform, nodded approvingly, adding the occasional "Amen!" for punctuation.

Warming to his theme, Norris referred to his meeting in San Antonio that previous May, sponsored by that city's First Baptist Church, led by his longtime friend Dr. I.E. Gates. It was a ten-day crusade and very effective in winning converts; in fact, the church received several hundred new members as a result of J. Frank's visit.

The preacher yelled, "And a lot of fellows came to give me warning, and said, 'You better look out how you are talking about the Catholics,' and so I just announced I would preach on them for ten days." The crowd burst into applause. He continued, "And I did. Now, I have never before told this publicly, but there was a meeting down in Beethoven Hall, the Ku Klux Klan hall, and they couldn't get in that night, and something happened — I don't know just what it was — but there were six thousand men there that night that lifted their hands and swore to Almighty God that if a hair falls from the head of that preacher, every black-bosomed priest in San Antonio will be hanging on the Alamo Square before daylight." This was followed by sustained applause.

Incendiary stuff.

Norris was so proud of it that he had it printed on the front page of the next *Searchlight*. For the next few years, this would be his message. The Klan itself would soon fade as an organization, but the ideas and attitudes that drew people to it would remain. And J. Frank Norris knew just how to cultivate and manipulate these sentiments in service to his ambition to become a major player in America's religious, and political, life.

CHAPTER NINE

"The Largest Protestant Church in America,
a Weekly Paper and a Radio Network"

AS THE SUMMER of 1924 unfolded, J. Frank Norris was riding the rails and traveling around the country preaching and doing his best to make news wherever he went.

Norris fascinated students at Southwestern Baptist Seminary across town from his church. Though they were discouraged from associating with the preacher because of his antagonism toward the denomination, some found a way to see the controversial clergyman in action. And when one of them had the courage to try to visit Norris at his office, risking the wrath of seminary officials, J. Frank was gleefully accommodating.

Roy Kemp was one such gutsy guy. When he decided to pay a call on Norris, the ever-present secretary-gatekeeper, Miss Jane Hartwell, ushered him immediately into the preacher's office on the second floor of the church's Sunday school building.

"Roy, I take it you have come up to find out how I run my business," Norris said, looking fiercely at Kemp.

"Yes, sir."

The preacher then pointed to a portrait on his wall — one of a locomotive — and told his visitor that he was like that powerful lead car on a train forcing all in its way off the tracks. He pointed to another picture on another wall — Napoleon Bonaparte — and said:

Roy, do you know that man's philosophy? One: he believed — and said so — that no man ever served another man except for personal gain. Two: Or, out of fear. He would never have a man around him for long who had his first allegiance to any other man or woman. Full and unconditional allegiance had to be to him and him personally. That's the way I run my business!

Earlier that year, in January 1924 to be exact, one popular periodical of the day, called *World's Work* — a monthly publication devoted to national and international news written with a reformist bent and a penchant for muckraking — profiled Norris as a prospective leader of all fundamentalists in the country.

> Potential leaders abound, and among them the strongest, shrewdest, and most romantically adventurous is J. Frank Norris, of Fort Worth, Texas.
>
> In Fort Worth, opinion regarding Norris is divided. One faction says he "totes a gun," the other says he "totes two guns."
>
> Many of Frank's former foes adore him, as does half the community. Buildings covering a block and more attest his success, and his auditorium, when alterations are complete, will hold six thousand applausive adherents, with a choir of seven hundred.
>
> Prince of crowd gatherers, paragon of advertisers, and a sensationalist of the first order, Norris has created a new profession, that of church-efficiency expert, and is its most brilliant practitioner. Heralded as "the Texas Cyclone," he will enter any city you choose to name, lay hold of some doddering, dead-and-alive downtown church, draw crowds into it, galvanize them, get the gloriously revivified institution financed, and erect a living, lasting monument to his abilities. After witnessing his performance in Cleveland, Dr. W.W. Bustard declared that in the service of a business corporation Norris' genius would be worth $50,000 a year. He understated the case.

Norris tended to get a kick out of that whole "gun toting" thing. Whenever it came up, he would smile and tell folks that it was just so much legend because of Fort Worth's Wild West heritage.

WITH NO IDEA that they were creating and arranging the kindling for an eventual community-wide wildfire, many of the movers and shakers of Fort Worth began to think about how their city could be reinvented to become friendlier to a broader and more diverse business base and to plot a course for long-term prosperity. If the city could be better organized, it would be less vulnerable to control by *certain* groups — in other words the Ku Klux Klan.

The local titans of commerce leading the effort to reorganize their community in ways designed to manage recent growth and facilitate new expansion included oilmen, industrialists, businessmen, lawyers, and bankers who met regularly at the exclusive Fort Worth Club. There they talked about their town, the times, and local politics, while reserving an ample amount of time for the accepted misbehaviors of poker and, though technically illegal, drinking.

These men typified the kind of boosterism featured in the popular Sinclair Lewis novels *Main Street* (1920) and *Babbitt* (1922). They wanted to see their city grow, which meant make money, a lot of it for them. These local aspirations fit the national zeitgeist. President Coolidge's pronouncements on American business qualified him as the country's leading practitioner of boosterism.

In Fort Worth the distinction of being the biggest booster went to Mr. Amon G. Carter. His unbridled civic passion was given voice through his newspaper, the highly successful *Fort Worth Star-Telegram* — well on its way by the mid-1920s to becoming one of the nation's largest newspapers. Carter was its charismatic creator and publisher. And it was said, "No Caesar ever thumped his Rome as energetically as Amon peddled Fort Worth." It was also about this time that he began using the phrase on the paper's masthead that would become so familiar to so many for so long: "Fort Worth, Texas — Where the West Begins."

By the mid-1920s the *Star-Telegram* had a vast circulation that reached people living as far as seven hundred miles away, spreading news of Fort Worth's cultural and commercial achievements throughout the region.

Carter was "a stunning salesman" who "had the glibness of a snake oil peddler, the dogmatism of a saved-again evangelist, and the sincerity of a first-term Congressman." For all practical purposes, and for several decades, Amon Carter "ran Fort Worth. He loved it, lauded it, lavished gifts on it when it was good, punished it when it was bad."

It all began, at least for Mr. Carter, one particularly cold winter day back in 1905, when he heard about a curious business opportunity. Although it had the feel of a get-rich-quick scheme, he decided to check it out. It had to do with the idea of exploiting two resources in abundance around Fort Worth. One was oil, though this was long before serious quantities of the black stuff would be found thirteen years later. The oil was merely a support player for the local commodity whose potential Carter found most intriguing: cow manure.

The idea was to market excrement from the local stockyards. A quarter million head of livestock moved through the Fort Worth stockyards each year, second only to Chicago. The cattle's presence in the city was undeniable, especially when the breeze shifted just right. Some entrepreneur thought it would be possible to mix bovine waste with a little oil and sell the product as a fuel usable to heat local homes and businesses.

So Amon donned his coat and hat and, braving brisk wind and frigid temperature, made the three-mile trek to the fragrant area where two relatively new-to-Fort Worth companies, Swift and Armour, processed meat that was then shipped all over the region.

The demonstration of the new fuel that day had drawn a little crowd and some investor interest, despite the weather. There were even a couple of newspaper reporters on hand just in case there was something to it all. With great ceremony, a sample of the fuel was lit. It was quite amazing, at first. Just look at the stuff burn, people thought. Maybe this *would* be a profitable venture.

Then came the smell. And it kept on coming.

In hindsight, it seems incredible those gathered that day thought this new discovery could be viable. The crowd dispersed quickly. There would be no investors, just a small group of unhappy and slightly nauseated people feeling more than a little foolish for having been there in the first place.

No quick money would be made via oil-soaked cow chips, but while the air was still filled with incredible foulness, Amon Carter struck up a conversation with the two reporters who had long since put their notebooks away.

They talked for a while about a favorite subject for the journalists, how nice it would be if there could be another evening newspaper in town to compete with the *Fort Worth Telegram*. Local residents also had access to a morning paper, the *Fort Worth Record*.

Carter seized the moment. By the time the air had cleared and the three men parted company, they had shaken hands on a deal to start such a newspaper. It would be called the *Fort Worth Star*. In that odd and odoriferous moment a multimillion-dollar communications empire was born, and the city would never be the same.

The *Star* would struggle for the first few years of its existence. Fort Worth had been hard on the newspaper business; forty papers had failed since the early days of the city's history. Three years after founding the *Star,* Carter found himself being lured to a new job at the more prosperous *Telegram*. He turned them down and, instead, decided to try to buy out the competition. He later said famously, "We were failing, so we decided to expand." So came into being the journalistic institution known forever after as the *Fort Worth Star-Telegram*. The wheels were now in motion that would ultimately transform Carter into the most influential and famous citizen in the history of Fort Worth.

The only man in town who could come close to rivaling Amon Carter in the ego-driven departments of ambition and audacity was J. Frank Norris. But he would not be an official part of the group plotting and steering the city's plan for growth. Despite the fact that thousands of local citizens considered him to be their leader in all things great and small, Norris never would be one of the boys. He attacked too much. They didn't like him. And worse yet, they really didn't know what to do with him.

The city's ascendance had mirrored the preacher's personal rise to prominence, and many around the country, when hearing of Fort Worth, thought of Norris, not Carter. Amon was more influential, but the fiery and flamboyant pastor of the First Baptist Church was becoming more famous, and notorious.

Even though he had literally once said to an adversary, in true Wild West fashion, "This town isn't big enough for the both of us," Amon Carter kept a wary distance from J. Frank Norris.

This is not to suggest that the two larger-than-life personalities ignored each other — quite the contrary. J. Frank Norris watched with keen interest, for example, as the famous and powerful newspaper tycoon William

Randolph Hearst tried his best to acquire Amon Carter's publication for his empire in the early 1920s. He was rebuffed at every turn. At times Carter teased the mogul and strung him along, only to ultimately resist the advances of his powerful suitor.

Once he was finally convinced that he couldn't buy Amon Carter out, Hearst decided to do the next best thing, and in 1922 he acquired the struggling *Fort Worth Record* for $150,000. The paper's anemic circulation at the time was somewhere around twenty thousand. Norris, fully immersed in the publishing of a weekly paper, was thrilled about this development — seeing the move as the beginning of the end for Amon Carter's reign as king of Cowtown. Writing in the *Searchlight,* Norris said: "Amon has plenty of enemies in Fort Worth. The complaint is that Amon irritates quick. He has a violent dislike for some citizens, who return it with usury. The Anti-Amonites look forward with great joy to Amon's impending ruin at the hands of the Hearst organization. The big show is on. When newspapers fall out, the public always gets a square deal. One newspaper owes a million dollars. The other has a hundred million dollars. It won't be long now."

When the *Record* decided to run large advertisements in Norris's tabloid, the preacher could not help but gloat: "At last Fort Worth has a great paper, and the future will show even a greater paper." Reminding his loyal readers of his expertise in the business of publishing, the preacher said, "These words are said by one who is in a position to know, one who owes allegiances to no set, clique, clan, or faction, but as one who has an unselfish interest in the welfare and growth of the city. But the thing that this note is to call attention to is to show the good sense the *Fort Worth Record* has in taking a whole page advertisement in the *Searchlight.*"

In the end, though, Citizen Hearst had underestimated Carter's staying power, and within two years he sent a representative to room 1316 of the Texas Hotel to sign the papers as Amon Carter bought the *Fort Worth Record* for the amount Hearst had originally invested. In the words of one observer, "The *Star-Telegram* merged with the *Record* like a toad with a fly."

William Randolph Hearst had badly underestimated Amon Carter. So had J. Frank Norris.

A few years later *Time* magazine reported that Carter had threatened to "beat up J. Frank Norris" in Houston in a dispute arising out of Democratic

Party presidential politics. Carter indignantly denied this and in a letter to the periodical (one that was published full-length in the magazine) called what had been written "pure fabrication, false, slanderous, libelous and vicious." But one suspects that, even if he didn't actually threaten to rough up the preacher, he probably wished he could. And he wasn't the only one in Fort Worth who felt that way.

A major component of Amon Carter's power in the city and accumulation of personal wealth was his early investment in radio, with his station WBAP ("We Broadcast A Program") taking to the airwaves in April 1922. J. Frank Norris champed at the bit for a station of his own, and when he was able to purchase a five-thousand-watt transmitter in May 1924, he was in business. He set up his studio in the church building, and eventually tall radio towers appeared near Fourth and Throckmorton. The station's call letters were KFQB, and the best Norris could come up with for a catch-phrase was "Keep Folks Quoting the Bible."

Over the next couple of years, with the new medium largely unregulated, Norris was able to enhance his signal and develop a primitive network of affiliates throughout the South. Quicker than most, he understood that radio offered far greater potential for his kind of populist demagoguery than *any* newspaper.

So by the middle of 1924, J. Frank Norris had the largest Protestant church in America, a newspaper that went into more than fifty thousand homes, and a radio station and network that could potentially take his voice to millions.

CHAPTER TEN

"Is the City Manager a Czar?"

THE GREAT GALVESTON hurricane disaster of 1900 killed six thousand and rendered thousands more homeless. It also forever dashed the hopes and dreams of its visionary civic leaders who thought their community was poised to emerge as the premier Gulf Coast city. Before the monstrous storm roared ashore that fateful September day, Galveston "stood on the verge of greatness." The city was well on its way to achieving the stature of "New Orleans, Baltimore, or San Francisco." One New York City newspaper had already dubbed Galveston "the New York of the gulf," and it had an emerging reputation as "the Wall Street of the Southwest." Galveston was very much in competition with another city, Houston, located just fifty miles to the north, to become the great coastal city in Texas. And by all accounts, in the summer of 1900 "Galveston had the lead."

But one day changed everything.

In the aftermath of the storm, and as the coastal community began to recover and rebuild, the leaders who survived knew that along with obvious things such as building a seawall, they needed to improve on the flawed system of municipal management that had, in effect, exacerbated the disaster. This gave birth to the commission form of city government, known for years as "the Galveston plan."

Fort Worth followed suit in 1906.

By the 1920s the city on the Trinity had grown from a population of about four thousand to around one hundred thousand. It had become the leading cattle market and terminal grain market of the South and also the South's greatest meatpacking center. There were four hundred factories in the city, and they turned out products valued at $185 million per year. The railroad industry, which had been so crucial to the city's growth at the beginning, had grown to the point where nineteen lines came through the city. In fact, nearly half of the freight entering the state of Texas went through Fort Worth.

And on top of all that, it was a principal oil center in north Texas.

The commission form of government put in place in 1906 was no longer up to the task of managing the city's affairs. Explosive growth combined with the factionalism that arises whenever more is at stake pointed to the need for a new order.

One being instituted in other cities was a council-manager form of government. So around the time that the nation was mourning the sudden death of President Warren G. Harding, the people of Fort Worth began to read and talk about adopting the kind of municipal government that, in those halcyon days of civic and cultural optimism, promised to lead the city to the "land of milk and honey."

More and more, as local citizens sat down for breakfast in the coffee shop of the Westbrook Hotel, or ate a quick, cheap lunch at the Quality Cafeteria on Houston Street, or maybe enjoyed one of the popular "down south plantation dinners" at the Texas Hotel — "soup, fried chicken, candied yams, corn fritters, and strawberry shortcake for just 75 cents" — ideas for changing how city government operated became the talk of the town.

The most serious discussions, outside of the official debate on the record at city hall, took place against the backdrop of the luxurious confines of the Fort Worth Club. By 1924 this exclusive club had been part of the fabric of the city for thirty-nine years.

In practical terms, adopting the reorganization plan would mean that the number of city council members would increase. They would then elect a mayor from their own ranks and hire a full-time professional who would oversee the day-to-day operation of the city's business. Centralized government and efficient management were the watchwords of the day.

As the city prepared for a referendum on a new charter that would reorganize the government, scheduled for December 11, 1924, J. Frank Norris used his pulpit and paper to endorse the plan. Speaking to his congregation a few weeks before the election, he said, "The day of small-town stuff is past in Fort Worth. We have become a great metropolitan city. We have no longer need for or time to lose with cheap peanut politicians running a $150,000,000 corporation. We need a city manager that is worth $25,000 a year."

The very next Friday, the *Searchlight* ran a full-page advertisement: "Why Adopt the New Charter — Reasons Given — Objections Answered." It listed "17 reasons why the citizens should vote for the new charter on December 11." Another article answered the question: "Is the City Manager a Czar?"

When the good citizens of the city went to the polls, they agreed with Norris and Fort Worth business leaders, overwhelmingly approving the new form of government. Shortly thereafter a council was elected, and the members chose Henry Clay Meacham as the first mayor of Fort Worth under the new system. He was the highly successful owner of one of the large department stores in the city and a popular resident.

H.C. Meacham was a serious and successful-looking man in his mid-fifties. His full head of hair was graying at the temples; he combed it to the side across his forehead. His face was accented with horn-rimmed glasses, giving him a professorial look.

Described as "a lusty man, with courage," it was also noted that like most men of courage and energy "he picked up enemies along the way." He was "hard-headed, hard boiled," with a "clear-eyed faculty for looking a fact in the face." He would long be remembered as a man who was seldom "swayed by sentiment" except in cases of "intimate friendship."

The future mayor of Fort Worth was born on October 10, 1869, in Senatobia, Mississippi. H.C. Meacham didn't know much about his own family background. He knew that they were originally from North Carolina, but having been orphaned before the age of five, he had to piece information together over the years. He knew that his father's name was Henry Banks Meacham and his grandfather was simply known as Banks.

He received his early education at the Tate County Country School in Senatobia. His fondest memories of that time are of a devout Methodist couple, the Reverend T.H. Porter and his wife, Annie Echols. He went on to college, but just for a year at Mississippi A&M in Starkville. Over the years, largely because of his run-ins with J. Frank Norris, it was common to see Meacham referred to as a Roman Catholic, but there is no evidence that he was ever anything other than a nominal Methodist.

At the time he became mayor, Meacham's Department Store employed 157 people and had thirty or more departments. It claimed to be the largest such store in Fort Worth, occupying a four-story building spanning a city block on Twelfth Street between Main and Houston.

The first significant task for Mayor Meacham and the newly elected council was to find the right man to be Fort Worth's first city manager. They conducted a nationwide search and narrowed it down eventually to two prime candidates, Earl C. Elliot of Wichita, Kansas, and Ossian E. Carr of Dubuque, Iowa. Elliot withdrew his name, likely because he knew he was mismatched against Carr, who already had quite a reputation in the emerging field of city management.

Ossian Carr, or O.E. as he preferred, grew up on a farm in rural northwest Pennsylvania, but he was determined to leave agriculture behind. He pursued his degree in engineering at Allegheny College in Meadville, graduating with a bachelor of science degree in 1900. He spent a few years with the US Coast Geodetic Survey, then moved on to a job with the Baltimore & Ohio Railroad.

His interest in the application of his engineering ideas to the work of urban governments began when he took a job with the City of Pittsburgh on a project involving the construction of a new water filtration plant. From there, in 1906, he took an assignment with J.G. White and Company in Olongapo, Philippine Islands, as the assistant superintendent over the construction of a mechanical coal handling plant. After that he moved around a lot, but always with glowing references. He worked in Seattle, Washington; Cadillac, Michigan; Niagara Falls, New York; Springfield, Ohio; and Dubuque, Iowa. While in Iowa he also served the national City Managers Association, first as secretary for a couple of years, then as its president. He had a résumé that sold itself, along with extraordinary letters of reference. From the minute H.C. Meacham heard of Carr and saw his record, he knew that he had found his man.

So when the newly installed mayor of Fort Worth opened his mail on April 20, 1925, and saw a letter from Carr, he tore the envelope open and was thrilled to find the words: "It happens that I am free to accept early employment. This year's program finishes the larger needs of this city for its present population." The personal interview was a mere formality. O.E. Carr would be Fort Worth's first city manager, and he would whip into shape the municipality's planning and implementation for streets, parks, police, and fire departments, as well as all other aspects of the governance, helping the city on the Trinity to become even greater.

The city manager's salary, however, was not even close to the twenty-five thousand dollars J. Frank Norris had suggested the job was worth. Carr's starting pay for managing the burgeoning business affairs of Fort Worth was set at $13,500 a year.

O.E. Carr was "a pleasant but very efficient looking man in his late forties." He wore a bow tie with most of his suits, and his hair was slicked back with a part near the middle. He moved to Texas and hit the ground running.

CHAPTER ELEVEN

"A Deep Laid Conspiracy"

JOB NUMBER ONE for the new city manager was to analyze Fort Worth's tax situation, collect past-due taxes, and look for sources of new revenue. His first few moves to fix what he saw as inequities plunged O.E. Carr into a front-page controversy. After conducting a preliminary study a month or so earlier, O.E. Carr determined that Fort Worth Power and Light Company had not been paying enough taxes to the city. He was convinced an error had been made assessing the value of the utility's assets. Carr ran his own numbers and conducted a quiet investigation. He then sent a notice to the utility that the city was reassessing them and that their taxes would increase.

Almost immediately Carr found himself at war with the chief counsel for FWP&L, former Texas state senator W.A. Hangar, the man who defended Governor Jim Ferguson during his 1917 impeachment trial and one of the most popular and powerful lawyers in town. Hangar was as politically well connected as they came in Fort Worth. In fact, his son Robert had recently been elected district attorney for Tarrant County.

Hangar fought Carr tooth and nail over the rate increase, and along the way the lawyer threatened the new guy in town with a particular kind of political pressure. It was not a very well-kept secret that Bill Hangar was also an important member of local chapter number 101 of the Ku Klux Klan, the group that held regular meetings in its large and newly rebuilt hall on North Main Street. And though the Klan's candidates for public office had been soundly defeated at the polls the year before and the national Klan had been disgraced just that April by the sordid story of Indiana Klan Grand Dragon D.C. Stephenson's rape and mutilation of a girl — who then committed suicide — there was still a sense in Fort Worth that the hooded citizens had some clout.

Hangar conveyed to his brethren his displeasure with the new city manager. As Klan members contemplated how to apply pressure, they saw another action by Carr as provocative. The city manager had, as part of his general efficiency-driven housecleaning at city hall, dismissed several employees. And some of them *happened* to be Klansmen. To them, Mr. Carr must have fired the Klansman as an act of retaliatory persecution, obsessed as they were with conspiracies. The Klavern gathered at its hall on Friday, July 31, and voted to "refrain from cooperating with the present city administration." There was also talk of trying to organize an effort to recall the members of the city council.

Later that night Fort Worth citizens saw the ominous image of fiery crosses burning at several locations around the city.

Mayor H.C. Meacham was in New York City that week, staying at the Vanderbilt Hotel. He received a two-page letter from O.E. Carr on Monday, August 3, informing him of developments in Fort Worth. Carr wrote to Meacham: "The air is full of rumors and talk. Our mutual friend, J. Frank, states that a joint major operation is to be performed on you and I here in September . . . he feels I am very culpable on account of my associations with you." The city manager then told his boss, "The Klan held a meeting here last night." He described the meeting as an anti-Meacham and anti-Carr affair and also wrote the mayor that the matter of the dismissed city employees had been discussed at the Klan Hall. Sensitive to the charge that he had somehow dismissed the employees unjustly, Carr spent time in his missive to Meacham insisting that these terminated "parties in the Health Department" just *happened* to be members of the Klan and that he was completely unaware of that affiliation.

The way he saw it, Carr told Meacham, W.A. Hangar was in "cooperation with J. Frank" and that the three "elements" banded together — the utility company, the KKK, and J. Frank Norris — will "make life really worth while and quite interesting." He probably smiled as he wrote with sarcastic flourish, but Meacham most likely did not as he read it. The mayor hated conflict and did his best to avoid it.

Carr indicated that "J. Frank is the most formidable element in that fraternity, inasmuch as some people are inclined to think he is an angel of light, instead of one of darkness." He told the mayor that he was determined to stay the course and see it all through.

The same day Meacham was reading his letter in New York, Carr told reporters who had gathered around his desk in his city hall office, "When the power behind the Ku Klux Klan dictates the policies of the city government, there will be another city manager. It shall not be done while I am here."

M.R. Toomer, editor of the *Fort Worth Press,* wrote that morning: "For being an ill-advised move, the *Press* believes the Ku Klux Klan attack on the city government takes the prize." He was sure that "the Klan's action will receive no support from the city at large, and that the attack launched by the burning of fiery crosses will die a perfectly natural death."

Toomer reminded readers of the *Press* that the taxpayers of the city had, by opting for the new form of government, "forcibly decreed an end of Klan domination in Fort Worth politics and a beginning of business government." He gave high marks to the new city manager and to the form of government that was now in place. He reminded subscribers that the new municipal paradigm "was created as a means to rid the city of selfish domination of government by the Klan, government which ran this city into debt."

At city hall, however, Carr was noticing that his support from those who had hired him, the city council, was not as stalwart as he might have hoped. Of the five men on the council, only two made statements publicly supporting the new city manager; the other three were silent. The Ku Klux Klan was still feared by many.

Mayor Meacham always seemed to be out of town when controversy flared up. With the Fort Worth Power & Light back-taxes controversy and the Klansmen city hall firings controversy both raging, one newspaper suggested, mockingly, that when he got back to town "from his business trip in the east he'll be surprised again." He was.

Meacham's new headache had to do with a decision O.E. Carr had made with regard to First Baptist Church and its infamous pastor, J. Frank Norris. While the nation was still mourning the death of William Jennings Bryan, and as Norris was waging a concerted campaign to become heir to the mantle of the Great Commoner, Carr was going after Norris and his church for taxes he claimed they owed to the city of Fort Worth.

Following the devastating fire in 1912 and the various trials that ensued, First Baptist Church rebuilt. The new building was much larger and designed for a growing membership. As the church grew over the next decade, improvements were made and new construction added to the point that the campus took up an entire square city block in the heart of Fort Worth — not to mention a five-story building that the church also owned across the street.

The main sanctuary was the largest auditorium in Fort Worth, the venue of choice for school commencements, concerts, and big-name events. William Jennings Bryan spoke there, as did Colonel Billy Mitchell — even former president William Howard Taft. The famous Irish tenor John McCormack, of "It's a Long Way to Tipperary" fame, gave a concert at First Baptist Church. It was described by one Norris detractor as "a great place for shows and shams, for concerts and confabs." He added that the building was usually for rent "when Frank isn't using it for rant."

In 1925 the newly reorganized Fort Worth Symphony Orchestra, under the direction of conductor Brooks Morris, who would hold that position until 1957, gave its first of several performances in the auditorium of First Baptist Church. Brooks Morris was a member of the church and by 1926 its choir director, a role he would fill for several decades.

Probably the most famous entertainment event in the First Baptist Church auditorium, outside of the regular J. Frank Norris show, happened in November 1925. Will Rogers was in his prime as a cultural icon, having emerged on the national scene just as the modern mass media age began shortly after World War I. The decade after the November 1918 armistice "saw the development of radio, phonograph records, newsreels, and syndicated newspaper features." Rogers was tailor-made for this new era, "being inclusive, accessible, amusing, and marketable."

He was already famous when concert promoter Charles L. Wagner signed Rogers for a seventy-five-appearance national tour in the fall of 1925, promising the cowboy an unprecedented fee plus expenses.

Arriving by train at Fort Worth's Texas & Pacific passenger station on Thursday, November 12, 1925, he was met with a "reception as unique as it was rousing." Facing the crowd, the cowboy "smiled and shuffled from one foot to another" while a band played. He told those gathered: "It looks like the old gang from the movie lot."

Someone asked Rogers about the lecture tour. He replied: "Havin' the time of my life. 'Cept I don't like some of the ball parks they stick me in." He complained that "they don't give a fellow a chance to get intimate with his audience — it's hard to be funny."

He wouldn't have any problems that evening, though. Norris had designed the stage at his church to be conducive to showmanship and sensation. The standing-room-only crowd at First Baptist that night witnessed a vintage Rogers performance.

Ever self-conscious on the stage, the entertainer took a while to warm up, but eventually he rolled through some set pieces that always worked. "The children of Fort Worth are taught two things," Rogers said, "to fear the Lord and hate Dallas." He would poke fun at the city's richest citizen: "He got by on his pluck and perseverance. The trouble is we can't find somebody to pluck like he did." Along the way he would talk about "the Klan, Prohibition, the Florida land boom, aviation, evolution, and his own meetings with Coolidge and the Prince of Wales." He had a kind word or two for J. Frank Norris and the church and refrained from poking fun at the preacher.

Clearly, the spacious church facility at Fourth and Throckmorton was more than a church. It had become a theater, a town hall, and an all-around multipurpose building for the city. The church also leased prime street-level space to several business concerns — generating a handsome profit.

The entire area around First Baptist Church was flush. Monnig's Dry Goods Company had just announced that they would be moving from Fourteenth Street to a spot near the church. The Westbrook Hotel, just a block away, was in its heyday. Stripling's Dry Goods was nearby, as were the Fort Worth & Denver Railway and Burk Burnett office buildings. And Sanger Brothers Department Store was making plans to build a facility one block east. First Baptist Church was located where the action was, and the value of its property had increased exponentially.

President Coolidge had declared that "the business" of the country "was business," and one of the ways the boom of the 1920s played out was through the growth of large chain stores. Woolworth's added more than seven hundred stores nationally, and A&P grew from just over four thousand outlets to more than fifteen thousand.

As the J.C. Penney Company expanded by more than a thousand stores across the United States, it targeted the Fort Worth market, a fact sure to have displeased competitors such as H.C. Meacham. Penney's leased prime retail space at 406–8 Houston Street with plans to expand their store so that it would run through to Throckmorton and have an entrance directly across the street from Norris's office. The building Penney's occupied belonged to First Baptist Church. Though the church profited enormously, it paid no taxes whatsoever on the rent proceeds. Furthermore, it paid no property taxes even on buildings and space not being used for religious purposes. Businesses had operated for years out of properties owned by the church, but no one in city government, before Carr, had the fortitude to tangle with Norris.

The new professional city manager, however, saw revenue owed to the city and had no reservations about calling the pastor on the matter. His job was to manage the city's business, and that involved making sure all taxpayers were paying their fair share. Clearly, Norris never anticipated such an outcome when he advocated for the new form of governance.

When Carr finally visited the preacher he had heard so much about but never met, it did not take him long to realize that he had taken on someone quite unlike anyone he had gone up against before. He sat in Norris's office and received a tongue-lashing.

The preacher refused to acknowledge that the church should be taxed. In fact, he was adamant that it was completely exempt. He pointedly reminded Carr of all the things he was doing for the city and that his church building was regularly used as a prime venue for civic and commercial events that enriched the cultural life of Cowtown. The two men parted company determined to win. Carr told one reporter, "I have dealt with the red-light outfit in New York state when I was city manager of Niagara Falls and with crooked contractors when I was city manager in Dubuque, Iowa, but I have never met a man who, in my judgment, used his intellect more viciously against the betterment of the community in which he lives than J. Frank Norris."

Norris, for his part, changed his stance on the new charter and began publicly to belittle Carr, often sarcastically referring to him in sermons and in print as "our imported city manager."

Carr formally recommended to the city council that the portion of the First Baptist Church property being used for clearly nonreligious purposes be placed on the tax rolls. Such practice is commonplace today. Churches across America regularly pay taxes on income derived from bookstores, rental properties, and such. But the proposal was a first in Fort Worth. In July 1925 the city council voted to send a tax bill to First Baptist Church. Though the entire property of the church plant was said to be valued at more than $1 million, the city asked for tax on just $63,750 worth of the property.

Norris saw this as declaration of political war, and he prepared to do battle with Fort Worth's city government for the second time in fifteen years. The first time he had taken on a mayor and municipal powers his church had burned down and he had been indicted for arson and perjury. But those memories were no deterrent. He began to denounce city officials, accusing them of prejudice against him and First Baptist. He saw the issue in conspiratorial terms, and himself as a crusader fighting corrupt interests and bad government. His megachurch congregation agreed.

In August 1925 he told the readers of the *Searchlight* that "about September first a major operation will be performed upon the city management" — cryptic but clearly threatening language. Nothing happened immediately. Ever prone to jump from one issue to another, J. Frank spent a month preaching in New York City, decrying that city's ills from the pulpit of Calvary Baptist Church on West Fifty-seventh Street.

Though Norris loved to play the persecuted martyr, he was much more comfortable on the offensive. The tax issue had put him on the defensive. So before he would escalate the conflict he needed something, maybe an issue to spin or twist — anything he could turn around and use against the mayor and his city manager. He waited and wondered.

Meanwhile, the tax bills kept coming, with late notices and fees, all ignored by the pastor and his passively complicit church board. In January 1926 the taxes became delinquent. The bill was for less than $1,500, a small part of O.E. Carr's larger campaign to collect nearly $750,000 of back taxes owed to the city by businesses from June 1925 to June 1926. But to J. Frank Norris it wasn't about the money; it was the principle of the thing. Never mind that Carr was going after establishments large and small across the city for back taxes and new taxes. Norris saw the tax bills presented to the church as part of a "deep laid conspiracy."

In May 1926 City Attorney Rouer announced that he was preparing an opinion about the church-property tax issue in light of a recent ruling by the civil court of appeals in San Antonio having to do with property owned and operated by the YMCA and YWCA. The court had struck down a law passed by the Texas legislature in 1912 specifically exempting those two organizations. That law was voided "on the grounds that it granted special privileges that made it class legislation."

Rouer's report would cover "parsonages, churches and lodges holding property from which income revenue is received." Newspaper accounts of this announcement noted that "the city's course of action brought the officials into conflict with Rev. J. Frank Norris and other ministers and lodge members."

As Rouer prepared his opinion, one that was widely assumed to be a formality with the outcome a foregone conclusion, J. Frank Norris kept his eye on city hall and the newspapers, waiting for something to emerge that could be represented by him as fishy enough to use in a new attack. Then he would go on the offensive. He had put out the word to well-placed sympathizers who reveled in rumor and innuendo, stringers who would be more than happy to feed the preacher gossipy morsels. He knew something would break; it was just a matter of time. The new city manager and all in the municipal government would, he fumed, rue the day they ever decided to tangle with him.

CHAPTER TWELVE

"The Grand Champions of the Fort Worth Club"

THE FORT WORTH Club was the center of power for the city on the Trinity. The "top dogs of the city ate lunch everyday" at the club, and Fort Worth's "power elite" gathered there to "get a haircut, a massage, play a game of pool, read the *Wall Street Journal* and *Oil and Gas Journal.*"

It was no secret that a small and powerful group of unofficial oligarchs, men such as "Amon Carter and his cronies," virtually ran Fort Worth from the club's luxurious confines. It was "where presidents and princes of the corporate, social, and entertainment world" gravitated while in the city. Will Rogers, who never met a man he didn't like, simply *loved* the Fort Worth Club. The resident chef "even knew how to prepare chili the special way" America's favorite cowboy preferred it.

When its towering new twelve-story building at Seventh and Throckmorton Streets opened in March 1926, it instantly became the most prestigious and famous address in Fort Worth. The club was located a few blocks down from where the First Baptist Church dominated the intersection of Throckmorton and Fourth. The two entities would often converge awkwardly when VIPs visited Fort Worth, such as when Will Rogers came to town, hanging out with the local boys at the club before speaking to several thousand in the church's auditorium.

Under the leadership of its dynamic president, Amon Carter, the club's membership had swelled to seven hundred by the time it made the move to its new high-rise facility. Carter's *Star-Telegram* boasted that the new edifice "will rank with those of any club in the country," adding that the building "is one of the most graceful on the skyline of Fort Worth."

On April 15, 1926, Amon Carter hosted what was then described as "easily one of the most gala evenings in the history of the city." It was a dinner for "the Grand Champions of the Fort Worth Club" and "in appreciation of the support given in building the new club." Approximately 225 of the most influential movers and shakers dined "on choice cuts of the grand champion steer of the 1926 stock show in the main dining room." Mayor Meacham, though a club member himself, gave an official welcome as the top politician in town; other speakers talked about the growth of their exclusive club and the city they hovered above.

Between bites of some of the best steak the club's members and guests had ever eaten, the table conversation drifted to an unpleasant subject. Though no one wanted to spoil the evening with such unpleasantness, there was something almost morbid about how the chatter came back around, again and again, to what J. Frank Norris was up to.

Almost to a person, the city's elite gathered for the festivities wished the cantankerous preacher would just go away. They especially took issue with his chronic criticism of public officials such as Mayor Meacham. Couldn't the minister leave this good man alone? Norris seemed to delight in stirring controversy and conflict, inflicting discomfort, causing trouble. They all knew that H.C. Meacham had health problems, and J. Frank Norris just didn't seem to care.

A few days later a famous guest paid a visit to the club. Jack Dempsey was more than the world's heavyweight boxing champion; he was a cultural icon. He had also become a movie star and had married actress Estelle Taylor, who played Moses's sister, Miriam, in Cecil B. DeMille's 1923 version of *The Ten Commandments*.

Dempsey had not defended his title in more than three years, so the public was clamoring for a big fight. Jack thought he had found a good, safe opponent in ex-marine Gene Tunney, so his promoter, George L. "Tex" Rickard, worked out the details and Dempsey traveled to Fort Worth to sign for the fight. Amon Carter and Rickard were boyhood friends, and Carter knew a thing or two about publicity himself. On April 20, 1926, the champ came to Cowtown and "was immediately whisked to Carter's suite" at the club — 10G, where he was one of the first to sign the new register. He hung out with many of the good old boys, and the men were excited to meet one of the most famous people in the world.

The next day Dempsey signed the contract in Amon's *Star-Telegram* office, using the same pen that had been used to sign "the first bond for the construction of the monumental new Fort Worth Club building." The big fight would take place in Philadelphia five months later, and many of the boys would travel by special train to see it. Those who couldn't make the trip would listen to it on the radio at the club.

CHAPTER THIRTEEN

"The Time Was Ripe for a Full Airing"

AS J. FRANK Norris marked time, looking for the opportunity to go on the offensive, he revisited a story he had been sitting on, one that, at least for him, began one otherwise normal day in the church office in 1920, long before Fort Worth reinvented itself and he and the new mayor began crossing swords in civic conflict.

Back then, Jane Hartwell, Norris's longtime secretary, affectionately (and by some, fearfully) known to congregants as "Miss Jane," entered the preacher's office to let him know that a man named S.L. Mock was in the anteroom and wanted to talk to the pastor. She reminded the preacher that, though Mr. Mock did not attend the church, his wife did. Her name was Julia, and for a while she had been a teacher in the large church Sunday school.

Miss Jane was J. Frank Norris's gatekeeper. She knew where everyone worked, which pew they sat in, and also where the proverbial bodies were buried. It was rare for anyone to gain access to the preacher's office without her consent and introduction. She was the daughter of missionaries to China, and it was said that "if she were a Catholic she would be a nun." Highly regarded by church members as sort of a congregational "big sister," she was described by one outsider as "gracious and bleak, narrow-minded and sensitive, emotional and repressed." She ran the office of the church with a quick mind and a flair for efficiency. There was little doubt, on the part of insiders or outsiders, that "she would go to any length" to help the church and her pastor.

This devoted woman saw the greater cause of the gospel and the work of J. Frank Norris as virtually synonymous. She was Norris's trusted assistant as well as his eyes and ears throughout the church's premises and its membership. "A tall, thin, dark-haired, dark-eyed, dark-skinned, long-chinned, angular, intense woman in her forties," she was the consummate "true believer."

Norris agreed to see Mr. Mock not knowing what the conversation would be about. After the introductions and a bit of small talk, the visitor plunged into his story full of sadness and anger. The previous night when he came home from work, instead of finding his wife home and waiting for him, she was absent. So were her belongings. All she left was a note. Trembling, the distraught husband reached into his suit coat pocket and withdrew the paper, handing it to the pastor.

The gist of the note was that Julia had left her husband and did not plan to return. She insisted that he not try to find her. The pastor drew the full story out of the heartbroken man.

Julia had been unfaithful to her marriage vows, the kind of story clergymen have been hearing for generations. But Norris listened with enhanced interest when Mr. Mock revealed the name of the other party in the affair. He, too, was married and a prominent citizen of Fort Worth.

Mrs. Mock had fallen in love with her boss at the department store where she was employed, the wealthy businessman H.C. Meacham. She had been working closely with Meacham on store business, traveling with him as he went to places like New York and Chicago — even Niagara Falls.

Weeping and devastated, S.L. Mock asked Norris what he should do. Interestingly, by all accounts the preacher spent little, if any, time dealing with the various spiritual and emotional aspects common to a pastoral counseling session. Instead, J. Frank Norris matter-of-factly suggested three potential courses of action: "He could leave it alone, resort to violence, or consult an attorney." They agreed that the latter recommendation was the wisest course, and Norris encouraged Mock to contact local attorney Marvin Simpson to initiate an action against the wealthy businessman for "the alienation of affections of his wife."

Mr. Simpson filed suit: *S.L. Mock v. H.C. Meacham*. Meanwhile, Julia Mock filed for divorce. The matter had the potential to become a scandal.

The venue for all of the legal wrangling, the alienation of affection suit and the divorce action, was the Forty-eighth District Court in Tarrant County. Local citizens simply referred to this as "Judge Bruce Young's court." Bruce Young ruled his courtroom as a benevolent and popular despot. By 1920 he had been at his post for six years and was already well on his way to legend status. Quick-minded, often to the point of abruptness, he would "frequently cut short a tedious hearing by announcing that he had already made a decision and there was no need for further testimony." A fearless man, he once faced an angry mob on the steps of the county jail. They had gathered to lynch a murder suspect but dispersed after hearing the judge's plea.

He was best known, however, for sorting out marriage and family matters. The judge was very "outspoken on the bench against quick remarriages after divorce." He saw the potential for "neglect of children of the first marriage." He regularly admonished recently divorced women to "know a man longer than two months before you marry him." He was a well-known friend to mistreated wives and children and would not flinch at the idea of sending a man to jail for failing to pay child support. He would tell the deadbeat dads, "Pay up, go to jail, or leave the country." They usually paid.

To defend himself against S.L. Mock, H.C. Meacham hired high-powered attorneys William "Wild Bill" McLean, Walter Scott, and Sam Sayers. Meacham's attorneys sought from early on to find a way to settle matters out of court and spare their client a public airing in Judge Young's courtroom.

One day in 1920 J. Frank Norris happened to be walking on Twelfth Street near Meacham's Department Store, and he encountered H.C. Meacham on the sidewalk. Meacham confronted the preacher and asked: "What do you mean by interfering in my affairs?" Norris played dumb and asked what he meant.

"I refer to the Mock suit."

Norris deflected the issue by minimizing his role to that of simply telling someone to get an attorney.

Ultimately, rather than have the case be brought to trial — and therefore, presumably, become an issue in the separate but related divorce proceeding — a settlement was reached. On March 23, 1921, S.L. Mock agreed to drop his suit against Meacham in return for a cash settlement of $12,500. Additionally that same day, Julia Mock signed a "ratification" of the settlement, joining with her estranged husband. There was no way she wanted her affair to be brought up in her divorce case. Adultery carried a lot of legal weight in those days, particularly when standing before Judge Young.

Meacham reportedly paid at least ten thousand dollars to his attorneys for their work keeping the matter quiet. He knew that J. Frank Norris had the whole story and was capable of using it against him. So when Meacham decided, at the urging of many friends in town, to put his hat in the ring for a seat on the newly reorganized city council in early 1925, he was concerned the story would be put into public circulation. In fact, there was a whispering campaign under way, mostly by women, questioning whether Meacham was a man of sufficient moral character to be elected. Rumors were flying around about his "moral delinquency," with some people using the specific epithet *home-wrecker.*

Meacham decided to pay a visit to J. Frank Norris to try to persuade the preacher not to fan the flames of gossip with what he knew. Norris claimed that he was not behind the rumors. Meacham reportedly said, "I believe your statement." At least that's how Norris remembered the conversation.

Now, however, things were different. J. Frank Norris had been sitting on this story for several years, and it seemed that the time was ripe for its full airing and exploitation to destroy a political leader and enhance his own reputation as a guardian of morality. No matter that doing so involved a serious breach of pastoral ethics, not to mention things the Bible clearly taught. The trick was in the timing.

As Norris continued his written tirades in the *Searchlight,* he teased his audience and taunted Meacham and Carr, warning that additional details "will be given from the pulpit of the First Baptist Church, over the radio, and in this paper, and if anybody doubts that it will be given he is simply a newcomer or a fool." Norris then added, "and the city manager could qualify under both heads."

He ended this attack piece with a reference to a sarcastic remark "one of the most highly educated men in Fort Worth" had recently made about Mr. Carr: "All this talk about the missing link, and all the discussion that is going on about it should cease at once, for if the evolutionists should go to city hall and look at the city manager for one second, the whole argument of the missing link would be settled forever."

CHAPTER FOURTEEN

"When the Lid Is Taken Off"

IN NOVEMBER 1925 the citizens of Fort Worth approved a large revenue bond for an assortment of city improvements, including the widening of certain downtown streets to accommodate increased traffic flow. This was pretty much business as usual and drew little notice, except from J. Frank Norris. He decided to watch how the details unfolded. One of the projects planned was the expansion of an alley into a one-way street. Norris pondered its potential as something he might be able to use against the mayor and his "imported" city manager.

A few blocks from the center of the fundamentalist world in the American South, the empire being built by J. Frank Norris at First Baptist Church, stood St. Patrick's Church and St. Ignatius Academy. The latter was a venerable Roman Catholic school. To widen the nearby street, the city needed a right-of-way, which would require acquisition of some of the land owned by the local Catholic diocese. The local Real Estate Board of Trade appraised the value of the land needed at $62,000. This would purchase a portion of the property, but not the entire plot.

However, when the city council met in June 1926 to approve the purchase of the right-of-way, they decided to purchase the entire property, with the intention to resell at a profit what they did not need or use. They added another $90,000 to the transaction, bringing the total for the purchase of the property held by St. Ignatius Academy to $152,000.

This was the issue J. Frank Norris had been waiting for, one tailor-made for him. He saw this as nothing less than a vast conspiracy involving the city government, led by its mayor, to support the Church of Rome. For someone known for his provocative messages about the "Great Roman Catholic Conspiracy" to control America, this was too good an issue to ignore, not to mention that it appeared to be a generous subsidy to the Catholic diocese at the very time the city was going after his Baptist church for taxes.

In fairness, Norris was not alone in seeing something that did not pass the smell test. Before the preacher could even begin to use the issue against his enemies in city government, a heated debate erupted in the city as many citizens accused the council of using taxpayer funds to, in effect, subsidize a Catholic parish. And to make matters even more suspect, the whole deal had a net benefit for the mayor and his department store, making it more accessible.

As June gave way to July, a suit was filed in the Forty-eighth District Court seeking to restrain city officials from paying for the St. Ignatius property. Filed by "J.B. Davis et al," Joe Greathouse, the attorney representing the plaintiffs, claimed that he "knew his clients only thru statements made in affidavits."

Calling the price that the city was paying for the property "exorbitant and in excess of market value," Davis and the other five plaintiffs alleged that City Manager Carr and the council "are not purchasing a large part of the lots for municipal purposes and for the widening and improvement of Twelfth Street, but for the avowed purpose of having city funds used and invested in the real estate business." The petition criticized the initiative as a "speculative transaction unauthorized by law." Carr was further charged with engaging in a "wasteful campaign of expenditure of the city's funds."

Mayor Meacham was criticized for being "greatly instrumental in procuring purchase of said properties for his own private use and benefit." Noting that Mr. Meacham's department store was located at Twelfth and Main Streets, and that the major shopping business in the downtown area had shifted to "the vicinity of Fifth and Taylor Streets," the suit charged the mayor with an abuse of his official position. It said that Meacham, in effect, was placing "his store in the path of traffic from the residential districts over Jennings Avenue."

Many Fort Worth citizens, including City Manager Carr, saw the hand of J. Frank Norris behind the suit. Carr referred to the matter as "just some deviltry on the part of J. Frank Norris." Norris, always delighted to respond to critics, especially if his words found their way to page one of a newspaper, remarked in a written statement: "This seems to be the characteristic attitude of Mr. Carr toward all people who differ from him. That may be the method of dealing with citizens in the North, where he hails from, but it is not the method that the citizens of the South and West use."

The conflict between Norris and O.E. Carr escalated during the first week of July as the nation marked its 150th birthday. The preacher claimed with typical bravado, "I have a pulpit that reaches 8,000 people, a paper that goes into everybody's home and a radio that covers the air." An editorial in the *Fort Worth Press* said, "In other words, say what you want to Mr. Carr, and 'I' Frank Norris, will be tickled to death to come back at you." The editorial referred to the fight as "a fine example of mid-summer madness," adding "personality has no particular place in the argument."

City Manager Carr was proving to be a stubborn and formidable adversary to Norris, who was accustomed to people caving under his pressure, usually out of fear. One journalist said: "The plain fact is that the people of Fort Worth are afraid of Frank Norris. From newspapermen to merchants and bankers he has them bluffed. They are afraid of him in precisely the same way in which one is afraid of an insane man or one who is violently drunk." The reporter added: "There are no tactics they feel, to which he will not stoop, nothing too low or vile, true or untrue, that he will not say about his enemies."

Carr, however, had not been in town long enough to develop such a fear of Norris. This made him a more effective foe, and Norris knew it. Defending the action of the city council to tax part of the property of First Baptist Church, Carr said: "The law demands that all property be taxed equally for the support of government, it matters not to me whether property used for business purposes be owned by J. Frank Norris or the most obscure citizen, it should be taxed." When the city manager's statement was reported to Norris, the preacher replied, "No hand that had ever been raised against the First Baptist Church had ever prospered."

In fact, Norris redoubled his efforts: "Why bring in the First Baptist Church as a smoke screen in his efforts to misapply $152,000 of the taxpayer's money? On some Sunday night when the weather gets cool, the entire administration of the imported manager will be reviewed, as also the career of the Mayor."

That same week in early July 1926, with the opulent April Fort Worth Club dinner and Jack Dempsey's visit now distant memories, Mayor H.C.

Meacham presided over a closed-door "off the record" and informal meeting of business leaders and political sympathizers at the new club headquarters. Among the topics of discussion that night was what, if anything, they could or should do about the city's J. Frank Norris problem. The thirty or so men present were very concerned that the out-of-control preacher was causing great harm to their community.

Meacham admonished the group that "he regarded Norris as a menace to the town and that he should be supported by no one." The mayor was using one of Norris's pet words, *menace,* deliberately. He particularly scolded the bankers in attendance, suggesting that Norris was close to being insolvent financially "and that if the bank would cut off his credit and quit loaning him money that it would be a good thing for the town."

Henry Zweifel, the future prominent Texas Republican committeeman, sat and listened as the mayor went around the room rebuking those who were doing nothing about Norris and giving specific suggestions about what might possibly be done about the preacher. Zweifel, a "short, stocky, and wiry-haired" man, had been appointed to the US Attorney's Office in Fort Worth in 1921, making something of a name for himself going after oil industry swindlers. The mayor had advice for the lawyer, telling him that the preacher was circulating his tabloid, the *Searchlight,* "under second class postage to people who had not subscribed to it." This was a violation of postal regulations, and the mayor told his prominently placed friend that Norris "ought to be prosecuted for fraudulent use of the mail."

One man at the meeting said, "If Norris were to make statements about me as he has made about you, and they were untrue, I would take my shotgun and kill him." The mayor acknowledged the sentiment but said, "On account of my physical condition, I cannot do it." More moderate voices, including that of Amon G. Carter, advised Meacham that the best thing he could do was to leave Norris alone, to which the mayor replied: "I will be damned if I will do it."

A fellow in the room named Dexter Elliott Chipps didn't say much, but he took it all in. He was in the lumber business and lived at Fort Worth's elegant Westbrook Hotel. Chipps was a large, mostly bald man, weighing about 230 pounds. Friends suggested that, but for the receding hairline, he looked a lot younger than his age. Born in Bedford, Virginia, in 1876 at the foot of the Blue Ridge Peaks of Otter, he had moved to Texas, apparently via Tennessee, in 1905 to start a lumber mill in Diboll, a small town in Angelina County built largely around an abundant supply of local pines for lumber.

Having made some money, he moved three years later to Fort Worth, where he made more money and soon took his place as a bit of a minor player in the emerging commercial life of Cowtown. He was a Shriner, a Mason, and a member of the best civic organizations in town, including the Fort Worth Club, where he regularly rubbed shoulders with the big boys, played poker, and took more than an occasional drink. He was also a member of the River Crest Country Club, where he would often play a round of golf with his friend H.C. Meacham.

These days he lived the life of a bachelor at the Westbrook, having been divorced from Mae, his wife of twenty years, in October 1925. They had a son, Dexter Jr., who was fourteen years old. Mother and son lived in the family home out on Lipscomb Street, but they all saw one another regularly. Some who knew Dexter and Mae believed that it was just a matter of time before they were man and wife once again.

Chipps and Meacham had been working closely together on a project for the Fort Worth Club. The mayor had been appointed to collect funds to have a portrait of Amon Carter, the driving force behind the club's new $1.5 million headquarters, commissioned for display in the building's lobby. Meacham, having reluctantly agreed to spearhead a fund-raising campaign for the portrait, quickly found himself not wanting to deal with the details. As he thought about someone to help, he decided to enlist the help of his friend D.E. Chipps.

It wasn't just that Meacham was a busy man with a department store to run while serving as the mayor of Fort Worth. Actually, under the new city management model, his mayoral role was largely symbolic and ceremonial. No, something else was at play. There had been a feud simmering for a while between Meacham and Carter, and the tension made fellow club members uncomfortable. Perhaps some had thought asking the mayor to head up the portrait fund-raising effort would help repair the relationship.

It is uncertain what caused the bad feelings between the newspaperman and the department store owner. Carter was known for his feuds, and he had them throughout his career. Meacham, on the other hand, avoided conflict. His sensitivity no doubt contributed to his ill health.

Some said Carter and Meacham fell out because they had bought a ranch together and had "quarreled over mineral rights." Another version of that story was that Meacham had never paid for his half of the ranch in the first place. There were whisperings that they had "argued over the favors of a woman," or "about the division of a case of gift liquor." One popular rumor was that Amon and H.C. had "disagreed over payment of a planeload of illegal liquor flown to Fort Worth from Mexico."

All that is really known is that before their relationship cooled, the pages of the *Fort Worth Star-Telegram* would carry "at least ten pages of advertising each week" for Meacham's Department Store. But by the time H.C. Meacham was campaigning for office, the paper "editorialized on the front page against his candidacy." Following the election, Meacham told his department store staff, "There will never be another ad in the *Star-Telegram* as long as I live."

Now he had to raise money so that a giant portrait of Carter could stare at him every time he entered the lobby of the Fort Worth Club. D.E. Chipps was more than happy to take some of the stress out of his friend's life. The two men had, therefore, been meeting on a daily basis, tracking the donations. Beyond that, with the mayor's wife taking time away from Texas, as was her habit during the hottest part of the summer, they would dine together often, either at one of the local restaurants or at Meacham's home at 1100 Elizabeth Boulevard. And there was always the chance for Chipps to report on his club work as they played golf at River Crest, now that the weather was warm.

As D.E. Chipps listened to Meacham that July night at the club, and as he saw how the group was receiving what his friend had to say about J. Frank Norris, Chipps began to seethe with anger. Although he had never met Norris, he knew enough about him, as did all the citizens of Fort Worth, to form a definite opinion about the man and his methods.

The meeting broke up with everyone even now further convinced that Norris was a toxin to the city. It was around this time that Chipps began to think about confronting the man he saw as a fraud. Perhaps he could teach the troublemaker a long-overdue lesson.

It was announced that Norris would speak at a vacant lot not far from Meacham's store the very next Sunday night, July 11. Having months before promised to perform an "operation on the city management," Norris finally got around to making good on the threat, beginning with an article he wrote for the July 9, 1926, issue of the *Searchlight* titled "The Meacham-Carr Graft on the Taxpayers of Fort Worth." In this stinging attack, Norris, equating the recent real estate transaction with graft, argued:

> The taxes are already exorbitant in Fort Worth and now it has been decreed to take $152,000.00 of the taxpayer's money and give to St. Ignatius Academy and Mr. Meacham's store. There can be no other interpretation. Let the citizens go and look at that alley and see the old, ramshackle building which it is proposed to pay three to four times its value. And then let the citizens see how the street is to run in order to catch the traffic coming north on Jennings Avenue, making an obtuse angle and turning said traffic into Mr. Meacham's store.

But the vitriolic preacher did not stop there. He insinuated that there had also been a misuse of city funds in the amount of thirty-five hundred dollars for a "grafted" trip Mayor Meacham had made to New York City. He then accused the mayor of having a bad attitude toward the churches of Fort Worth (presumably with the exception of the Catholic Church). He also went after O.E. Carr, telling readers that the city manager had, in previous jobs, profited by being "the main stockholder in a corporation whose chief business" was buying up properties that had gone into foreclosure for nonpayment of taxes. The preacher had been doing homework and digging up dirt.

Then he hinted at another bomb he would throw. Writing about Mayor Meacham, he referred to the fact that "he is good at figures as one $12,000 item to a former lady employee thoroughly attests, but the facts concerning this item will be brought out when the lid is taken off Mr. Meacham and his imported manager."

That *when the lid is taken off* phrase was one of the preacher's favorites, and he used it again that Friday evening when he spoke at the regular weekly meeting of the Ku Klux Klan in their auditorium on North Main Street. The event had been advertised in Klan circles for several days. He talked at length about the proposed purchase of the Catholic property by the City of Fort Worth. His audience drank in every word of the latest diatribe. It was a very friendly crowd. Local Klan Grand Dragon Lloyd P. Bloodworth introduced Norris to the crowd as his friend and pastor.

Norris also told the Klansman that Meacham had been up to something that very day. The preacher told the assembled they should come out to the church on Sunday morning when he planned to "take the lid off."

CHAPTER FIFTEEN

"Mr. Meacham's Record Is Well Known"

ON FRIDAY, JULY 9, H.C. Meacham was in his office at his department store when the store manager, Mr. L.B. Haughey, approached. He was clearly agitated about something. Haughey was relatively new to his post at Meacham's. Hired in the summer of 1925, Haughey brought twenty-six years of experience with him when he moved from Springfield, Ohio, where he had managed an upscale department store for Edward Wren and Company. Prior to that, Haughey had worked in Indianapolis, Pittsburgh, and Terre Haute, Indiana. The Fort Worth job was his first in the South. But the man from the North and Midwest was impressed with the city on the Trinity River. He noticed "a fine spirit of congeniality" in the town and was impressed, surprisingly so, that it was a place of what he called "unusual progressiveness." He quickly assimilated to Texas life, including affiliating with a local church.

But in matters of religion, L.B. Haughey found himself in a minority. He was a Roman Catholic in a city dominated by Protestants.

H.C. Meacham looked up from his desk and immediately asked Haughey what was wrong. The manager informed him that several young men were out in front of the store selling copies of Norris's paper, the *Searchlight*. This particular edition included the preacher's latest diatribe about Meacham and Carr. It also contained a teaser about that little "personal" problem Meacham had dealt with six years before: his affair with Julia Mock.

J. Frank Norris had printed several thousand copies of his paper that week, beyond the nearly fifty-five thousand paid circulation, for the express purpose of saturating the city and creating interest in his next Sunday pulpit exposé. He had mobilized a platoon of newsboys and instructed them to aggressively hawk the paper to anyone entering or exiting Meacham's Department Store. In fact, some of the enterprising young go-getters were actually *inside* the store.

Meacham was outraged. Never one for confrontation, in part due to his weak heart and chronically upset stomach, he felt the need to retaliate, but how? He needed to hit Norris and hit him hard in a way that wouldn't be expected. Then an idea came to him.

Meacham asked Haughey if any members of Norris's church worked at the store. The manager told his boss that he thought there were several, but he would look into it and get back to him quickly. He hurriedly conducted some research and reported back to Meacham that seven women and one man in the employ of Meacham's Department Store were known to be active members of First Baptist Church. The mayor then directed his store manager to give these eight workers an ultimatum: They could either quit the membership of their church or look for new jobs. Neither man seemed to be at all concerned that Haughey, a practicing Roman Catholic, was being tasked with firing Baptists. And these weren't your garden-variety Baptists; they were dyed-in-the-wool, fundamentalist, J. Frank Norris–idolizing Baptists.

One by one the store workers were called in. They were quizzed as to their church affiliation and level of involvement with Pastor Norris. And during the course of an hour or so, one man and five women chose to remain faithful to the church, no matter what. They were terminated on the spot. The other two women indicated that they could certainly find membership in another Baptist church. They were kept on the Meacham payroll.

As soon as J. Frank Norris heard about how some of his loyal church members were fired, solely on the grounds that they supported their pastor, he was almost gleeful. He knew he now had a fresh issue to exploit in the escalating conflict. And this one would be received with broad sympathy. For a sitting mayor to fire some faithful Baptists because of their church affiliation — well, Norris could hardly believe the opportunity that had been handed to him.

The firings quickly turned into a big story, and when the fact came out that the man the mayor had tasked to terminate the workers was a Roman Catholic in a city where the Ku Klux Klan had significant influence, all the necessary elements were in place for a political firestorm. All through the next day, Saturday, July 10, Norris did everything he could to spread the word that he would be speaking the following day at First Baptist

Church on the subject: "Six Members of First Baptist Church Fired By L.B. Haughey, Roman Catholic Manager of Meacham Dry Goods Company."

Meanwhile, at the mayor's store, Meacham and his manager Haughey tried to respond to the consequences of their colossal tactical blunder. "The telephone has been busy with persons asking if it is true that we have asked members of that organization to make a choice," Haughey informed his boss. "When told that it was, they have threatened to do everything to injure our business. We only reply that they may do that, but we will still retain our self-respect." At the heart of the Meacham position was the idea that anyone who believed what Norris was saying about the owner, their employer, could not "conscientiously wish to retain positions" with the store. The mayor himself declined to comment, suggesting that to do so would be "below the dignity of his office."

He also began to get very nervous.

Usually Norris delivered his more sensationalist sermons at the Sunday-evening service, but this time he was going to talk about the matter during the morning worship hour. It would also be broadcast live on the church's radio station, KFQB, and a network of affiliates all over the South. That Sunday, First Baptist Church would report a combined attendance exceeding fifteen thousand for all services. The *Searchlight* later reported that seventy-one people became new members of the church that day. Norris always emphasized additions to his church as evidence of divine favor.

J. Frank Norris turned the Sunday-morning service into a trial of sorts, interviewing the so-called Meacham Six who gave their jobs for their church and pastor. He had six chairs placed in a prominent place on the auditorium stage and invited the newly unemployed members to come up from the audience and join him. "Is Mr. Cecil Ellis present? Mrs. Cora Dobbs? Mrs. C.K. Baker? Miss Hyacinth Burns? Mrs. R.R. Crosson? Mrs. Dolly Boyles Shepherd?" One by one the six made their way to the front of the church, where the pastor directed them to the chairs.

Norris then admonished the congregation: "Now, I am not going to detain you unusually long, but maybe a little longer than usual this morning, so if you cannot stay until I pronounce the benediction, depart now." Then following a reading from the Old Testament book of Daniel, chosen to associate the six stalwart church members with the three Hebrew children, Shadrach, Meshach, and Abednego, who would not bow to pressure at great potential peril, he offered a long and pious prayer before beginning his attack on Mayor Meacham, City Manager Carr, and store manager Haughey.

"I am going to give you a testimony this morning that I would have not believed, an incident that I would not have believed could have occurred in this free land of ours." He then let the crowd know that they need not worry about catching every word, reminding them "this entire sermon will be printed in next week's *Searchlight!*"

Stenographer L.V. Evridge was in the front row, taking it all down.

After a few more introductory comments, delivered in a business-like and low-key manner, Norris asked Mr. Cecil Ellis to stand. At that, the massive overflow audience burst into applause. Norris said, "This young man is a member of the First Baptist Church. How old are you?"

"Twenty-three years old."

"How long have you been a member of the First Baptist Church?"

"Nine years."

At this point, several voices yelled: "Louder!! Louder!" Norris answered, "We will get it to you all right, so don't get impatient. You will hear more than you can take home!"

Turning back to Ellis, the pastor continued, "Where were you working up to a certain day last week?"

"At the H.C. Meacham Company."

"What position did you hold there?"

"In charge of the men's furnishings department."

"How long have you been working there?"

"Two years and a half."

"Tell this audience whether or not you were fired out of that store last week?"

"I was certainly fired." At this point he asked the preacher, "Do you want me to just tell the whole story?" Raising his voice, Norris replied, "Who called you up — who did it — what's his name?"

"Mr. L.B. Haughey, the manager of H.C. Meacham's store, called me to his office. I went up there, not knowing what he had in mind to say to me. When I entered his office he started in saying different things about Dr.

Norris, and said I would have to take my choice between the two and he asked me what my choice would be. I told him I would take Dr. Norris." The audience went wild, bursting into applause.

Mr. Ellis added: "He told me that I would have to resign, and I told him I wouldn't resign, but he could fire me, which he did."

For the next hour Norris kept the audience enthralled as he peppered questions at the six now-unemployed church members. Mrs. Dobbs indicated that the store manager advised her that there were other Baptist churches in town where she could transfer her membership, telling the audience, "I told him that the First Baptist was my choice." Mrs. Baker testified that she told Haughey, "I wouldn't give up my Sunday School class for any job." The others shared virtually the same account.

Following the testimonies, the preacher warmed to his theme, and with the audience hanging on every word he launched into another attack on city leaders: "I don't believe now in this city that is so overburdened with taxation — taxes so high that legitimate business is groaning under it, and so high it is a hard matter for the average homeowner to pay them — I don't believe that it is the proper thing for the gentleman — the imported manager — and Mr. Meacham, the mayor, and others that may join with them, to take $152,000 of the taxpayers money of Fort Worth and give it to St Ignatius Academy (a Roman Catholic School), and open an alley in order to benefit Mr. Meacham's business!" At this, the audience erupted in lengthy applause.

Norris pleaded to his congregation and the audience listening all over the South on the radio that these church members had been treated unjustly simply because of their pastor. Challenging Meacham and Haughey, "If I am the one they have it against, why don't they walk out like true, brave, Americans and settle the issue with me?"

Norris railed against the mayor of Fort Worth, calling him "un-American" and added "it violates every fundamental of freedom and free speech. It is cowardly, for it is the position of a powerful employer holding the big stick of a position over a breadwinner."

Earlier in the week Meacham had told a reporter that the idea of Norris's messages going out to thousands via the airwaves "worried him."

Norris referred to Meacham's published remark and reminded all listening to his voice that "this is going out, too." Then he shared some news: Just the night before, it was discovered that someone had been tampering with the church radio equipment. "I want to say that we have got guards on this thing night and day and orders to shoot to kill the first man that lays his hand on it." This warning was received with thunderous applause.

Later in his diatribe, Norris referenced a recently published photograph of the mayor with a local beauty pageant contestant. "The man who occupies the high position of mayor of the city of Fort Worth has no business having his picture taken with his arms around young women who are dressed in one-piece bathing suits." More applause. By modern standards the content of the photograph was rather tame. In fact, the swimsuits the young women wore would be standard apparel in Amish country these days, but Norris loved to exploit the modesty issue in the age of the flapper.

This moralistic, somewhat Victorian rebuke of Meacham was the perfect setup for Norris to play the other card he had been holding: Meacham's affair with Julia Mock. He told his audience, "Mr. Meacham's record is well known. Up there in Judge Bruce Young's court a few years ago, it is a matter of record that H.C. Meacham had to pay to one of his employees — a young lady — $12,500 and he gave the lawyers $10,000 besides to settle it."

Pausing for effect, he said: "My friends, I say to this great audience, it is a shame on the name of Fort Worth that a man of that kind should be mayor for one minute's time." The audience roared with applause. When the crowd finally quieted, Norris continued, "There is no dispute about it. It is a court record. And if he wasn't guilty as hell, why did he pay it?"

He summed up the issue and his feelings about it: "If he paid it, he isn't fit to be mayor of a hog pen." And to dig the knife in even farther, he reminded everyone that the mayor was "listening in to what I am saying this morning, and I am glad he is. I am not going to reflect on the mayor's character, for a man has got to have one before it can be reflected on."

H.C. Meacham *was* listening, as were many of his friends and supporters. In the wake of the broadcast, the mayor threatened to sue Norris for libel if he printed and distributed the "sermon" in the *Searchlight*. Norris would welcome such a suit and moved full speed ahead to put out the paper, planning again to have newsboys near the doors of Meacham's store the next Friday and Saturday.

Norris conducted another large service that evening, this one in the open air on a vacant lot at Lipscomb and Morphy Streets. It had been advertised as the meeting where Norris would give the record of the mayor and his "imported" city manager. A newspaper report suggested that more than twelve thousand were in the crowd. One man would later observe that he "had to park blocks away" and that city buses arrived every few minutes with more and more people who wanted to hear what Norris would have to say that night.

Norris rehearsed again the matter of his dispute with the city. And he intimated that the mayor himself was "as I am speaking — he is out here at Lake Worth, in a car, with another man's wife." Some time later, recalling his remarks that hot summer night, Norris told an associate, "You know what? That fellow was — sure enough — with that woman in his car out here at the lake. And he had his car radio on. And both of them heard me. And she jumped out of the car and fled, screaming through the thicket! And he was so scared he ran off in the car and left her!"

As Fort Worth went to work on Monday, July 12, the offices of the *Searchlight* and First Baptist Church were hives of activity as staff members went through the telegrams and messages that were coming in from radio listeners. People from all over Texas, Oklahoma, and throughout the South wrote in to express support for the preacher's latest crusade. Many of the testimonials found their way into the pages of the *Searchlight*. The Friday, July 16, edition promised to be a page-turner, complete with a transcript of Norris's anti-Meacham sermon and other things that might develop during the week.

Although he had played right into his ferocious adversary's hand, H.C. Meacham remained adamant, though a bit defensive, about the firing of some of his employees because of their affiliation with J. Frank Norris and First Baptist Church. He wrote on Tuesday, July 13, to Garfield Crawford, a friend who worked in the F&M Building, "Some of my friends have told me that I made a serious mistake in allowing to be discharged from this store several members of the First Baptist Church, and it may be that I was, but those who know me know that I could do no other thing and keep my own self-respect."

He suggested that he had only gotten involved in city politics and now served as mayor "at the solicitation of my friends" thinking that "I might be of service to the city that has been so kind to me." He also indicated that he expected a certain measure of criticism to come with such a position. But he felt the fact that Norris was putting "all this on the radio" crossed a line. He wished they could find "some way to shut this off and that for the good of the city." He thought it to be the most objectionable thing that a preacher should be able to denounce "city officials, members of the school board, and even a great religious organization" (a reference to St. Patrick's Church and St. Ignatius Academy). He hoped that "some day some way can be found to stop this."

CHAPTER SIXTEEN

"If You Do, I'll Kill You"

IN ADDITION TO catering to a steady stream of out-of-town guests, the elegant Westbrook rented rooms like apartments to a number of local citizens. A regular-sized room went for about forty dollars per month, and many residents split the cost as roommates. Dexter Elliott Chipps was one such resident. The Westbrook was his home.

Chipps entered the Westbrook lobby Saturday afternoon, July 17, 1926. As he walked toward the front desk, the lumberman's mood was noticeably foul, a marked change from the night before when he had a simply wonderful time on a date with his ex-wife, Mae. Though she had divorced him, largely over issues having to do with his drinking and womanizing, they remained close. Described as "a dark-haired, slender woman of fine dignity and gracious presence," and "exquisite as a lovely orchid," Mae had agreed to meet Dexter for dinner the night before. They talked long into the night, even nurturing a thought about getting back together. Their son, Dexter Jr., was fourteen.

Described as a "dark, handsome lad . . . a high-spirited, lovable young chap, of the sort who would always be popular," he very much needed "the firm hand of a father." Mae, however, was determined to proceed with caution.

D.E. Chipps had awakened early that Saturday, another seasonably hot, if overcast, summer day. He had to meet a contractor at his office a few blocks away, tend to some fund-raising business for the Amon Carter portrait project at the Fort Worth Club, and connect with H.C. at the store.

Maybe he could persuade Mae to catch a movie with him that night. Several were showing in town. The new Cecil B. DeMille picture *Silence* was at the Capital, a film about a petty crook about to be hanged for a crime he did not commit. If that was too serious for a date, perhaps they could see the new Gilda Gray movie called *Aloma of the South Seas* at the Palace;

word had it that the actress actually wore seaweeds in one scene. Or maybe they could catch *The Blind Goddess,* a story about a powerful politician who was murdered, possibly by his estranged wife.

A lot of local folks were planning to spend the afternoon out at the new Panther Park, a stadium built for the local Texas League baseball team. Mayor Meacham planned to be there. Fort Worth was a big baseball town and in love with their Panthers, or "Cats" as they were affectionately known. The new facility was the first in the league to be built with steel as well as wood. The Cats had won six straight Texas League titles but were struggling this season en route to what would be a disappointing third-place finish. There would be a large crowd this day, though, as the home team hosted the Waco Cubs.

Dexter Chipps, however, would not be attending the game. Earlier that afternoon, Meacham had called him through the hotel switchboard. The operator listened in and heard the mayor vent about the fact that J. Frank Norris's "damned *Searchlight*" was being sold in and around his store with its word-for-word transcript of Norris's rant from the Sunday before. The operator later recalled hearing Mr. Chipps offer to pay a visit to Norris, but he was discouraged by the mayor, who said, "No, you'd better come down here a moment."

En route to Meacham's store, Chipps had to stop by his office located in the Wheat Building at the corner of Main and Eighth Streets to meet a friend named Frank Conley. Conley was coming by to pick up some money Chipps owed him. After this, Chipps made his way over to Meacham's Department Store just a few blocks up Main Street at Twelfth. He noticed newsboys on just about every city street corner distributing Norris's latest *Searchlight*. Chipps was infuriated.

Entering the store, he made his way past sale tables where men's broad-cloth shirts were marked down to just $1.59 and women's shoes to less than $5 per pair. Business at the store had fallen off sharply during the week as the feud between Meacham and Norris escalated. Controversy may have been boosting the size of Norris's crowds, but it was depressing customer traffic at the store. Chipps took the elevator to the top floor, where Meacham had his private office.

As he entered Meacham's office, he noticed a copy of the *Searchlight* in his friend's hand. Meacham began a nervous and animated diatribe about Norris and how much harm he was doing — waving and shaking the newspaper as he spoke. Chipps did his best to change the subject. He did not like to see his good friend, with his poor health, so upset.

They moved on to Fort Worth Club fund-raising business, and Chipps fumbled for his reading glasses. He was holding a small package, something he had picked up along the way, and he set it down on the desk so he would be free to take up papers Meacham was handing to him. Meacham had a good idea what the package contained but ignored it. Chipps then found his spectacles in one of his pockets and put them on as he reviewed the material Meacham kept passing to him. At one point Meacham gave Chipps an envelope, and the lumberman put it in his pocket.

Meacham kept returning the focus to Norris. And as he vented, Chipps began to boil. The mayor later said that Chipps "had often talked to me about the way in which Norris spoke and wrote about me, and while in my office said something more to me about it," but Meacham could not "recall a single thing that might be interpreted as a sign that he intended to approach Norris" that particular day.

The mayor told his friend that he was going to see the Cats game and could be reached out at the stadium. As Chipps left the office, the two men shook hands; Meacham glanced at the clock on the wall and noted the time. It was now ten minutes before four o'clock.

Chipps walked briskly back to the Westbrook and approached the front desk to ask for the key to room 341. As the clerk handed it to him, he observed an "oblong package under his arm," and as was the case with H.C. Meacham, he was pretty sure he knew what it was. Those suspicions were confirmed when Chipps called down to the desk a few moments later, requesting that some ice be sent up to his room.

About five minutes later, Chipps rang the hotel's switchboard. Mrs. Fannie Greer answered. When not at her usual post routing telephone calls at the Westbrook, she spent a lot of time around First Baptist Church. She was a church member and loyal follower of J. Frank Norris. Mrs. Greer was also an accomplished eavesdropper and had handled the earlier call from Meacham to Chipps, as well as many other calls between the two friends over the past several days. Knowing full well about her pastor's quarrel with the mayor, she kept an ear on things, letting some of her friends in the church office know what was going on.

This time, however, Mr. Chipps did not want to be connected to Meacham's Department Store. Instead of Meacham, Chipps tersely instructed Mrs. Greer to connect him with First Baptist Church and the Reverend J. Frank Norris. Her curiosity fully aroused, Greer dialed the church, lingering on the line after the call was completed. She heard Chipps ask, "Is this Dr. Norris?"

"Yes, what do you want?" came the abrupt and staccato reply.

"Are you going to be in your office?"

"Well, I was just fixin' to go out."

"Well, will you be there in 30 minutes?"

"I'll be here two hours and 30 minutes, but who is this?"

"That doesn't make any difference. I want to see you."

J. Frank Norris then insisted on knowing the identity of the caller but was put off again: "It isn't any of your God damn business who this is, but I want to see you."

Then the caller identified himself, declaring, "This is Chipps."

Norris covered the receiver with one hand and urgently motioned to one of his staff stenographers with the whispered shout: "Get this down." About this time, Fannie Greer had to take another call, but within a few moments she plugged back into the potentially juicy conversation. At first Norris thought the man had called himself "Litts" or "Hitts" but quickly came to understand the man's name was "Chipps."

"Well, I'm coming up there," Chipps said.

With that, the call abruptly ended, and Norris looked over at Mr. L.H. Nutt, who was seated a few feet away. A lay leader in the Young People's Department of First Baptist Church, he had dropped by the church office, as was his Saturday habit, to confer with Norris about plans for the next day's church program. Norris asked Nutt, "Do you know Chipps?" After a moment's reflection, Nutt began to nod and replied, "I think he does business down at the bank." Though he committed a great deal of time to the work of his church, Nutt was employed as an auditor at Farmers & Mechanics Bank. He also sat on the church board of deacons. "A gray haired, almost bald man in his late forties," Nutt was highly regarded in the community as a man whose "business integrity" was reputed to be "unimpeachable." He and Norris soon changed subjects and began to talk about church matters.

Meanwhile, D.E. Chipps left his hotel room and soon exited the lobby onto Fourth Street. He turned right and began walking toward First Baptist. He crossed Houston Street and came next to the corner of Fourth and Throckmorton. He looked across at the church building and for a moment paused, trying to figure out how best to enter. There were several doors, and he was unfamiliar with the facility. He crossed over Throckmorton and climbed the stairs to the main doors of the church, trying to open them. They were locked. He walked back down the steps and looked down the block toward Third Street, where he saw some people and moved toward them.

About fifty feet from the entrance of the church office building, the door leading to Norris's office, Chipps stopped, unsure of exactly where to go. He saw a black man by the name of Balaam Shaw. Chipps asked Shaw where Norris was. Shaw had for years worked for First Baptist as a janitor or, as many called it back then, a porter. Because of the color of his skin, he was barred from church membership. This fact was scheduled to be, at least partly, remedied the very next day, as Pastor Norris had announced to readers of the *Searchlight* that Shaw "has joined a colored Baptist Church" and has made the "unique request that the pastor of the First Baptist Church baptize him." Norris added: "Notwithstanding the certain criticism that will come, the editor of this paper has agreed to baptize this colored janitor whose skin is as black as tar, but whose heart has been made white by the blood of the lamb."

Shaw pointed Chipps in the direction of a door leading to a stairway to the church offices in a building barely separated by a walkway from the church proper. Called the Sunday School Building, the four-story structure housed the offices of the *Searchlight* as well as Norris's study. Chipps came back a moment later with a confused look on his face and said, "I can't find that goddamned preacher and his goddamned office." At this point, a young man in a short-sleeved shirt indicated that he was going that way and that Chipps should follow him. Shaw grabbed his mop bucket and trailed behind both men up the stairs one flight to the office area. He was already a bit late to clean up the area, having been summoned earlier by the ever-demanding Miss Jane Hartwell.

When Chipps got to the top of the stairs, he went through a door into a reception area where several secretaries in the office pool were at work, even at this late hour on a Saturday afternoon. Then he entered a small anteroom, about twelve by eight feet in size. He made it to this point so swiftly that no one challenged him or asked to help him. But his presence and pace did not seem to be noticed. He said nothing until arriving at Norris's study just off the anteroom. Chipps entered the partially opened door without knocking and announced, "My name is Chipps."

Although he had phoned, Norris and Nutt were mildly surprised by his appearance, though not especially fearful. At any rate, they both knew that there were plenty of people nearby in case there was any trouble they couldn't handle. Norris drove himself hard and worked long hours, demanding the same commitment from his staff. And of course, Mr. Nutt was right there in the office seated in a wicker chair; any tussle would presumably be two against one.

The preacher's office was a rectangular room described as "pleasant but unostentatious." The floor was covered with a "taupe-colored Wilton rug," named for the city in southern England where these woven carpets were originally made. Several wall bookcases filled out the rest of the room. At the end of the room sat "a couple of wicker rockers" accompanied by a "long wicker sofa" on the left wall. Over against the right wall, right in the middle, sat Norris at his oak rolltop desk, which bore a sign that said: LIFE AINT IN HOLDING A GOOD HAND, BUT IN PLAYING A BAD HAND WELL. A picture of William Jennings Bryan hung on the wall directly above him. One visitor described the room as "quite comfortably full," adding that "another piece would make it crowded."

Nutt, who was seated along the right wall between Norris and the door, rose to his feet upon seeing Chipps and said to his preacher, "I know this man, I know him down at the bank." To which Chipps replied, "Yes, I know you."

They shook hands.

Chipps, continuing to address himself to the familiar Nutt, said, "I'm D.E. Chipps and I sell lumber. I sell lumber all over and lots of it." He then turned to J. Frank Norris, who was seated at his desk across the room, and said, "I've got something to say to you and I mean it. If you say anything more about my friends, I'm going to kill you."

Norris asked, "Who are your friends?"

"Meacham, Carr, Austin, and Roach," Chipps replied angrily as he clenched his fist.

The preacher looked over at Mr. Nutt and shrugged. "Who is Roach?" And the banker gave Norris a clueless look accompanied by a slight shrug.

Austin was one of the members of the city council and Roach was, apparently, a mispronounced reference to City Attorney Rouer.

"Dr. Norris has had men say these things to him before," Nutt replied, trying to distract Chipps and deflect his anger.

Norris then remarked to his irate visitor that he was going to continue his messages about the city administration regardless of what Chipps or anyone else thought, adding, "You come out and hear me."

This curious invitation further provoked Chipps, who replied, "If you do, I'll kill you."

Norris rose and told his visitor, "I don't want any trouble with you," adding with a dismissive gesture, "There's the door."

But Mr. Chipps didn't budge. Only after a second, then third such invitation to leave did the lumberman begin to exit the study, very slowly. As Chipps was leaving, Norris, instead of just letting the man go, and for reasons known only to him, said, "I repeat everything I have said."

What happened next would be examined, analyzed, sworn to, debated, and rehearsed again and again over the following weeks and months. Did Chipps move toward Norris? Did the preacher feel that his life was threatened?

What is certain is this: In the next few fateful seconds, at 4:40 PM on July 17, 1926, J. Frank Norris, the leading fundamentalist in the nation, heir to William Jennings Bryan himself, and with the portrait of Bryan looking on, fired three shots into the massive frame of Dexter Elliott Chipps. The wounded man staggered and fell to the floor in the rear corner opposite Norris's desk, blood spilling from his body and soaking into the loops and weaves of the Wilton rug.

CHAPTER SEVENTEEN

"Hello Chief, Let's Go"

AS DEXTER ELLIOTT CHIPPS fought for his life in the corner of J. Frank Norris's book-lined office, bleeding profusely from several gunshot wounds, the preacher, with cool detachment, handed the gun, a .38-caliber Smith & Wesson, to someone. He would never remember to whom. One of the bullets had entered Chipps's body, just under the heart. Another went into his breast. Yet another went through the fleshy part of his arm. That same bullet also entered his breast.

Norris, not even going near the dying man on his study floor, shouted, "Call an ambulance." He then quickly left the study. He would not reenter it until the next day. Incredibly, no one else in the office went near the dying man's body and not a single attempt was made to administer aid or even comfort Chipps in any way.

L.H. Nutt was in shock. He heard the command about calling an ambulance but later described himself as "flustered" while events unfolded. At first, he couldn't even think of the name of an ambulance company, and when he finally did he couldn't find the number. About this time he overheard secretary Jane Hartwell calling an ambulance from the other room. She had been in the large office area with the other secretaries when Chipps went in to see Norris. Usually the protective gatekeeper, she was away from her post near the study door at the crucial moment. Her biggest priority in the moments before the shooting had been to find a way to get Balaam Shaw, who had arrived with mop and pail, in to clean the pastor's study. In fact, seeing D.E. Chipps beginning to exit, she told Shaw, "Now's our chance." But seeing Chipps start back and turning, she threw up her hands in dismay and said to Balaam that they would have to wait. Then came the gunshots, and Norris's office had become a crime scene.

Norris went to another part of the suite of rooms and found a telephone. Miss Jane observed this from across the room and wondered why the preacher had not asked her to place the call for him, as was their custom, but then hearing him say "Sweetheart" as he began the conversation, she knew he was calling his wife, Lillian.

After telling his wife about what had happened, he instructed that no one should come downtown. He would be home later and explain everything in detail.

Several minutes went by and no ambulance arrived. Police officers, however, were on the scene within five minutes of the shooting. Upon arrival at Fourth and Throckmorton, it took them another couple of minutes to locate the office area. Chief of Police W.H. "Henry" Lee led a team of four other officers: C.D. Bush, C.R. Rabb, W.B. Hinkle, and A.L. Ford. Mr. Lee was a "tall, broad-shouldered, well built, middle aged, dark haired, and dark eyed" man, with a surprisingly kind face for "a man of his position."

When Norris saw Lee, he said, "Hello Chief, let's go." They walked down the stairs and out the door, with Norris turning left toward Third Street and the courthouse several blocks away on Weatherford Street, where he thought he would tell his story to District Attorney Robert K. Hangar, the son of longtime friend W.A. Hangar. "I'll walk to the courthouse and everything will be all right." Lee countered that they needed to go the police station first. He pointed Norris in the other direction, and they walked up Throckmorton toward Fourth near the main entrance to the church. A crowd had begun to gather, and Lee and Norris could hear the whispers as they made their way toward city hall at Throckmorton and Tenth Streets. But by the time they reached the next corner, a patrolman pulled up in a touring car. Norris and Lee climbed in and rode the rest of the way.

As they entered the ornate city hall building, a four-story structure built in 1893 and accented by a tall clock tower, the chief noticed that Norris was "just as cool as a cucumber," unusual for a man who had just shot someone. The eighteen-year homicide veteran didn't notice any real emotion on the preacher's part until the desk sergeant at the station, who didn't know the notoriously famous preacher, asked his name. The parson answered: "Rev. J. Frank Norris, Pastor of the First Baptist Church," after which "he kind of bit under his lip."

Back at the church the other officers went about their business of investigating what had happened. C.D. Bush, a city detective, asked, "Well, what is the trouble up here?" when he arrived at the scene, just about the time Norris was leaving with Chief Lee. He inquired as to where "the other party" was and Norris pointed toward the door of his study, which was about halfway open. By this time the rest of the responding officers had arrived, and Bush entered Norris's study. Officer Hinkle entered right behind him. They observed Chipps lying on "his right side, kind of on his hands, his hands kind of back under him." Bush also noted "blood was kind of just oozing just a little out of his mouth."

About this time they noticed that no ambulance had arrived, and Officer Hinkle left the room to call one; for some reason the call placed by Miss Jane Hartwell a few minutes earlier had not resulted in the dispatch of an ambulance. The policeman phoned Robertson and Mueller, which also owned a mortuary, and Mr. F.W. Spreen, who doubled as an ambulance driver and an undertaker, was dispatched to the scene at First Baptist Church. A "typical hard-boiled, but good natured" young man, Spreen had the reputation of being "the fastest ambulance driver in that city." He raced toward Fourth and Throckmorton.

While Hinkle was placing his call, Bush searched the dying man's pockets. He found two one-dollar bills, a bloodstained envelope — the one Chipps had received from Mayor Meacham — a cigarette holder, and a tin of Prince Albert tobacco. Bush later recalled the cigarette holder as "about four inches long and couldn't weigh very much."

When the ambulance arrived, Spreen raced up the stairs to the office area, stretcher in tow. He noted that Chipps was still barely alive, but as he moved him on to the stretcher he was sure the lumberman exhaled for the last time. With the help of one of the police officers on the scene and with City Detective Bush watching from a few feet away, Spreen worked quickly to move the mortally wounded man from the scene. Bush, along with Officer Rabb, moved to the head of the stairs and watched Spreen and his helper make their way down and out to the street. Very quickly the stretcher was secured and the ambulance departed for the hospital.

By this time the crowd gathering outside had grown significantly. Directly across the street from the stairway to Norris's office, the newly expanded J.C. Penney Company store was a beehive of activity. For some months crews had been at work renovating the commercial building, owned by First Baptist Church. The store had been advertising its "Grand Opening of Our New Store" (meaning the new section on the church property) for Friday and Saturday, July 16 and 17, and was winding up a very successful two days of business. Store manager Garland H. Kanady was excited about the expansion and the grand opening festivities, which had included an "open house Friday evening from 6 to 10 PM."

For several days businesses in the community had been running ads in the newspapers congratulating the store for the new opening. Among the ads was one featuring a large picture of J. Frank Norris with the words: "The largest Sunday School in the world and the largest Young People's Department in the world, both of the First Baptist Church, welcome the new store of the J.C. Penney Company — a member of the largest chain of department stores in the world, as our downstairs section. We're glad to have you with us." Penney's had sponsored the radio program that aired July 15 at 8:45 PM on KFQB, Norris's radio station.

The new entrance across from Norris's offices featured window displays of various items from the ladies' department and shoe department, including hats, shoes, and even lingerie — the departments immediately inside that entrance. Shoppers gathered there Saturday afternoon at the start of the five o'clock hour all had their eyes fixed on the scene unfolding across the street at First Baptist Church. The road space between the store and the church office building was choked with police vehicles, an ambulance, and hundreds of bystanders trying to catch a glimpse or glean a morsel of information about what was happening.

CHAPTER EIGHTEEN

"Extra, Extra, Read All About It!"

AS THE POLICEMEN began taking statements from those inside the offices, Officer A.L. Ford approached Miss Jane and inquired as to the whereabouts of the weapon Norris had used. Since the shots were fired, she had been doing her best to keep the office girls "quiet and in their places during the excitement." Instead of volunteering the weapon immediately, Miss Jane asked respectfully, "Are you an officer?" When satisfied that Ford was indeed with the department, she quietly led the officer back into Norris's study and to his rolltop desk. She opened a drawer and pointed at the gun partially covered by a handkerchief. However, there were no shells found, empty or otherwise, and incredibly "no point was made of their absence."

Meanwhile, Fred Spreen's ambulance had arrived at the St. Joseph Infirmary, the city's oldest hospital, which was owned and operated by the Roman Catholic diocese. Spreen remained there, however, only briefly. After examining the body on the stretcher, the doctor on duty, a man named J.A. Goldberg, pronounced Dexter Elliott Chipps dead. Spreen, now assisted by a man named Carmichael, loaded the body back into the ambulance and drove over to the Robertson and Mueller mortuary. O.W. Phillips was waiting there, along with Judge Dave Shannon, a justice of the peace.

Phillips was "a tall, lean, matter-of-fact man" who had been an embalmer for many years. He made a thorough examination of the body, carefully studying each wound. He could not reach a conclusion as to which of the wounds caused the death of D.E. Chipps. In fact, any of the three could have been fatal.

As Phillips attended to Chipps's body, others began to arrive, including, notably, Mayor Meacham. He had received word of the shooting while watching the baseball game at Panther Park. The news quickly rippled through the stands, and attention shifted from the field to the mayor as

Meacham quickly left his seat. By this time his friend Dexter had been pronounced dead at the hospital, so the mayor made his way with a small entourage to the mortuary. When he saw the lifeless body of his fallen friend, the mayor became emotional, almost inconsolably so. "Oh Chipps, poor old Chipps," he sobbed. As he wept, he remarked in the hearing of everyone present, but to no one in particular, that he feared Chipps had lost his life because he was trying to defend him.

As those assembled watched the mortician examine Chipps's body, someone brought word that the dead man's funeral, with full Masonic rites at graveside, was already being planned for less than twenty-four hours later in the mortuary's chapel.

All the while, city newspapers were working feverishly to capitalize on the story with special extra editions. M.R. Toomer, editor of the *Fort Worth Press,* had been typing a letter in his office at Fifth and Jones Streets when he glanced at the clock and noted that it was a few minutes before five o'clock. He looked away from what he was writing, lost in thought, and observed that, "across the building folks were closing up the business of the day." A ringing telephone across the way in his office jarred him, and he made his way to it after a couple of rings.

"Press?" a voice on the other end of the line asked.

"Yes."

"There has been a killing at 404 Throckmorton."

"All right, and who is this calling?"

"This is the police."

Toomer placed the phone on its cradle and walked over to the circulation department. He announced that there had been a killing a few blocks away and speculated that it "might be good for an extra." Pete Hamilton, the newspaper's business manager, overheard the conversation and shouted, "I'll go over there. I'll phone back as quickly as I can." Toomer noted that it was unusual for Hamilton to work as a reporter but dispatched him nonetheless. Though the intersection of Fourth and Throckmorton was not too far away, the significance of the address hadn't registered with Toomer. A few minutes later Hamilton called back and spoke excitedly. At first, the editor thought his business-manager-turned-reporter said "Blank Burris" had shot a man.

This made no sense, so Toomer asked, "Who?"

Hamilton replied clearly, "J. Frank Norris."

The news made the editor "jump." And then as he thought more about it, he declared, "It has happened."

Toomer sprang into action and directed all those around him in the effort to put out an extra as quickly as possible. Before the night was over the *Press* would publish two printings. Its newsboys sold more than ten thousand copies in just a few hours at one cent each. People were devouring the story.

Over at the *Fort Worth Star-Telegram,* the city's much larger newspaper, things were much the same, as people scurried to get the details into print.

Having worked with lightning speed to publish special editions, the Fort Worth newspapers mobilized their mighty armies of newsboys and sent them out to every nook, cranny, and street corner in Fort Worth.

Though the time would come when the running of special editions of a paper to cover breaking news would give way to radio, then television as media for on-demand information, the newsboys — "a motley bunch, mostly poor, life-hardened, wise, and young, playing a hardscrabble game of survival on the pavement" — still used the famous cry heard in Pat O'Brien movies: "Extra, Extra, read all about it, D.E. Chipps, lumberman, slain by J. Frank Norris."

After booking him for murder at the police station, Chief Lee escorted Norris to the office of District Attorney Hangar at the Tarrant County Courthouse. They drove past First Baptist, where a crowd still lingered, and toward the pink Texas granite building on Weatherford Street. L.H. Nutt, who had been questioned by officers back at the church office, was already at the DA's office. Norris gave his statement to Hangar, and Nutt corroborated it with his own, quoting Chipps as saying "I am going to kill you." Norris was charged with murder. Bail was set at ten thousand dollars.

As Norris and Nutt gave their respective statements to Hangar, and as the news of the slaying swept through the city, a crowd began to gather at the courthouse, including a great number of First Baptist Church members. Thirty men in the crowd came forward voluntarily to sign the bond so that their pastor could be released. Before leaving the courthouse, Norris met with an informal caucus of church members, including elements of the

Finance Committee and board of trustees. By this time a dark mood had replaced Norris's calm, and he was described as "sick, disappointed, and weeping." He once again rehearsed the story, telling them "he had done a thing he never thought he would be called upon to do." He also on the spot submitted his pastoral resignation. The group refused the resignation, and it was shortly thereafter announced that he would fill the pulpit the following day — in less than eighteen hours.

Norris left the courthouse well after dark and returned to the safe haven of his home at 3213 Edgevale Street. The Norris family lived just outside Fort Worth on "a beautiful rolling twenty-five-acre tract." There he would gather his loved ones and await what he called "the demand of the pursuing Sunday." He was especially concerned about his daughter, a college graduate — soon to be married — who still lived at home. She would be particularly distraught. She had long feared that her daddy might become involved in something violent "because of his many enemies." But when he got home, young Lillian and her mother for whom she was named felt "overwhelming gratitude for his safety."

Not long after Norris arrived at his home, L.A. Wilke, a reporter from the *Fort Worth Press,* knocked on the door. He was invited in and talked with the preacher for two hours, with Norris telling the journalist that he was not "disturbed" over what the outcome would be. "I had to shoot him because I feared he was going to kill me." Wilke noted that Norris "talked as evenly of the killing, or probably more so, that I ever did over the first wild turkey I had killed."

As they concluded the interview in Norris's living room, the preacher agreed to talk to him again the next day — after morning church. They would meet in the very room where Norris had killed Chipps.

CHAPTER NINETEEN

"God Works His Will in Unusual Ways"

DOUBTLESS MANY FORT WORTH citizens had difficulty sleeping that night. The news about what had happened at Fourth and Throckmorton had shaken the city. J. Frank Norris had always been a polarizing figure, but those who disapproved of him tried largely to ignore the preacher as more of a nuisance than any real threat to public order. But a shooting of someone in his church office was something else entirely. As the first streaks of dawn crept into the eastern sky that Sunday morning, some who had never paid that much attention to Norris or First Baptist Church contemplated whether or not to join the inevitable throng of curiosity seekers downtown later that morning. Rumor had it that the preacher, though charged with cold-blooded murder, was actually going to preach a sermon at his church during the eleven o'clock hour, the time that is held to be nearly sacred in church communities. Everyone knew Norris had a lot of nerve. But this was surprising, even for him.

The story of J. Frank Norris killing D.E. Chipps had not only captured the attention of Cowtown but also made its way across the nation via the national wire services, into countless Sunday-morning newspapers in cities and towns, and onto the front doorsteps of American homes.

News was able to travel quite fast by 1926. The Scopes trial in Tennessee a year before had demonstrated what a media circus looked like. Wire services such as the Associated Press (AP) had taken advantage of what was regularly touted to be "the swift march of mechanical progress" in their efforts to disseminate news from coast to coast, and beyond. It was becoming a time of high-speed communication made possible by technical advances that "had given both telegraph and cable lines higher standards of reliability and efficiency."

Familiar nicknames for the decade of the 1920s included the Roaring Twenties and the Jazz Age, but it was also known then as the "Age of

Ballyhoo," where "new journalistic techniques demonstrated the power of the media to rivet popular attention." The nation moved rapidly from obsession to obsession, with famous golfers, boxers, movie stars, and even stories of murder. One "trivial person or episode" could become, in the media environment of the period, "an accidental hero" — or villain.

There were more than two thousand "daily" newspapers in America at the time. This figure did not include weekly tabloids (such as Norris's *Searchlight*) or monthly publications. About forty million newspapers reached the public at the rate of one copy "for every two literate persons over the age of ten" in the nation. And sensational stories sold papers.

This was also the age of tabloid journalism, something J. Frank Norris knew all about. He understood its popularity and power and how to exploit both. But even such a publicity seeker as the Fort Worth pastor could not have imagined what was happening overnight in the newsrooms and presses of the country. A preacher shooting an unarmed man in a church office was a headline that wrote itself. And tabloids such as the New York *Daily News,* then with a daily circulation of over a million copies after just a little more than five years in business, welcomed each detail of the sensational story coming in over the wire from Fort Worth, Texas. *The New York Times* had the story on page one, with the headline: "Texas Minister Kills Man in Church" and reminded its readers of Norris's various pulpit activities during his previous visits to the city. But it was in the smaller towns of America, places where fundamentalism had flourished and had more of a cultural foothold, that the news in the Sunday-morning paper had the most powerful and unsettling effect. The headlines told the story:
"Fort Worth Minister Kills Man: Well Known Pastor Gives $10,000 Bond
    Following Shooting" — *Galveston (Texas) Daily News*
"Critic Killed by Texas Minister After Quarrel" — *Fresno (California) Bee*
"Lumberman Is Fatally Shot in Baptist Church by Its Pastor" — *Kingsport
    (Tennessee) Times*
"Pastor Shoots Rich Texan" — *Ludington (Michigan) Sunday Morning News*
Virtually every Sunday newspaper in the United States carried the story.

As the overflow crowd gathered at First Baptist later that morning, faithful church members had to wonder how the previous afternoon's events would influence their service. Rites of baptism and communion were on the schedule. The fact that a Negro was to be baptized that morning had electrified the congregants. It was certainly out of the ordinary, especially considering the church's long-standing, if informal, relationship with the Ku Klux Klan, and the fact that the local Grand Dragon himself, the Reverend Lloyd P. Bloodworth, was a church member. The communion service, or as Baptists preferred to call it, the Lord's Supper, had been held over from the previous Sunday, as Norris simply had run out of time with his public interview of the church members fired from Meacham's store. Would it be postponed again? And if not, what would be made of the spectacle of a church participating in the most solemn of religious rituals, led by a minister who had just hours before shot an unarmed man to death not more than a hundred feet from where he would officiate the ritual? Norris had a loyal following, but certainly fidelity to this preacher was going to be tested.

Pastor and Mrs. Norris taught their massive Sunday school classes at ten o'clock. The ladies in Lillian's class presented her a small bunch of flowers before she gave a lecture on the trial and crucifixion of Jesus. Using what was described as "stoic poise," she guided the assembled women through a Bible study drawn from the Gospel According to Matthew, while some in the room "daubed their handkerchiefs to their eyes." Coming to the part of the story where Christ stood before Pontius Pilate, Mrs. Norris reminded her class, "We cannot wash our hands of questions and problems." She even oddly speculated about Christ's betrayer, Judas Iscariot, "I got the idea somewhere — perhaps from intuition — that Judas did not really believe Jesus would be condemned when he betrayed him." She added, "Judas had the grace — say that reservedly — to go out and hang himself." As she prepared to dismiss the class she referred to her husband's sermon of a week before, the one dealing with the church members fired from the store, as "one to always be remembered."

By the time the eleven o'clock morning service started, every seat in the vast auditorium was filled, with many standing and several hundred outside. The crowd listened and joined in as a mammoth choir sang hymn after hymn, accompanied by two pianos and several tag-team pianists furnishing the music. Fort Worth Symphony Orchestra conductor Brooks Morris led the chorus as usual. Cynics saw the music building to crescendo as an exercise where Norris's "minions have gathered about their shepherd in mesmerized faith," with "psychologically caressed" pianos furnishing "additional emotion."

As Norris rose to speak, pausing for effect, clearing his voice, arranging his notes on the pulpit, members held their breath awaiting the message from the messenger; something to help them understand it all. But if they came expecting to hear a detailed explanation or defense by the preacher, they were disappointed. They also very quickly noted that the pastor would not be delivering his sermon with his usual animation. Instead, "The discourse was delivered in a monotone, without the characteristic fire."

After what seemed to be an inordinately long period of silence, the only sound in the room being the cumulative noise of several thousand hand-held fans waving in rhythm on the already hot day, Norris began with an awkwardly long sentence: "I invite your attention this morning briefly to one of the great mountain peaks of scripture that is found from the first word of Genesis to the last 'Amen' of Revelation, a chapter as found in the book of Romans, the eighth, the depths of which we cannot fathom, the heights of which we cannot scale, the riches of which we will never know this side of the glory world."

What followed for the next several minutes was a methodical, and decidedly unemotional, exposition of his chosen text, starting with a declaration of "no condemnation" for the Christian and building to verse 28 and the point of his message for the day: "And we know that all things work together for good to them that love God and are the called according to His purpose." Then beyond, to its climax with language promising that God's children are "more than conquerors" and will be ultimately victorious in life and death.

As an American flag "hung motionless in the sultry atmosphere," and as Norris, himself feeling the heat, "used a large purple-edged pocket handkerchief" to wipe his brow periodically, the preacher stood virtually "motionless with his hands at his back." The message was a comparatively brief one, and following it Norris led the congregation in communion as several dozen laymen distributed bread and grape juice throughout the auditorium.

As the service drew to a close, Norris, while not mentioning the shooting specifically, "made a declaration of unshaken faith" and "asked the prayers of the congregation and asserted that 'this begins a new day.'" Then he did what he always did at the end of a service. He called for converts. On a typical Sunday anywhere from twenty-five to fifty people would "come forward" to profess faith or join the church membership. This day, however, must have given Norris pause, because only "two men and three women" answered his call. The preacher even felt the need to comment on the small response as if sensitive to the criticism that his antics had finally hurt him where it counted most. Describing so few supplicants as "a little unusual," the preacher put the best face he could on it, saying, "But the unusual is the expected around the First Baptist Church. God works His will in unusual ways. My faith is stronger today in the living faith of the living God than ever before."

Norris stepped back from the pulpit, and an associate made several announcements to the church, including that the promised baptism of Balaam Shaw was being postponed due to the "already heavy strain on the pastor." It was also announced that the church and Dr. Norris had received many telegrams of support "from admirers and sympathizers over the country." Of special note were messages from fundamentalist leader W.B. Riley of Minneapolis, Minnesota, and prominent Fort Worth attorney Marvin Simpson, who was vacationing in Los Angeles. He "offered his services to Norris, agreeing to return at once to defend him." It was also announced that Norris would speak that night, as was his custom during the summer months, in an outdoor meeting at 2008 Hemphill Street. Then, after the benediction, hundreds of members and friends swarmed the platform and approached Norris to shake his hand.

CHAPTER TWENTY

"If You Can Keep Your Head When All About You Are Losing Theirs"

WATCHING THE ENTIRE SERVICE that morning from his perch in the church balcony was *Fort Worth Press* reporter L.A. Wilke, who had just hours before sat in J. Frank Norris's living room talking with the preacher about the killing of Dexter Elliott Chipps. He had been promised a follow-up interview and had not yet filed his story, hoping for more exclusive time with the notorious preacher. As he watched Dr. Norris go through his ministerial motions, he pondered the questions he was going to ask. During the communion time, knowing that the service would soon be over, he slipped quietly from his pew and made his way down the stairs and outside to the sidewalk. He was supposed to meet Norris in the very study where the shooting had taken place, and he walked down the block toward the entrance to the office building. He self-consciously smoked a cigarette, then another, watching all the while for indications that the service had been dismissed. Norris would not approve of the smoking.

As the crowd began to flood out onto the sidewalk, Wilke made his way up the stairs to the second floor of the building to await Norris, who would likely emerge from a back entrance. As he stood in the open area, he looked into the anteroom and saw a small spot; a stain of sorts that had been cleaned up. Blood?

After a few minutes Miss Jane Hartwell appeared and told the reporter that the preacher would be over shortly and had not forgotten about the appointment. Eventually, Norris arrived and invited Wilke to follow him as he opened the door to his study. For the next hour the reporter and the preacher had a conversation about what had taken place in that very room slightly less than twenty-four hours earlier. As they sat down, Norris at his desk and Wilke in a wicker rocker nearby, the reporter surveyed the room noticing pictures of the preacher's family on the wall, as well as the large portrait of William Jennings Bryan hanging directly over the desk. He also saw something else hanging on the wall; some kind of poem probably, he thought. "I am not worried over the court end of it. The only thing I am worried about is the effect it might have on the church," the preacher asserted. Norris was no doubt more than a little disturbed by the fact that on this day above all others, when so much national attention was focused on him and the church, he could only muster five paltry converts. But the preacher quickly caught and corrected himself before the reporter, ever conscious of appearances, seeming to reverse himself in midthought: "Whatever fear I may have had Saturday night about the welfare of my church is gone now."

Wilke listened as the preacher talked about receiving "hundreds of telegrams from all over the country." His telephone, he said, had not stopped ringing, adding "I think the congregation showed it was still with me and believed in me." It was, in his thinking, all about him. Wilke drew out of Norris that the gun "was the same one which Norris had used several years ago in a difficulty with Bob Poe, constable, who was slain last December in a fight with Manuel Carson, Riverside." A few years before, Robert "Bob" Franklin Poe, a Tarrant County constable who died in the line of duty at the end of 1925, had taken issue with J. Frank Norris, who had counseled his wife. Poe, so the story went, "had not cared for the advice" the preacher had given to Mrs. Poe and one day took a swing at him on the street. Norris reportedly "pulled out a gun and marched Poe at the end of it down the street and into his church study." Soon the angry husband cooled off and "mutual explanations were offered." The story became well known throughout Fort Worth.

As Wilke pressed Norris about the gun, the preacher said that when the incident happened with Bob Poe, "he had been wearing it (the gun) at the time because of threats made on his life." "The church night watchman," though, "had been using the gun of late," leaving it in the preacher's desk drawer every morning after his shift was over. Guiding the conversation back to the shooting of Chipps, Wilke asked Norris about the ammunition in the gun. J. Frank replied: "I don't know how many cartridges were in it or how many times I shot." The preacher opened the desk drawer to show that there was no gun there. He then paused and reflected, "Lots of people will say I am cold-blooded, but they can't know what is in my soul. I don't claim to be a superman, but I am not a slinking coward, and when it becomes necessary for me to defend my life, I will."

As the hour-long interview drew to a close, the journalist looked over at the framed words. Was it a poem? he asked. Norris paused and began quoting the words from memory, written years before by Rudyard Kipling: "If you can keep your head when all about you are losing theirs." He listened as J. Frank Norris quoted the entire piece from memory to conclude the interview.

The preacher clearly felt comfortable with L.A. Wilke and told his guest that his door would always be open to him if he had any further questions.

Meanwhile, at the Robertson-Mueller Chapel, where D.E. Chipps's body had been prepared for funeral and burial, extra chairs were being put down for the overflow crowd expected that Sunday afternoon at four o'clock. Dr. J.K. Thompson, pastor of Fort Worth's First Presbyterian Church, had been asked to officiate. The list of pallbearers and honorary pallbearers who would be part of the ceremony had reached twenty: six active attendants and fourteen honorary escorts. The list was a who's who of local leaders, including Mayor H.C. Meacham, City Manager O.E. Carr, and *Fort Worth Star-Telegram* owner Amon G. Carter.

As J. Frank Norris sat in his comfortable house that afternoon, trying to nap in his easy chair, resting so he could be in top form that evening during the open-air service, a somber crowd gathered in the flower-adorned funeral chapel back in town. Last to arrive was Mae Chipps, widow of Dexter, who just two days before had been talking to her husband about reconciling, even marrying again. She was escorted down the aisle to her front-row seat on the arms of her brother, Jack Murphy, and a close family friend named W.D. Caldwell. Her fourteen-year-old son did not attend.

The service was short, yet emotional. Pastor Thompson talked about Chipps's "untimely death," though avoiding specific references to how he had died. He called on all those in attendance to "prepare for the inevitable call." Mayor Meacham wept openly at several points. When the service ended, and as the funeral cortege organized itself and made its way toward Greenwood Memorial Cemetery, the vehicles in the procession ran a gauntlet of "curious rubbernecks." Upon arrival at graveside, last rites were conducted by members of the Masonic Lodge number 148. Then D.E. Chipps was laid to rest long before sunset on the day after his tragic death.

And while the sun still lingered in the west Texas sky, a crowd began to migrate toward a large vacant lot on Hemphill Street for the 8:00 PM service sponsored by J. Frank Norris and First Baptist Church. On another lot not far from where the service would be held "an enterprising youngster had opened a parking ground in anticipation of the Sunday night jam." It was quickly filled, and people were fighting for parking spots for five and six blocks around the site of the service.

As he rose to speak in the evening air, J. Frank Norris seemed to have rebounded and "was in his usual sprightly mood." He announced his text from the first chapter of the Acts of the Apostles and preached on the second coming of Christ. At the conclusion of the message, "thousands filed by the rostrum to shake the pastor's hand." As the crowd dispersed late that night, J. Frank Norris made his way home, physically and emotionally exhausted.

CHAPTER TWENTY-ONE

"All the Symptoms of a Paranoiac"

MONDAY, JULY 19, the morning newspapers again had the Norris story splashed all over their front pages, and several pages deep. There were moment-by-moment accounts of the shooting and numerous editorials. The *Fort Worth Press* featured an opinion piece by editor Toomer on its front page:

> Compassion has never been a part of J. Frank Norris' make up. He has pretty generally struck out at any opposition that has arisen against him. And it is generally understood that he has never asked for any quarter, and has never offered any.
>
> In a controversy recently he declared he has "a pulpit, a news-paper, and a radio" and when the weather got a bit cooler he would use them all. While the denouement of tragedy has come to his experience rather suddenly, it is not a thing unexpected, either by Norris or by any other observer.
>
> This experience ought to be a profound lesson to him, and it ought to cause a change in his methods. He would be of no less service to his church if he threw away his gun and became more continually a preacher and less a fighter.
>
> He would be of infinitely greater service to his people if he would forget his continual personal bickering and approach more nearly "that mind which is in Christ Jesus" the example which I am sure it should be any man's greatest desire to emulate.

Having been arrested and arraigned on the charge of murder in the killing of D.E. Chipps, Norris now found his future in the hands of the current Tarrant County grand jury. And the list of names of the men on the current grand jury included some who had been named in news accounts of Chipps's funeral. Among the sixteen men listed for the grand jury were three who had served as honorary pallbearers: Al Donovan, W.T. Fry, and W.B. Ellison.

District Attorney Robert Hangar was at work early that Monday, having already met with some of his assistants the day before. He was aware of the potential perils of dealing with a matter involving J. Frank Norris. He had known Dr. Norris for many years and had observed him up close by virtue of the warm friendship the preacher and his father, W.A. Hangar, shared. He also knew that there was a great possibility the investigation and trial would bring up issues relating to the Ku Klux Klan — a potential problem for any DA, but particularly one whose own dad had been a prominent member of the order.

Very quickly, Hangar's staff developed a list of fourteen witnesses who would be the first brought before the grand jury during its investigation. The probe, it was announced, would begin the next day, Tuesday the twentieth. Among the witnesses to be initially called would be L.H. Nutt, the only known eyewitness to the shooting; Miss Jane Hartwell; Mrs. R. Bonna Ridgeway, advertising solicitor for the *Searchlight;* Karl Crowley, attorney and manager of the Lynch Davidson gubernatorial campaign in Fort Worth; as well as the men who responded to the call when Chipps was shot: Officers Lee, Hinkle, Bush, Ford, and Robb.

Passions ran high, and rumors were rampant. One version had it that a "mystery man" had been present at the scene, possibly in the company of Chipps. Norris's forces spread the story in their effort to reinforce the idea of a conspiracy against their controversial preacher. One of the witnesses appearing before the grand jury reported having seen such a man.

Otis Sullivant, a reporter for the *Fort Worth Press,* told his readers, "Police and county officers were searching Monday for the 'mystery man' who was with D.E. Chipps, wholesale lumberman, when Chipps was shot and killed by Dr. J. Frank Norris." He went on to indicate that DA Hangar "received a message over the telephone Monday morning, which probably would lead to the identity of the man." Norris said he saw the man, referring to him as "one of the conspirators to take his life." The preacher indicated that he witnessed the man "just outside the door of his study at the time of the shooting." Sullivant added that Hangar had said "one clue the officers were tracing down indicated that the 'mystery man' was a member of the church who merely directed Chipps to the study." He also reported that a cryptic telephone call had been received at the Fort Worth Club after the killing. He indicated, "The owner of that voice is believed to have been Chipps's companion." Of course, Chipps had been a member of the prestigious club, so news like this further fed Norris's sense of paranoia.

The first mention of a so-called mystery man had actually been made by Norris's associate R.B. Ridgeway. He had been sitting in an automobile on Throckmorton Street just outside the church offices waiting for his wife, who worked for the *Searchlight,* to get off work. He saw Chipps approach "with a smaller man." They stopped near his car, and Ridgeway overheard Chipps say to his companion, "How in the hell will I know him?"

Meanwhile, J. Frank Norris announced that he was planning to keep his long-scheduled speaking engagement at New York City's First Baptist Church on Seventy-ninth Street in Manhattan, led by his friend the Reverend I.M. Haldeman. His office also shared details of messages of support coming in from around the country. They were words of encouragement from, for example, the Reverend Dr. Mark Matthews, pastor of Seattle's First Presbyterian Church and moderator of the Presbyterian General Assembly, who wired: "My Dear Brother: I have just noticed from the dispatches your sorrow. You have my profound sympathy, confidence and encouragement. God bless you and bring you unscathed and in every particular vindicated. We are praying for you." The leaders of the fundamentalist movement, across denominational lines, initially stood with Norris publicly, regardless of whatever personal doubts or concerns they may have had.

Norris failed to take into consideration, however, that he was only hearing from those friends and colleagues who felt inclined to be supportive. Many did not. The leaders of New York's First Baptist Church felt pressure from the newspapers in the big city, not to mention members of the congregation itself, to cancel Norris's scheduled appearance. Church officials issued a statement that Monday afternoon saying: "If the facts are as reported, and Dr. Norris doesn't cancel the engagement, he will be asked to do so."

Norris turned the rejection by the Manhattan church into an opportunity to announce a new venture. At the regularly scheduled weekly workers meeting conducted every Tuesday at noon, it was announced that "all previous engagements" had been canceled and Norris was going to spend the next several weeks conducting meetings throughout Tarrant County. His stated goal was to "devote his entire energies to the giving of the whole gospel of redemption," but the more skeptical citizens saw it as an exercise in public relations in advance of an almost certain indictment and trial.

Norris was going to do his best to influence Fort Worth residents, some of whom would sit on a jury in judgment of the preacher. He didn't actually appear himself at the Tuesday meeting but rather had his publicity director, J.J. Mickle, read a letter from him — just one more example of the preacher's flair for drama. The afternoon before, Mickle had issued a statement saying there was "a diabolical conspiracy" to kill the preacher and promising that "evidence would be offered by unimpeachable witnesses."

The letter, like so many others written by Norris for public consumption, was saturated with lengthy passages of scripture, complete with pious pronouncements. He wrote: "I never thought it possible to witness on this earth such unity of spirit, such loyalty and devotion to a great cause, and such heroic courage as characterizes now the First Baptist Church." He referred indirectly to the Chipps story: "Because of the new and strange situation presented, I am canceling all out of the city engagements, for some time ahead." He pledged full use of "the radio" and "the printed page of the *Searchlight*" in this campaign. Though his stated goal was to promote the ministry, the effort, like almost everything Norris did, was about him.

As clergymen across the country processed the story coming out of Fort Worth, more and more began to speak out against what Norris had done. At a Methodist Episcopal camp meeting in Des Plaines, Illinois, the Reverend Morgan Williams told a crowd, "It didn't take me long to enlist in the late war, but it doesn't follow that a minister ought to take a revolver in hand and shoot a fellow man, even on the plea of self defense. If a minister is called upon to defend his wife he might be justified in shooting, but not in self-defense. It's the minister's business to give his life and not take the life of another." His audience responded with sustained applause.

Earlier that morning, shortly after ten o'clock, the Tarrant County grand jury began its probe into the shooting. The first witness called was

L.H. Nutt, who had been sitting in Norris's study when Chipps came in. He recounted the story he had told to the district attorney following the shooting on Saturday. He was followed to the stand by R.B. Ridgeway, who was asked about the supposed "mystery man" he had seen and heard with Chipps. The final witness heard from before the lunch break was City Detective Winston Lewis, one of the many officers investigating the killing.

As the lunch break began, word began to spread around the courthouse that the so-called mystery witness had been found. But when asked about this, DA Hangar denied it. After lunch, Miss Jane Hartwell and the five officers who responded to the scene of the killing gave testimony. It was also announced that Balaam Shaw, the Negro janitor of the church, was being summoned. The grand jury adjourned early in the afternoon after hearing testimony from Mrs. Fannie Greer and L.S. Grevenberg, the hotel operator and clerk from the Westbrook, and it was announced that it would reconvene the next morning at nine o'clock. The list of those who would give testimony had by this time swelled to thirty-four.

Also that afternoon, First Baptist Church announced that J. Frank Norris would baptize Mr. Shaw the following Sunday. In fact, Balaam Shaw, inexplicably, would never be baptized at the church.

Still, the biggest news of that Tuesday, less than seventy-two hours after J. Frank Norris killed Dexter Elliott Chipps, was something that the widow of the slain man, Mae Chipps, had done — though not quite on her own. She had engaged attorneys from the biggest and most famous law firm in Fort Worth to serve as "special prosecutors," assisting the district attorney in this case that promised to attract national attention. It would eventually come out that H.C. Meacham very early that previous Sunday morning, just hours after his friend Chipps had been killed and after being traumatized seeing the lifeless body at the funeral home, began to think about how he might help facilitate the conviction of J. Frank Norris.

While the mayor was contemplating his options, others around the country were pondering the issue as well. A sociology professor named Joseph L. Duflot at the West Texas State Teachers College in the Panhandle town of Canyon wrote to the mayor questioning Norris's mental state. "It occurs to me as I read the newspaper accounts of the killing of Chipps by Norris and of the latter's remarks upon the case — especially the suggestion in his sermon of Sunday morning — that we have a description of a person having all the symptoms of a paranoiac."

The sociologist continued, "The criminologist defines paranoia as a chronic, systematized, delusional insanity. The delusions are self-centered and revolve about ideas of personal persecution and personal grandeur. A paranoiac always regards himself as the object of conspiracies and at the same time the idol of a group of followers." The professor added, "I trust you will regard this as a personal matter as I do not care to be connected with such publicity."

Another man who had followed the story in the New York papers, Mr. James A. Cotner, the former mayor of Ardmore, Oklahoma, then living in Great Neck, Long Island, had some specific advice for the mayor. He recommended someone to help with the legal prosecution of the preacher: "Oklahoma's leading criminal lawyer," James H. Mathers. The famous attorney had been involved in the most important legal battles of the decade in Oklahoma, and the former mayor of Ardmore said, "I have heard him express himself on the Norris case, and he thinks it a cold blooded murder." He mentioned that Mathers had been involved with the defense "in the Clara Smith case, where she was tried for the killing of Jake Hamon."

By the time that he read Cotner's letter, though, Meacham had already decided to contact some local talent and offer to fund a special investigation and prosecution of Norris. Interestingly, the Fort Worth attorneys he had in mind had themselves worked with James H. Mathers of Oklahoma in that case involving the killing of Jake Hamon. H.C. Meacham persuaded Mrs. Chipps to obtain the services of the firm of McLean, Scott, and Sayers. They were hired to "help round up every angle of the evidence," according to one of the attorneys, Sam Sayers. In a statement he said: "Mrs. Chipps has full confidence in the District Attorney's office, and she wants to cooperate with the officers in every way, but at the same time she believes a special counsel will assist in the matter." Mayor Meacham would write the checks, with a little help from his friends.

Mrs. Chipps refused to answer any questions about the effort, likely because she didn't want to disclose who was really paying for the high-powered legal muscle. It would eventually emerge that Meacham's contribution to the effort was more than fifteen thousand dollars from his own pocket. The mayor had contacted the firm that Sunday, just before heading out to Chipps's funeral. Sayers acknowledged a longtime friendship with Chipps, "whom he knew while county attorney at Lufkin." These were the same lawyers H.C. Meacham had engaged when dealing with the matter involving his affair with Julia Mock several years before. They were also somewhat famous for success in some of the celebrated cases of the decade, including that Oklahoma murder case.

W.P. McLean was already a courtroom legend. Described as "southern of speech and dynamic," he was "one of the best-known and most invincible lawyers in Texas." Sam Sayers, "with his black hair brushed straight back from a good forehead," and Walter Scott, "tall, blue-eyed, blond, and long-headed," worked as a formidable, though at times oddly formed, team. McLean was the senior member of the firm. His father, also a famous attorney, was one of the signers of the Texas constitution. The nickname "Wild Bill" attached itself to him because of "his dynamic technique in the courtroom." He was "a gallant, colorful figure," who had practiced law for thirty years out of the same offices "on the old square around the courthouse" in Fort Worth.

Years before, McLean had become entangled in a Norris-related legal web. He came forward to defend three young men who were falsely accused of burning the old First Baptist Church in 1912. He won release for all three. More recently, he had defended Earle B. Mayfield, who had been elected to the US Senate as a Democrat backed by the Ku Klux Klan. The loser in that 1922 election contested the outcome, and the case dragged out for nearly two years before Mayfield was seated, helped in large part by the crafty legal work of Wild Bill.

He was known as something of a judge baiter. Once when asked by a judge if he was trying to show contempt for the court, McLean replied: "No your honor, I'm trying my best to conceal it." On another occasion, when he was fined fifty dollars for a courtroom outburst, he said, "I got it right here in my pocket. It was worth it." The judge then sentenced "Wild Bill" to three days in jail, asking the lawyer, "Do you have *that* in your pocket?"

But McLean's greatest claim to fame had to do with his work in what was, up to that time, the most celebrated murder trial of the decade in the West. It was a case that had all the ingredients to capture the public's imagination: sex, gunplay, and even presidential politics. Wild Bill was the guy who won acquittal for Clara Hamon in a case where it looked to everyone as though she was certain to be convicted.

That Clara had shot and killed Jake Hamon, the "Oil King of Oklahoma," in 1920 was not disputed. But why had she done it? Not only was Jake one of the wealthiest men in the West in the heady oil-boom days immediately following World War I, he also backed the right candidate for the Republican presidential nomination in 1920. He put his efforts, not to mention his millions, behind the popular senator from Ohio, Warren G. Harding. And when Harding won in a landslide, the president-elect was planning to reward Hamon with the plum job of secretary of the interior. This would give the Oklahoman control of the vast Teapot Dome Naval Oil Reserve in Wyoming, an oil supply worth several hundred million dollars. It would also put the oilman in a position to wield tremendous power.

But there was one problem. It had to do with something Harding's wife, Florence, could not bear. Clara wasn't actually Jake's wife. He already had a wife. Clara was the "other" woman. The last name was not a fake. She had "married" Jake's nephew Frank, who was paid ten thousand dollars for participating in the ruse, to give her the Hamon name as cover. Having the same last name made it easier for the couple to travel and check into hotels together.

Even before his election, Mr. Harding broke the news to Hamon in a letter that his new job hinged on his getting back together with his real wife. Jake told Clara all about it the day after Harding won the presidency, indicating that he was choosing the big job in Washington over her. The day after that Clara bought a gun. And early one evening a few days later, after Jake came in from an afternoon of hard drinking, she came to him, stroked his forehead with one hand, and shot her lover in the chest with the other. Before he died six days later, she had fled the country, eventually surrendering to authorities in Mexico and coming back to stand trial.

McLean and company, including Sayers and Scott, won her acquittal by arguing, "Clara had acted in self-defense." It was a sensational trial with an unexpected verdict. Now they would be on the other side of the courtroom, using their skills to help convict someone of murder. What motivated them? Well, beyond the money and the obvious publicity flowing from such a case, potentially even more famous than the Hamon case, they shared with many in the city on the Trinity utter and long-standing contempt for J. Frank Norris.

The new "special prosecutors" got right to work investigating the case, but the initial purpose, at least in part, of their work was to counteract the Norris public relations campaign. They knew that he was a master of manipulation and that he could bend the truth and even some people to his will. They had to fight back and try to get ahead of the preacher before he poisoned the jury pool, making it harder to gain a conviction. So as J. Frank Norris talked about "a deep laid conspiracy" to kill him, they countered by encouraging Mayor Meacham to issue a denial, calling the preacher's charges "silly." Meacham said that his friend Chipps was "an unarmed man" and "had no intention of attacking Norris when he went to his office that day." But how could he know?

The biggest news McLean and company made public was reported in *The New York Times*. There had been "discovered after the shooting a pool of blood twenty feet from the spot where Norris said he stood when he shot the lumberman. It was stated that a possible deduction was that Chipps might have been just outside Norris's office when shot, rather than in the office." This possibility cast early doubt on the preacher's account of the story.

CHAPTER TWENTY-TWO

"The Shooting Salvationist"

MEMBERS OF THE national media began arriving in Fort Worth within a few days of the killing. Though the story had been carried by the wire services, ambitious journalists from out of town began interviewing citizens and digging for details. The smartest of the bunch tried to find a local reporter to follow around, someone who knew the beat.

Part of this invasion, a serious-looking lady with ample round eyes and a large toothy grin, left the Westbrook Hotel on Wednesday morning, July 21, in the company of *Fort Worth Press* reporter L.A. Wilke. The pair made their way to Fourth and Throckmorton Streets and toward the office of J. Frank Norris. Wilke had already conducted two lengthy interviews with the Reverend Norris, and he was excited about the prospect of helping his companion gain access to the preacher. She was well known in journalistic circles, and her articles were widely read across the nation. She dressed conservatively from hat to shoes, but this attire was not indicative of her personality or her writing. An avowed socialist, she represented one of the most influential and widely read magazines of the day, which she jointly owned with her equally "radical" husband. None of this seemed to faze Wilke; he was in the company of a star.

Working in a trade dominated by men, the lady reporter hoped to get a word or two from Norris himself. Given she wrote for a publication known for its hostility toward religion in general, and fundamentalism in particular, she hoped that the local guy could help get her foot in the door.

Her name was Marcet Haldeman-Julius, co-editor of the *Haldeman-Julius Monthly* or, as it was better known, *The Little Blue Books.* She had been in town for a couple of days, talking to locals about the Norris story, and had a title already picked out for the piece: "J. Frank Norris — Shooting Salvationist."

Marcet was at the pinnacle of her success as a writer, due in large part to the metamorphosis that had recently taken place in the world of books and periodicals. Among the most important and longest-lasting economic booms of the 1920s was the exponential growth of the publishing industry. More and more people were buying and reading books, and in 1926 the Book-of-the-Month Club was born. A year later came the Literary Guild. What was "once a cottage industry" became mainstream. Along the way, innovators developed what were clearly "sophisticated techniques in book production." It was a revolution of sorts, a "mass market for books."

One of the best known and read of the innovators was maverick publisher Emanuel Julius, who exploited new methods to reach an emerging market. His popular little books were "among the most widely read in the 1920s."

Born in Philadelphia, Pennsylvania, to Jewish parents who had recently come to America from Odessa, Russia, Emanuel rejected the faith of his parents and remained an adamant atheist throughout his life. His father was in the bookbinding business, even once doing some work for Theodore Roosevelt, so although as a young man his schooling was at best haphazard, books surrounded him at home and became his life. His political leanings were leftist. He joined the Socialist Party in Philadelphia before his twentieth birthday and was soon interacting with "some of the giants" of the movement. He worked here and there as a reporter and journalist before moving to tiny Girard, Kansas, to work on the socialist journal *Appeal to Reason*. A few years later Eugene V. Debs, already a perennial Socialist Party candidate for the US presidency, moved to Girard to write for the periodical. During his early days in Girard, Julius met a girl named Marcet Haldeman, the "daughter of an affluent banker." Described as "a no nonsense, rather hard-nosed social worker who was trying to write while addressing the needs of the poor," she fell in love with Emanuel, and they married in 1916. A year later, as America joined the war raging in Europe, complete with a surge of patriotic Americanism that was the antithesis of what the Socialist Party stood for, the young couple bought *Appeal to Reason*. The banker's daughter put up the money, and her husband donated his "managerial and editorial skills." From that point on their work appeared under the egalitarian hyphenated surname Haldeman-Julius.

They created a periodical modeled after "a German publisher, Universal Bibliothek, which successfully published a list of seven thousand inexpensive small books in red paper covers": the *People's Pocket Series*, eventually renamed *The Little Blue Books*. The socialist couple produced the monthly periodical for "a penny a book," selling them for a nickel, with the price eventually climbing to fifteen cents. All in all, it became pretty successful business for a couple of wide-eyed socialists. In fact, by 1927 more than a hundred million *Little Blue Books* had been sold. The operation in the southeastern Kansas town "became the largest mailorder book publishing company in the world." When challenged about the apparent conflict between his business savvy and his socialist politics, Julius remarked: "I invested my capital in the *Little Blue Book* idea because I thought it was a sound business venture," adding "I was as interested in making a profit as Henry Ford."

The books often contained material not typically found in popular periodicals. Readers could find information about ways to improve "sexual techniques" and overcome "sexual dysfunctions." The publication regularly flirted with the censorship rules of the Post Office Department. One subject the outspoken couple regularly wrote about was religion — especially fundamentalism. Certainly J. Frank Norris was aware of *The Little Blue Books* and their regular attacks on his faith. So when Marcet Haldeman-Julius climbed the stairs of the church office building on Wednesday morning, July 21, with L.A. Wilke, and the duo approached Miss Jane Hartwell to ask if they might speak to the preacher, she had no reason to expect that he'd consent to meet them, much less grant an interview.

The Reverend Norris surprised her.

Curiously, Hartwell did not ask the visitor for her name, seeming to trust Wilke, who was a familiar face, and the lady journalist did not volunteer it. Norris had been free with interviews throughout the week. He had no lawyer as yet to caution him about talking too much, and his door was open. Only after entering Norris's study, the very room where the tragic shooting had taken place just four days earlier, did she formally introduce herself. The preacher at once recognized her name and presumably the significance of having an on-the-record conversation with one of the country's most widely read writers. J. Frank Norris shook hands with his guests and pointed them to seats. Marcet sat in a low wicker chair. The preacher started the conversation by speaking kindly about Emanuel Haldeman-Julius, indicating that "he was very curious to meet him." Norris's openness came as a surprise. Later Marcet reflected: "Dr. Norris was quite willing to discuss freely both himself and the shooting." It didn't take long for Marcet to form the opinion "that he was quite one of the most complex characters I ever had met."

She took charge of the interview by asking Norris right off how he was able to "proceed about his routine business" after the shooting. She told him that "a part of the world was aghast at the coolness." Norris pointed at the poem on the wall and asked her if she knew Kipling's "If."

Marcet interrupted Norris before he could launch into verse. She wasn't about to let the parson filibuster her, and she immediately began the first lines herself: "If you can keep your head when all about you are losing theirs and blaming it on you?"

Norris looked at her for a moment, as if annoyed.

Haldeman-Julius pressed the issue. "But," she asked, "how could you preach before a great congregation with the man you had killed still unburied?" It was a blunt question and was met with brief silence as Norris stared at her "in a quiet, detached sort of way." Finally, he began to reply slowly and methodically: "When a man is in trouble he wants to be with people he loves — with his family." He went on to say that his congregation was part of his extended family and that they had "come through much stress together" over the years. His verbal cadence quickened as he warmed up to a subject near to his heart and his rhetorical comfort zone. "The relationship between me and my flock is a most unusual one," Norris said, "a very personal, a very intimate one.

"I knew my big family was shocked and grief-stricken," Norris declared, "and needed me just as my little family did." The idea of his not occupying the pulpit that day was never really a serious consideration. "I had a prepared a sermon," he said. "They expected it. Not to have preached it would have been weak — when they needed my presence, my strength." He continued, "Of course some people came out of curiosity, but it wasn't for them that I preached."

The reporter wrote feverishly as Norris talked and posed her next question. "Even so, most people simply couldn't have done it. The average person would have been too unnerved, too filled with regret, too tortured with remorse — when he found that he had shot an unarmed man."

The preacher replied quickly that "remorse" and "regret" were two different things. He did "regret the necessity that had confronted him." But he added that he did not feel any remorse. "I am not a sentimentalist," he continued. "Whenever it becomes necessary for me to defend my life, I will."

Marcet Haldeman-Julius decided to leave this line of questioning and move on. She asked Norris, "Do you know Chipps' boy?" The preacher shook his head and said no. He then asked the reporter if she had met him and how old he was. "About 15," she said. She described the son of the man Norris had recently shot to death as a good-looking boy who had impressed her. Norris seemed moved by the description, as if lost in thought for a moment about the larger impact of what he had done. But he quickly snapped back to form. He told the reporter that he "felt deeply for the boy," but that it was not he himself, "but the people who had sent Chipps there" who were responsible for this young man no longer having a father to look up to.

J. Frank Norris recognized that he would be mistaken to underestimate the lady in his office. She was a savvy adversary. He determined to shift gears and try to take control of the conversation, changing the topic to Mr. Chipps himself, describing the man who came into his office that preceding Saturday afternoon as a virtual giant, someone intimidating even without a weapon.

Norris then shuffled through a pile of papers on his desk. After a few moments he found what he was looking for and handed a document to Marcet, saying, "Read this." The reporter took the paper. It was an affidavit from a house detective at the Westbrook Hotel, where D.E. Chipps had been living at the time of his death. The document described how "intractable Chipps was when he had been drinking." It was also an early indicator of how Norris and his emerging defense team were going to characterize Chipps in the coming weeks and months. The page read:

> TO WHOM IT MAY CONCERN: My name is Ollie Stanley. I was house detective at the Westbrook Hotel for five and a half years, up to about November 1, 1925.

During that time I had ample occasion and opportunity of knowing D.E. Chipps. He lived at the Westbrook for about three years. As house detective it was my duty to preserve order in the hotel and keep down trouble. I was forced to go to Chipps' room several times during the time he was there because of trouble that he caused.

On one occasion I was called to his room and went in and found him stripped naked and a woman in the room, and he drew back a chair and said, "Stanley, I'm going to kill you."

Thereupon I drew my gun on him and backed him up against the wall and checked him out.

He went to the Metropolitan and stayed a few hours and came back and registered again in the Westbrook with the promise and understanding that he would behave himself.

He was the most profane man I ever heard use profane language and the vilest. He would call up the telephone operators of the Hotel and curse and abuse them so that the proprietor and myself would have to intervene to protect the girls.

He was a hard drinker and was under the influence of liquor most of the time. I considered him a very dangerous man when under the influence of liquor. He was one of the most powerful men physically I ever saw. I had occasion to handle him to take hold of his arm. I weigh 225 pounds, and he was heavier than I and weighed 240 to 250 pounds.

Heavy as I am and stout as I am, in the difficulties I had with him I would not allow him to get hold of me for I was afraid of him.

Judging from firsthand knowledge and actions I considered him a very overbearing and dangerous man.

Marcet handed the affidavit to Mr. Wilke, who perused it while she asked the pastor the obvious and relevant question, "Had he been drinking Saturday?" Here Norris stumbled. His immediate reply was, "No, he was sober." Then, catching himself, he quickly added, "That is, he appeared to be sober." He went on to assure the reporter of his expertise in reading people and that "there was a certain type of man who could carry a good deal of liquor before anyone would suspect that he had been drinking at all."

Throughout the interview, Marcet Haldeman-Julius noted the cool, detached, although far from harsh fashion in which Norris discussed the events from the previous weekend. At this point she could resist no more the concern welling up inside her. "I understand, of course, that you feel you were absolutely justified," she told the preacher, "but even so, I cannot see how you can seem so unperturbed. If I had killed anyone, I don't care whom, nor how justly, I would be shaken — crushed."

J. Frank Norris tried to assure his office guests that it was actually very difficult to ascertain from a person's outward appearance how he or she really felt on the inside. "I know," he said, "a minister who preached his own wife's funeral sermon, and yet he was heartbroken." He further added, "I know men who sobbed and almost collapsed when their wives died, only to marry again in six months." The preacher tried to get his visitors to understand "that the whole experience was for him a bitter ordeal." Haldeman-Julius looked for signs of "emotional and mental strain" but could not find any. She observed that Dr. Norris "does not believe there is one chance in a million that if brought to trial he will be convicted." She saw this as "consistent with his claim of self-defense."

Norris shared his view that "all life is precious." He said, "I never hunt, I would not even kill a dove." By this time Marcet Haldeman-Julius was sure that Norris was someone who quickly sized up an adversary and had the ability "to sense the moods and personalities of others." She was sure that "he realized in all sincerity that I found his self-righteous attitude quite incomprehensible." Nothing he said had altered the reporter's view that Norris's shooting of Chipps was "one of the most cold-blooded and unnecessary killings in many a day."

The journalist had done her homework before venturing to talk to Norris himself. Not only had she talked to numerous local citizens, including the very civic leaders the preacher was opposing, but she had also read with great interest Norris's own words in the pages of the *Searchlight*. She had especially noted something the preacher had said back on Sunday, July 11, as he was "interviewing" the First Baptist Church members who had been fired from Meacham's store. During that fiery message he mentioned that someone had tampered with the church's radio mechanism. Norris threatened that day: "I want to say that we have guards on this thing night and day with orders to shoot to kill the first man who lays his hands on it." While the crowd thundered in applause, he added, "Some of you low-down devils arrange for your undertaker before you come around here," which was met with yet greater applause.

She asked the preacher, "How could you say a thing like that?"

Norris gave a rambling reply to the effect that "men who would molest valuable property were thugs and gunmen and, in doing so, deliberately took their lives in their own hands."

Haldeman-Julius countered with, "I don't think any old radio is worth a human life."

Before Norris could respond, the journalist shifted gears and directed the conversation to events of the previous Saturday. She listened as Norris repeated the same story he had been telling since his visit to District Attorney Hangar's office immediately following the shooting. He described a threatening call from Chipps and then how Chipps burst into his study a few minutes later. As he recounted the conversation with Chipps and how he'd asked him to leave, Norris demonstrated to Haldeman-Julius how he'd showed Chipps the door. When he reached the door of his study, he pointed to the anteroom and told the reporter that Chipps left the room and went "out past the desk there." Norris then reenacted how he had started back to his desk, only to turn and see Chipps "lunging" at him and looking like "a wild-man." The preacher then opened the drawer to show where the gun was and described the shooting.

When Norris finished, the journalist asked, "What on earth was Nutt doing at the time?"

Norris shrugged at the question, indicating that he had no idea. "It all happened so quickly."

Haldeman-Julius pressed with the blunt opinion, "I should think two grown men could have handled an unarmed man."

In reply Norris launched into a monologue about human nature and response during a crisis. He told the story of a young woman who was driving a car much faster than her passenger, a man, thought was safe. In a split second he reached over and grabbed the wheel, resulting in the car turning over, and the girl's death. "People asked," Norris continued, "why in the world he grabbed the wheel. It had cost the life of the woman. Those same people, I suppose, ask the same sort of questions about me. On the spur of the moment, when you think your life is in danger, you do what you think is best."

"Did he say anything after he was shot?" the reporter asked.

"No," Norris replied.

"What did you do? Didn't you rush over to him? It seems to me that would have been the first thing I should have done."

Norris said calmly, "What he needed was an ambulance and medical aid. I had that sent for."

As the interview drew to a close, Wilke jumped in with a couple of questions of his own, beginning with Norris's health. The preacher replied that he had been considering an operation for appendicitis "and was in poor condition to defend himself." He described how weak he felt and how he "watched every movement of his (Chipps') hands and tried to talk calmly with him, although he was using the vilest of language. I knew with me sitting down and he standing up and being the powerful man he was I would have no chance with him."

Norris rambled on: "I was glad when I thought Chipps was going to leave and when I got him to the door to go out again. When he started back at me though, it was as a wild man and my first thought was to defend myself. When I saw him make *as if to get a gun* I stepped back to my desk and grabbed my gun and shot. I don't know how many times I shot."

This was the first mention or note of Chipps making "as if to get a gun," part of the story that would become more and more important in the days and weeks to come. In fact, by this time the essence of Norris's defense before the courts of Texas and of public opinion was beginning to take shape. It would be a two-pronged argument: There was a conspiracy against him, and Chipps looked like he was going for a gun — "the hip pocket move."

In the Texas court system, the phrase *hip pocket move* had significant meaning. It was a surprisingly successful defense for a person shooting someone who turned out to be unarmed.

Three years earlier, a set of essays called "These United States: Portraits of America from the 1920s" was published in the national periodical *The*

Nation. It was a popular series and featured writers such as H.L. Mencken, Sinclair Lewis, and Theodore Dreiser. A lawyer-journalist by the name of George Clifton Edwards wrote about Texas. Norris, who was a voracious reader of newspapers and periodicals, would most likely have followed the series and read the piece about the Lone Star State, if only because it mentioned him. Writing about the Fort Worth preacher, Edwards referred to Norris as "the most lurid of our Texas Baptists," though admitting that he was "very successful."

Elsewhere in the essay, Edwards commented: "The best preventative against conviction in a Texas murder case is money. The best trial defenses are the 'unwritten law' and the '*hip-pocket move*,' both, generally, based on pretense and perjury."

The "hip-pocket move is pleaded against a person who after death by shooting is shown to have nothing in his hip-pocket." The writer then chronicled three "recent Texas cases" where the defense was used successfully — including one situation where a man was sitting at his desk with a "fountain pen in hand" when he was shot.

Did J. Frank Norris begin to hint about "the hip pocket move" — something he had not mentioned in his statements to police and the district attorney — as part of a calculated invention designed to avoid conviction, having read about how effective it was?

With this, the preacher indicated that the interview was over. The journalists left his study and walked to the outer office, via the anteroom. Marcet noted the "dark stain" on the carpet, which was nowhere near where Chipps's body had been found by the police when they arrived at the scene.

As the reporter left the anteroom she encountered Miss Jane Hartwell once again. This time she engaged Norris's secretary in conversation. After a brief exchange of small talk, Hartwell bluntly asked the reporter, "Are you a Christian?"

"No, I cannot say that I am."

"Then you would never understand. Only those who have faith in the Living God can understand!"

"I realize, of course, that you are convinced Dr. Norris must have felt it necessary to act as he did, but what I want to know . . ."

"We have faith in the Living God!"

"Yes, but what I am trying to find out is . . ."

"We have faith in the Living God!"

At this point the journalist tried to steer the conversation to some common ground. But just as soon as Hartwell seemed to come down from her soapbox-pulpit and looked "as if she would talk" to the reporter, Mr. J.J. Mickle, the man in charge of publicity and public relations for Norris and the church, walked past the door and called Miss Jane out to him. When she returned, she said "sweetly, but firmly" that she would not have any more to say.

MEANWHILE, THE GRAND jury had gotten back to work at the courthouse. The Wednesday session opened with a report that a "mystery witness" had appeared at Hangar's office. His name was Frank Conley, a contractor who had regularly done business with D.E. Chipps. He had been in Breckinridge, Texas, for a few days when he was told that the authorities in Fort Worth were looking for him as the possible mystery man who had reportedly accompanied Chipps to Norris's office. When he arrived at the district attorney's office he gave a statement saying that he did not go with Chipps to the church and "did not see Chipps later than 2:00 *pm* on Saturday, when they had dealings relating to his contracting work."

That same day the First Baptist Church publicity machine — under the direction of Mr. Mickle, but obviously approved by J. Frank Norris — issued a statement saying that "Chipps was an attendant at a Catholic church, 'though not a member, but his entire family were members.'" In fact, this was partially true. Though Mr. Chipps himself never attended St. Patrick's Church in Fort Worth, his wife Mae did on occasion, and their son had attended school at St. Ignatius Academy a few years earlier. When asked about this, Mayor Meacham angrily said that all the talk from the Norris camp about some kind of conspiracy was "silly and ridiculous." He bemoaned the fact that his friend Chipps "was now dead and cannot talk for himself."

As evening fell that Wednesday, and as the faithful of First Baptist prepared for their regularly scheduled midweek prayer service, J. Frank Norris issued a statement declaring that he wished to be indicted:

"Notwithstanding there is no evidence to return an indictment on, for every fair-minded man will agree it is a case of self-defense, yet it is the wish of the pastor and the church that an indictment be returned in order that all of the issues involved may be tried out, and most of all that the deep, dark laid conspiracy be given to the American public."

CHAPTER TWENTY-THREE

"The Inevitable Tragedy That Was Forced upon the Pastor"

"I WILL AGREE THAT if he leads me by one vote in the primary I will immediately resign without waiting until next year if he will agree that if I lead him by 25,000 in the primary on July 24, he will immediately resign." So said Texas governor Miriam A. "Ma" Ferguson in the early summer of 1926 in a challenge to her nearest rival, Dan Moody. It was an odd wager even for rough-and-tumble Texas politics, but Mr. Moody accepted the dare.

Almost, but not quite, forgotten with the Norris story dominating the news was the fact that one of the roughest Texas political campaigns in memory was under way and would culminate in a primary election that next Saturday. The big prize on the fall ballot was the governor's seat in Austin. Winning the Democratic nomination was the equivalent of complete victory. The general election in November usually saw barely token Republican representation. Three were running for that nomination: Lynch Davidson, Moody, and Mrs. Ferguson. Mrs. Ferguson was the incumbent, having been elected in 1924 as a "front" for her husband, Jim Ferguson, who after his impeachment when he was governor ten years earlier was barred from holding that office again. When she ran in his place in 1924, her initials M.A. were soon morphed into the familial "Ma," and not long after that Jim became "Pa." The folksy "Ma and Pa" image was far from reality; they were two crafty political operators.

Texas attorney general Dan Moody, however, was emerging as a new political star. If elected, he would become, at age thirty-three, the youngest governor in state history. He was an ambitious young man in a hurry and was running an effective campaign. He was described as "tall, rather thin, boyish-looking, with reddish hair inclined to curl," as well as "a hearty, ruddy complexion and pleasing, soft drawl"; what he lacked in the eloquence department he made up for with "seriousness carried with conviction."

His campaign found its way to Fort Worth and the platform of the First

Baptist Church just three days before the primary election. Inclement weather dictated that Dan Moody would deliver a speech from the same platform J. Frank Norris regularly occupied, less than a hundred feet from the scene of the shooting. But it would not be the last awkward convergence casting a shadow over Mr. Moody at key moments.

The plan had been to have a large open-air rally at Marine Park, just north of the downtown area, at 8:15 PM. A crew had been working all day to put a platform together and set up appropriate amplification equipment. As they worked, they kept one eye on the sky. The weatherman was predicting possible thundershowers for one of the biggest rallies of Moody's campaign. "Delegations from Dallas, Wichita Falls, Denton, Weatherford, Mineral Wells, and other nearby cities" were expected to attend. Hours before the scheduled start of the rally, the rains came, accompanied by thunder and lightning.

The backup plan, arranged long before the shooting, was to hold the rally at Fort Worth's largest and most conducive venue: the auditorium of First Baptist Church. Any connection to the events of three days prior was of course problematic for Moody. And to add another complication, J. Frank Norris was backing long shot Lynch Davidson in the campaign. Davidson's ads had been prominent in the *Searchlight*, and the candidate had been broadcasting almost nightly from the church's radio station, KFQB, prompting a protest from the Moody campaign about the propriety of that kind of involvement by a church in a political campaign.

Davidson was rumored to be the candidate for governor backed by the Klan, though there was never an official endorsement. In addition to Norris's *Searchlight*, the *Fort Worth American*, a Klan periodical, wrote favorably of his campaign and unfavorably about the other candidates. Both publications contained ads suggesting that "a conspiracy of oil and booze was going to elect Dan Moody." Thus the stage was literally set for an awkward convergence of Norris's church and a candidate he opposed.

Following an introduction by Douglas Tomlinson, president and publisher of the *Fort Worth Tribune,* Moody came to the pulpit and gave his stump speech. He attacked the Fergusons while responding to criticisms that he was slinging mud. He told the crowd, "I am not. Everything I say or have said about Jim Ferguson has to do with either the record in the courthouse or admissions which he has publicly made and never denied. I do not know anything about his private life and I care a thousand times less. I am slinging facts, not mud."

One observer in the crowd noted, "It was a real speech, given in a fine way and with fine spirit, and there is no reason to believe other than that the 6,000 who heard it were impressed with Dan Moody's genuineness. He was not in the slightest degree discourteous to any person who heckled him, and hecklers must have enjoyed the meeting as much as anyone else. Dan spoke like a winner."

J. Frank Norris did not attend the rally. He was across the street in the "Young People's Building" auditorium, a room that itself could seat nearly twenty-five hundred people. It was located on Throckmorton directly across from the Sunday School Building. The lower two floors were leased to J.C. Penney, while the upper floors were dedicated to the ministries of First Baptist Church. The scene was the regularly scheduled midweek Prayer Meeting and Bible Study — a gathering designed for the paid and volunteer staff of the church and Sunday school. The format was simple: Norris would give a homily, in effect the lesson that all teachers in the Sunday school would teach the following Sunday. Then there would be a time of prayer. It was a weekly motivational session during which the preacher inspired his followers to go out and, as noted by one of the faithful, "sell J. Frank Norris to the masses."

Dr. Norris would use this particular Wednesday meeting to rally the faithful behind him. In his lengthy address he exhorted the most faithful of his flock to rise up and seize the moment, capitalizing on the attention focused on him. He assured the crowd, "The church is witnessing the largest results during any summer in our history." More than two thousand heard Norris that night, "notwithstanding the rain and the fact that Dan Moody, candidate for Governor was speaking just across the street."

Norris affirmed what had been previously announced, that he would undertake "a perennial evangelistic campaign." He also reassured his people of the support they were all receiving from a vast throng of sympathizers around the country: "In this hour of sore trial the entire congregation deeply expresses its profoundest appreciation for the hundreds of telegrams and letters that are pouring in from every part of the earth concerning the inevitable tragedy that was forced upon the pastor and people."

Norris then confidently declared: "As never before people are seeking membership in the First Baptist Church." Certainly the results of the previous Sunday's service did not indicate as much, but Norris had a gift for shaping perceptions to suit his ends.

Following this meeting, and as the political rally in the church sanctuary ended, Norris accompanied the man he was backing for the governor's chair, Lynch Davidson, to the radio room of the church. The candidate had been across the street in the main church auditorium listening to young Dan Moody speak, taking notes and preparing for his radio rebuttal.

When the transmitter was fired up, station KFQB was on the air featuring a broadcast by the gubernatorial candidate, who was by now an also-ran. The businessman-turned-politician "berated Moody as a complete failure" to anyone listening at that late hour. One newspaper editorial called Davidson's radio address "bushwacking," adding, "I doubt that there is any good to be rendered to Lynch Davidson by such a system of broadcasting."

Most of those present at the church to hear Moody had by now decided, "Dan's the Man!" And Texas citizens seemed to agree by giving him 126,000 more votes than Ma Ferguson. She didn't keep her bargain and resign, though. His resounding victory notwithstanding, Moody no doubt noticed that his visit to Fort Worth was not the big story in town that week. He could only take comfort in the fact that he wouldn't have to worry about the preacher actively campaigning against him, due to the fact that he was facing a possible indictment for murder.

CHAPTER TWENTY-FOUR

"The First Law of All Is the Law of Self-Preservation"

THE THUNDERSTORMS OF the night before gave way to milder, cooler weather on Thursday, July 22, 1926. Shortly after nine o'clock that morning, the grand jury resumed its work in the Tarrant County Courthouse. It had fallen to Assistant District Attorney J.B. Young Jr., son of Judge Bruce Young, to work most closely with the jurors, making the case against Norris. It was a monumental job. Before beginning that morning, a stenographer advised him that the pool of those who were transcribing testimony from the numerous witnesses that had been called already had fallen woefully behind. It might be several days before they could catch up and have an accurate transcript prepared. Nevertheless, Young pressed ahead and recalled L.H. Nutt to the stand to go over the details of his earlier testimony, the first given, in light of what other witnesses since had said. Also recalled were Chief Lee and City Detective Bush. Then came Justice of the Peace Dave Shannon, who had conducted the inquest on Chipps's death, as well as Dr. J.A. Goldberg, for more information.

Also called that morning were Ralph Ridgeway and *Searchlight* employee Frances Turner. By noon the stenographers had become overwhelmed, and it was announced that the grand jury would adjourn until the following Tuesday, July 27. District Attorney Hangar told reporters that "four additional witnesses" would appear. He declined to comment on "whether or not they were additional eyewitnesses to the tragedy." Obviously, his actions and words had the effect of creating some speculation about the real reason for the adjournment and delay. But he dismissed this emphatically: "The state thinks it is highly improper to discuss the facts or merits of this case while it is pending before the grand jury. The grand jury called for a full stenographic report of all the testimony submitted to it in the Norris case. That cannot be available before Tuesday by reason of its length and the inability of the court reporter to complete it. In addition, there are more witnesses to be heard."

Over at First Baptist Church, J.J. Mickle, the ministry's publicity director, was peppered with questions as to when Norris would announce his defense team. He replied, "There was no announcement to be made as to the retention of counsel," and that he wasn't sure if Norris was going himself before the grand jury.

Norris, even with his love for publicity, was feeling the pressure of the scrutiny being given to him, his church, and every aspect of his life and work. He exhibited some thin skin by accusing one of the local papers, the *Fort Worth Press,* of publishing purported quotes he claimed to have never made. Possibly he sensed that he had been too free with comments to reporters such as L.A. Wilke and Marcet Haldeman-Julius. Whatever the reason, he sent notice of his demands to the paper, which published them on the front page, along with a response:

"Please do me the courtesy to cease publishing in your papers statements which I do not make. Kindly publish this. Thank you. Signed, J. Frank Norris."

The editor replied: "That courtesy asked by Rev. Norris has never been denied him. The statements attributed to Rev. Norris in the *Press* have been obtained in good faith by reporters. Signed, Editor."

Though the grand jury would not reconvene until well after the coming weekend, the special prosecutors hired by Mrs. Chipps and paid for by Mayor Meacham and friends were busy conducting their own "unofficial" probe. On Friday, July 23, they announced that they were "in possession of evidence which will tend to show Dr. J. Frank Norris did not kill D.E. Chipps in the study of the First Baptist Church last Saturday in self-defense." They promised to issue a statement "covering these investigations" after the grand jury report was made.

Norris certainly expected that, at the very least, his good friends in the Ku Klux Klan would stand behind him. Yet that Friday the *Fort Worth Press* reported that Norris would "not receive the backing of that organization in his case." In advance of their regularly scheduled Friday-night meeting at their auditorium on North Main Street — a meeting similar to the one Norris had spoken at just two weeks earlier — it was announced that "discussion of the case will be kept down." Lloyd P. Bloodworth, the local Klan Grand Dragon, as well as a member of Norris's church, said, "It was decided several weeks ago that politics and other such matters would not be made an issue in this Klan and I am sure the Norris trouble will not be taken up."

Bloodworth, however, assured Norris of his personal support and that he would be in the front row at church on Sunday. J. Frank told him that he should come to the platform and lead the congregation in prayer, and he agreed to do just that. Moreover, an Associated Press report quoted Bloodworth saying almost exactly the opposite of what was reported in the *Fort Worth Press*. According to the AP version of events, Lloyd Bloodworth had returned to Fort Worth on Thursday, July 22, from a Grand Dragon conference in Chicago "and went immediately to Dr. Norris' office." While there, Bloodworth assured Norris that "the order would lend any assistance it could." Norris reportedly asked Bloodworth if the Grand Dragons had discussed his case in Chicago, to which the Fort Worth Klan leader replied, "We talked about little else."

Bloodworth was quoted in *The New York Times* as saying, "I have known Dr. Norris for seventeen years, and in that time he has been an outstanding crusader for Protestant Christianity. In every moral fight that has taken place in the city of Fort Worth, Dr. Norris has ever been ready to champion the cause of right." He added, however, "I am not attempting to speak officially for the Klansmen of Texas, but I presume to know their attitude in regard to free speech, free press, free conscience and the freedom of worship. The first law of all is the law of self-preservation, and it has been so since the beginning of time. Therefore a man must defend himself in a time of emergency." He finished with the comment, also picked up by the AP: "In conclusion, I wish to say I have a very high regard for Dr. Norris and it is my sincere belief that the Klansmen of Texas are with him in his fight."

That Friday, subscribers, church members, and the simply curious awaited the publication and distribution of the latest edition of Norris's *Searchlight*. What would the tabloid, the first one printed since Norris killed Chipps, have to say about it all? Newsboys were hired to distribute copies throughout the city. Readers saw the banner headline on page one, which was simply a quote from Paul's epistle to the Romans, chapter eight, verse 28, "And We Know That All Things Work Together for Good to Them That Love God, to Them Who Are the Called According to His Purpose."

This was also the text of his sermon the previous Sunday. That message was published in the *Searchlight* in its entirety with the lead, "Sermon Preached in Most Solemn Service in History of the First Baptist Church."

Also on the front page was an editorial that described the grand jury, then investigating the Norris case, as rife with "Roman Catholics and enemies of Dr. Norris." The article began with the question, "Is it an accident that certain Roman Catholics and certain bitter enemies of Dr. Norris are on the present grand jury?" It continued, "The evidence shows that one of the main purposes in the formation of this present grand jury was that an indictment for criminal libel should be returned against Dr. Norris." Declaring that "an open trial will bring out all the facts," the editorial hinted that the reason so many were out to get Norris was that he had "been preaching against Romanism and bootleggers." And as if to add more drama, the article stated: "As we go to press we have just learned of a certain meeting on a certain night this week, at which a very large sum of money was raised to hire well-known criminal lawyers to prosecute Dr. Norris, lawyers who always take the side of the defense — names of parties participating in this conspiracy to raise funds to job the pastor of the First Baptist Church will all come out when we come to an open trial."

Readers of that Friday's *Searchlight* also saw a written statement from B.F. Bouldin, an attorney who served as the First Baptist Church's chairman of the board of trustees: "The pastor and entire church deeply regret the tragedy in the church office last Saturday afternoon, but being in possession of all the material facts and knowing conditions, as perhaps no one else knows them, we know that Dr. Norris acted in his necessary self-defense and that he did nothing but what any other reasonable, sensible man would be compelled to do. We believe all thinking people will come to this conclusion when all the facts are fully revealed."

There is no doubt that J. Frank Norris saw a silver lining in the cloud surrounding him as the one-week anniversary of the shooting approached. *Searchlight* readers were informed that, "We Have Just Started." This was a reference to a new contract that had been signed just the day before with the Metsker-Griffin Syndicate, "one of the largest subscription campaign organizations in America, to put on a real subscription campaign" for the tabloid. It was also announced that "several thousand dollars in automobiles and other premiums will be given in the national and worldwide campaign."

This particular edition of the *Searchlight* also contained several pages of paid political advertisements, with the Democratic primary only a day away. Of particular note were ads for criminal district court judge George E. Hosey, who was already rumored as likely to oversee a Norris murder trial should the preacher be indicted, and county judge Dave Shannon, the justice of the peace presiding over the inquest into D.E. Chipps's death.

The next day, Saturday, Fort Worth newspapers featured paid advertisements by the First Baptist Church detailing the ministry schedule for the next day. Announcing, "Dr. J. Frank Norris speaks as usual in all three services. 10 AM The Resurrection and Great Commission, Matthew 28; 11 AM Four Steps in Salvation." And at an 8 PM open-air rally, Norris would speak on "The Menace of Roman Catholicism. All services broadcast over radio KFQB."

CHAPTER TWENTY-FIVE

"No Ordinary Preacher of Brotherly Love"

MARCET HALDEMAN-JULIUS, her research on the story virtually complete, was ready to return home to Girard, Kansas, to put the finishing touches on her essay, "J. Frank Norris — Shooting Salvationist." She looked forward to telling her husband in great detail about Norris and was already planning to be back in Fort Worth whenever the trial was scheduled, harboring no doubt that there would be an indictment.

Before leaving town, though, she wanted to experience a Sunday service at First Baptist Church. Haldeman-Julius had heard descriptions of the services the previous Sunday: how Norris had been reserved — even somber — the day after the shooting, with a little more fire on Sunday night but still not the preacher his people were accustomed to hearing. She wondered if he would be back in regular form now.

Marcet arrived a little late for the eleven o'clock morning service, while the vast audience was singing the venerable hymn "Stepping in the Light." She was struck by the almost surreal irony of being in a church whose pastor had recently killed an unarmed man and hearing the swells of *"Walking in footsteps of gentle forbearance, footsteps of faithfulness, mercy and love."* While the crowd joined the chorus, *"How beautiful to walk in the steps of the Savior,"* she found a seat in one of the areas in the balcony. Looking around, she noted that "the church was one of the ugliest" she had ever seen. In fact, she would describe it as "downright dirty looking. Its gray and ivory woodwork needs painting badly, and the whole place needs to be swept, scrubbed and dusted." As she looked around she tried to gauge the size of the crowd. Having heard from many that the building could seat six thousand in its pews, she acknowledged that it "was full, but by no means packed."

She had been interested in visiting the church even before the shooting occurred, this congregation and pastor being so immersed in the fight against the teaching of evolution in the schools of Texas. The fact was that "Norris, law or no law, has succeeded, with the help of his disciples, in having certain of the school books used by the Texas school children changed to read as he wishes them to read."

As the congregation repeated the chorus once again as a finale of sorts, Marcet watched a man walk on to the platform and shake hands with Dr. Norris. He was a large man with glasses, and she tried to recall where she had seen him or his picture. After a moment, it came to her: It was Lloyd P. Bloodworth, the Grand Dragon of the local chapter of the Ku Klux Klan.

With the end of the music, and as the crowd remained standing as if at attention, Bloodworth approached the pulpit. He paused and said: "Let us pray." In his prayer he thanked the good Lord for Dr. Norris, fervently so. He prayed for the pastor, that he might have what he described as "boldness in preaching God's word." The prayer lasted several minutes, and the supplicant waxed oratorical. Marcet cynically saw it as more of a sermon than a prayer. She did not close her eyes during the prayer and observed Preacher Norris sitting on the platform "leaning forward, elbows on knees, head in his hands."

After Bloodworth's "amen" — and the chorus of "amens" echoing in reply — the five-thousand-plus members of the crowd sat down noisily. J. Frank Norris approached the podium. As the preacher began to speak, first sharing some notices, the reporter was immediately struck by how different he sounded from the way he'd talked in his office the previous Wednesday. She remembered his private conversation as "very pleasant, almost musical," but as she listened from her seat in the balcony, she noticed his public voice was "twanging and rather shrill."

Norris reminded his congregation of his subject for that evening: "The Menace of Roman Catholicism." He also assured his church that he was conducting his work in a business-as-usual manner and would meet his usual engagements. Haldeman-Julius analyzed Norris as he talked to the crowd. The figure on the platform clad in a loose dark suit appeared a much smaller man than the one she'd encountered in his study. In fact, she thought he looked "positively frail" and was sure that "the memory picture of him which his congregation carries away Sunday after Sunday subtly adds to his appeal for them."

The ushers soon appeared and made ready to receive the collection, using what Marcet thought looked like ordinary tin cooking pans to accommodate the anticipated large offering. Following this, Norris launched into his sermon, but instead of his advertised topic "Four Steps in Salvation," he brought a message simply on "Faith." As he preached, the reporter noted that Norris was "essentially a man who can become absorbed in his subject and dismiss everything from his mind but the question of the moment."

Proclaiming: "The word of God never looks back. The religion of God is a forward looking religion," Norris talked about Moses, reminding his listeners, "Faith makes the right choice." The reporter hesitated to make notes but then looked around and saw many faithful congregants jotting down things the pastor was saying and realized that her note-taking would be inconspicuous. She wrote: "He is given to sharp, staccato exclamations, sweeping shoulder-movements which end abruptly in an upward jerk of the arm from the elbow, and quick little circular twists of the wrist."

"He moves about easily and takes the stage freely."

"There is no doubt that he chose his text as a vehicle for more than a religious message to his congregation."

"Once into his sermon, he thoroughly began to enjoy himself."

"He sketched scene after scene with gusto."

"He talked of miracles and became oratorical, declaring that God could take the shining firmaments and roll them up like a moth-eaten garment; that He who made the mountains could roll them away; that He had but speak and the tomb would give up its dead."

"When the Son of God comes — will He find faith?" To emphasize this question, Norris stepped forward "and rising on his feet he would ask the question with upflung arm and pointing finger."

The reporter wrote feverishly, trying to capture almost every word.

As J. Frank Norris began to conclude his message, he told the congregation, "I am as strong a predestinarian as there is. I believe God has set every man's race before him and that every man must make the race set before him." Then the preacher raised his right hand and used the testimony of a railroad engineer: "There may be dark tunnels ahead, there may be sharp curves that I cannot see. But I know that I shall make the landing in the Union Station." And nearly everyone in the church shouted back: "Amen!"

Then after a brief and deliberately pregnant pause, the preacher reached the crucial moment. A week earlier, when he needed it most, the invitation appeal failed to deliver but a token response, just a handful of converts. Today he hoped for a great and demonstrative vindication. Dr. Norris jumped down to a lower platform area in front of the pulpit and began to work the crowd, doing his best to bring many in the room to a place of decision. The choir began to sing, *"Just as I am without one plea..."* and Norris pressed his case: "The greatest people on earth worship at this church. Don't let timidity overcome you."

As Marcet Haldeman-Julius watched, and as the congregation stood to join with the choir in song, people began to move from all over the sanctuary. At first, because of the sheer numbers, the reporter thought they were just moving toward Norris to shake his hand, showing support for him. But no, she soon realized that "they were coming to profess their faith." Soon Miss Jane Hartwell and another man appeared near the platform. They greeted the converts and led them to Norris. This spectacle went on for several minutes. Then Norris came back to the microphone: "I want to ask, how many people live here in Fort Worth, but belong to churches in other cities?" Hands went up all over the room. "Don't be a bushwacker," he said. "Take your stand under Christ's colors! Today I want you to join this heroic company of men — be one hundred percent for the gospel of the Lord. Come on! Say you'll join the heroic throng! This is a church that has come through stress and storm, and stands today on the rock of the Lord. It has a more glorious future than ever before."

As Marcet Haldeman-Julius watched with great interest, she was struck by how Norris appeared at the moment, writing that "he wore a contented, paternal, almost an uplifted look." Norris was clearly back in the saddle that morning as sixty-three new members for his church verified. She was witnessing the work of someone with powerful skills of persuasion. He was, as she would write for thousands to read, "no ordinary preacher of brotherly love. No, not J. Frank Norris."

Not long after the service, she boarded a train for Kansas. Her article would appear in the September issue of the magazine she copublished with her husband, and it would cause quite a stir.

That evening, another very large crowd gathered at the vacant lot in the 2000 block of Hemphill Street in Fort Worth to hear Norris's diatribe against the Roman Catholic Church. Before Norris spoke, First Baptist's publicity director, Mr. Mickle, made a lengthy statement to the crowd. It was the first public mention of the pastor's case in one of the church services. Telling the members of the church to "stay steady in the boat," he commended the congregants for their "magnificent spirit of loyalty and union that has been developed in this, the best church in the world." The audience applauded Mickle, and themselves. He continued, "In the present trying emergency you can do just as the children of Israel did when the sea faced them and Pharaoh was in the rear. Stand still and see the salvation. There is a diabolical plot to take the life of our pastor."

Speaking of cards not yet played, he said, "When the propitious moment comes, I can substantiate this with irrefutable testimony of unimpeachable witnesses. We are not going to be forced to display anything by innuendo or insinuations of the enemy.

"You need not for a minute lose faith," Mickle continued. "When the time comes you can bet your sweet life that we will be Johnny on the spot."

As Norris then delivered his broadside against the Church of Rome, he took a shot at the grand jury. Noting that George Kreyenbuhl, the secretary of the local Knights of Columbus, was a member of the body hearing testimony in his case, J. Frank said, "I don't think any secretary of the Knights of Columbus should be allowed to hold any position in the courts of this land." The crowd shouted "Amen!" and applauded.

The theme of his message was that "Romanism," his preferred nomenclature for Roman Catholicism, was more than a different interpretation of the Christian religion; it was a threat to the very life and security of the nation. He called it "the most colossal system of false teaching that has ever been known in all the annals of time." He shouted, "The particular system that I refer to is, the great menace of this hour, God grant that the American people may become more aroused than they ever have." In Norris's mind and messages the "Romanist" issue was tied together with the cause of Prohibition. And he wasn't alone in making this connection. In fact, a widely used and abused loophole in the Volstead (National Prohibition) Act "authorized the manufacture and sale of sacramental wine," in a concession to Roman Catholic ritual. It became a booming business, and many viewed the whole enterprise with suspicion because it seemed like "an awful lot of Communion wine" was being made.

Norris feared the increasing political popularity of New York governor Al Smith, who had nearly gained the Democratic nomination for the presidency in 1924, only to be blocked by forces loyal to William Jennings Bryan. Now with Bryan dead, Norris warned that the way was being paved for a Roman Catholic to be elected to the nation's highest office.

J. Frank graphically described a scene where Al Smith kissed the ring of a Catholic cardinal "in the Governor's room in New York." Horrified, the fiercely Baptist-Protestant crowd gasped. The preacher warned about "the terrible wave of liberalism today that is sweeping over this land, 'down with authority,' 'down with the Constitution,' 'give us our beer and our wine.'" He told of how one night, after he had finished a sermon at New York's Calvary Baptist on West Fifty-seventh Street between Sixth and Seventh Avenues, he exited the building and crossed the street to walk down the block toward Seventh to see what the crowd was doing outside of Carnegie Hall on the corner. The doors opened. He walked in and realized that he had happened upon an anti-Prohibition rally of sorts. He told the Fort Worth faithful, "It wasn't composed of the riffraff of the East Side but intelligent, beautifully gowned women and handsomely dressed men." The preacher continued, "I saw a man stand out there, who seemingly had good sense, and here's what he said: 'To hell with the Constitution, give us our beer.' That is what he said, and that fight tonight is on and as never before in all the history of the one hundred and fifty years existence of this Republic."

Ever the self-styled expert on foreign affairs, Norris talked about the potential for another great war, claiming, "We are in eminent danger, and if Mussolini and his ally, the Pope, are on the opposite side of the best interest of this Republic, they have such a powerful organization that they can largely checkmate the United States Congress, both House and Senate, and even the President himself."

J. Frank Norris concluded his nearly two-hour sermon that hot summer night with a dramatic quoting of a passage from the Book of Revelation; then he abruptly ended with a sharp and dramatic: "Good night!" No appeal. No prayer. No benediction. Just a crowd left at fever pitch. Norris was doing his best to turn the act of shooting an unarmed critic in his office into part of a larger war between the forces of evil and righteousness. He would defend himself in court as someone who feared for his life, but to his die-hard followers he was a warrior, prophet, hero, their prophetic voice crying in the wilderness.

CHAPTER TWENTY-SIX

"With Malice Aforethought"

AS THE LAST WEEK of July 1926 began, the national news reported the death of the last of Abraham Lincoln's children. Robert Todd Lincoln (age eighty-three) had been found dead at his summer home in Manchester, Vermont. He was the oldest son of the country's beloved sixteenth president, and the last of the descendants to bear the family name. In Texas, meantime, the big political news was the decisive victory of Attorney General Dan Moody in the Democratic gubernatorial primary. He had overwhelmingly beaten "Ma" Ferguson and Lynch Davidson, though he fell short of the vote count needed to avoid a runoff. She had famously declared that she'd resign if he beat her, and by Monday morning her office announced there would be a statement at nine o'clock that evening. People were actually betting on whether or not she would keep her word and step down, with the odds two to one in favor of it. But she would ultimately break her campaign promise and stay on to fight Moody in a runoff.

In Fort Worth attention focused on the grand jury as it prepared to reconvene on Tuesday, July 27. By now, the big question seemed to be not *if* J. Frank Norris would be indicted for murder, but *when*. Assistant District Attorney Young said that the probe into Norris's killing of D.E. Chipps would last several more days at least. He was emphatic that "every available witness will be questioned by the grand jury before any formal action is taken." That Monday was also a day for rumors and speculation about potential lawyers for Norris's defense should he be indicted and brought to trial. Rumors abounded that counsel had been retained by the preacher, but there was no confirmation from Norris's office.

Newspapers across the country contained growing criticism of Norris by other members of the clergy. In Lawton, Oklahoma, the Reverend James W. Baker, pastor of that city's First Methodist Church, articulated what so many other spiritual leaders were thinking and saying as they faced their congregations. "There is a question in my mind," said Baker, "whether Norris could not do more good by giving his life in righteous cause than to live under wrong conditions and circumstances, to be branded as a slayer, as he henceforth surely shall." The minister then quoted scripture: "Thou shalt not kill; love your enemies; bless them that curse you; do good to them that hate you; all they that draw the sword shall perish by the sword."

The public had enjoyed more than a week to discuss, process, and speculate about what really happened on July 17 in J. Frank Norris's office, and now opinion boiled down to three basic theories. First there was the account given by Norris and believed by his loyal followers: *Chipps had threatened the preacher and made a move as if to draw a gun, and Norris shot him in pure self-defense.* Another theory, and probably the one most widely accepted, was: *Norris feared that Chipps, who was bigger and stronger, was going to beat him up, and rather than risk that, he shot him.* In other words, it was a gigantic overreaction on the part of Norris. Finally, some held: *Norris simply shot Chipps as he was leaving, in cold blood, with little or no provocation.*

As the grand jurors settled in their seats for another presumably long and arduous day of testimony, the bailiff brought the pistol found in Norris's desk to be examined by the jurors. This was followed by a steady stream of witnesses, some new, some returning. Curiously, though there had been talk about a mystery witness, a fourteen-year-old boy who had been in the church office around the time of the shooting, after he was actually located prosecutors said he would not be called to give testimony.

Marvin Simpson, a prominent local attorney who had offered his services to Norris from his vacation in California in the immediate aftermath of the shooting, was seen in the courthouse. When asked if he was going to represent Norris, he declined comment.

The grand jury did not work that afternoon, waiting instead to reconvene Wednesday morning. Surprisingly, though, no witnesses were summoned the next day, and District Attorney Hangar announced, "The investigation is probably closed." He did not indicate when the grand jury would take action on the Norris case and suggested the body had already begun to work on other cases.

When the jurors reassembled Thursday morning, however, they were back on the Norris case. They heard testimony from Mayor H.C. Meacham and Justice of the Peace Dave Shannon. An announcement was also finally made about the mystery boy. He was identified as Carl Glaze, who lived at 1306 La Gonda Avenue. Glaze had told friends that he was an eyewitness to the shooting, having "gone to the church on some minor errand." But again, the D.A.'s office insisted his testimony would not be necessary. The jurors had already made up their minds.

Shortly after eleven o'clock on Thursday morning, July 29, the Tarrant County grand jury indicted J. Frank Norris, pastor of the First Baptist Church of Fort Worth, the largest Protestant congregation in the country, on a charge of murder for the killing of Dexter Elliott Chipps, lumberman. The wording of the indictment was unambiguous: "The Rev. Mr. Norris did unlawfully and with malice aforethought kill and murder one D.E. Chipps by then and there shooting said D.E. Chipps with a pistol."

Announcing the indictment, District Attorney Hangar made it clear, "Dr. Norris, like any other Texas indictee; will receive acquittal, a minimum of two years for manslaughter, or the maximum of death in the electric chair, depending on how the twelve good Texas jurymen decide." It was the first time any official indication was made about the potential for J. Frank Norris to be put to death. An editorial in *Time* magazine that week, referring to Norris as the "potent medicine-man of the Texas Fundamentalists," confirmed that there were many who hoped District Attorney "Hangar" would live up to his name.

Norris was at work in his office when the indictment was announced. One of Norris's attorneys, upon hearing what had happened, went to the courthouse to process the paperwork for a new bond. The previous ten-thousand-dollar bond had expired upon the indictment; a new one was quickly set at the same amount. Eleven citizens signed it: L.R. Barton, B.F. Bouldin, Marvin B. Simpson, W.B. Fishburn, A.F. Plunkett, A.L. Jackson, Charles Mays, Clyde Mays, P.K. Thompson, Dr. O.R. Grogan, and J.M. Lovett. Shortly after the indictment was announced, it was revealed that Norris had begun to put together a legal team. Marvin Simpson, B.F. Bouldin, and Clyde Mays would serve as counselors, and there was little doubt that additional attorneys would be hired.

Taking the initiative, Marvin Simpson made a public statement for the defense:

> Having been requested by the press on numerous occasions since my return to the city, for a statement as to my connection as an attorney for Dr. Norris, I have, up to this date, declined to make a statement for the reason that I desired to acquaint myself with the facts in detail before doing so. After a thorough investigation of the facts, I feel justified in saying as one of the attorneys for Dr. Norris, that it was a case of absolute, unquestioned self-defense where a man had to defend his own life in his own study. From the very beginning, Dr. Norris demanded that an indictment be returned in order that all that is back of this case might be brought to light. Upon trial of his case some of the most startling facts will be developed establishing beyond question the formation of a deep laid conspiracy to take the life of Dr. Norris. Dr. Norris is deeply grateful for the fact that more than 100 of the most reputable lawyers of the city of Fort Worth and throughout the State and Nation have tendered their services and assistance in his behalf. It is my candid opinion that if it had been anyone other than Dr. Norris, around whom there has raged a storm of controversy on well known issues, the grand jury would have at once voted no bill by reason of the well known facts in this case.

Sam Sayers, one of the special prosecutors in the case, countered that the state's "version of the killing differed from that given by Rev. Mr. Norris." He asserted, "The state line of evidence will seek to show that Chipps was not slain by Norris in the latter's necessary self-defense, but that the killing was unjustifiable."

The stage was now nearly set for one of the most famous murder trials ever conducted before the courts of Texas.

CHAPTER TWENTY-SEVEN

"This War Between Heaven and Hell"

THE NEWS OF NORRIS'S indictment produced predictable reactions. His loyalists felt it to be a travesty of justice, even though the preacher had virtually *demanded* it. On the other hand, Norris detractors were delighted. Maybe now they would be spared further Norris antics and controversies — maybe now their tormentor would receive his due.

One person who was very glad the grand jury took the action it did was Mae Chipps, widow of the slain lumberman. She discussed her feelings on the matter with reporters the day after the indictment: "The act of the grand jury in returning an indictment against Rev. J. Frank Norris charging murder is the first act of vindication toward my dead husband. It establishes the fact that he was unarmed. I am hoping and praying for justice and earnestly desire that the facts may be presented to an honest jury. I will accept its verdict, know that any wrong that has been done will be righted so far as it lies within its power."

Her reference to an honest jury was more than simple phrasemaking. It suggested something that was on the minds of many Fort Worth citizens: Could any jury be found in the county that would be unbiased about J. Frank Norris? Almost immediately after the indictment came down, rumors began to circulate having to do with a possible change of venue for a Norris trial. Some who wanted to see the man convicted and presumably executed for his crime wondered if any jury made up of locals could possibly be free of his influence. Others, who saw Norris as a spiritual hero, wondered if there could be a fair and impartial jury formed when there was so much hatred toward their beloved pastor.

Even before the date of the trial was known, the issue of venue became a hot topic. Marvin Simpson, Norris's lead attorney, was asked about it: "No such move is contemplated." It was the same with W.P. McLean who, along with the District Attorney's Office, indicated, "The State does not plan at this time to seek a change of venue." Yet the rumors persisted.

Another edition of the *Searchlight* hit the streets and mails on Friday, July 30, complete with a full transcript of Norris's recent anti-Catholic diatribe. In one week the paper had added five thousand more subscribers, its masthead now reading: "65,000 — Searchlight Average Weekly Paid Circulation Is Over 65,000."

On page three of the tabloid, readers found information about the man Norris had killed. He was described as someone "who attempted the life of Dr. Norris." The affidavit by Ollie Stanley, the former Westbrook Hotel house detective — the one Norris had shown Haldeman-Julius and Wilke — was published verbatim. In addition, another cryptic, unsigned letter describing threats D.E. Chipps allegedly made purportedly surfaced. It said, in part: "On Saturday, July 17, D.E. Chipps came into my place of business, he was angry and cursing before me and others, he swore that 'I am going to kill J. Frank Norris.' He said, 'The crowd I run with haven't got the guts to do it; I can kill any man. Tomorrow morning's headlines all over America will read, "D.E. Chipps kills Dr. J. Frank Norris." I'll rush on him and get him first.'"

The *Searchlight* article, written by the tabloid's business manager, J.M. Gilliam, concluded: "The above testimony is substantiated by other reliable witnesses and will come out in open trial." Gilliam further wrote, "Just a few days before [the shooting] a fourth-degree Knight of Columbus came into Norris' study threatening him, but we succeeded in avoiding trouble. Later, three other Catholics came for trouble and made threats. But they were quieted. They did not like the sermons Dr. Norris was preaching on Romanism."

J.M. Gilliam busily sought to exploit the situation to the *Searchlight*'s advantage. A large advertisement in the July 30 edition announced a "Double Investment" opportunity for loyal readers. The tabloid was "offering to its friends a fifty thousand ($50,000) issue of its Ten (10%) Per Cent Cumulative Preferred Stock (preferred both as to assets and dividends)." Said stock would be "sold in installments where desired" and "issued with a par value of Five Dollars ($5.00) per share." The ad continued, "To buy this stock you will not only, in our opinion, be making a good investment strictly from a financial standpoint, but will be making a contribution that will enable us to make this paper the largest single force in America in defending the truth against modern infidelity in all forms."

The idea was to turn the *Searchlight* into a player in the national media mix that would stand for "the fundamentals of the faith," "exposing hypocrisy," and shedding light on "the conspiracy of Rum and Romanism to elect a Catholic president to overthrow the Constitution and control this government." Achieving this goal would require the "employment of agents throughout the United States and Canada." It was heady and ambitious stuff — even for a publicity hound like J. Frank Norris. He sought nothing less than to leverage a murder charge against him into a national crusade for fundamentalist causes.

As the weekend began, all sides waited for official word about the date and place of the trial. Much of the delay was due to the fact that DA Hangar had to make an emergency trip to San Diego, where his father-in-law was very ill. But after his arrival there, his office released a statement that the J. Frank Norris murder trial would begin Monday, September 13, 1926, in the Tarrant County Criminal District Court and would be presided over by Judge George E. Hosey, who had just won reelection via his Democratic primary victory.

That Sunday, August 1, J. Frank Norris made a direct and specific appeal to his congregation. If his support was virtually nonexistent in certain quarters and described by detractors as on the wane, you would never know it from the happenings in and around First Baptist Church. The ministry reported "over 15,000" present at all services, the preacher speaking six times on the first Sunday of August, a little more than two weeks after he'd shot Chipps. In fact, the church boasted "one hundred and three additions to First Baptist Church for the day," or roughly twice as many as the week before.

Pastor Norris preached that hot Sunday morning on the subject "God's Answer to Satan's Conspiracy." Throughout the sermon, which was drawn from the story in the book of Daniel, chapter three, about the three Hebrew children enduring the fiery furnace, he identified himself with history's persecuted. He also talked about others in his camp being treated unfairly. "For instance," he shouted, "you take the office force of young ladies that you love, these good young women, most of whom are orphan girls, that now, by the underworld, by the powers of darkness, by hired, paid conspirators, and paid persecutors, that the names of these young women are now dragged in the mire and their characters attacked. Why? Just because perchance they happened to be in that office two weeks ago, the time of the unfortunate affair?"

He spent a great deal of time commending the congregation for being so solidly behind him. As the sermon wound down, he mentioned a letter he'd received from a lady in Kentucky, who had enclosed a check for five hundred dollars to help with expenses related to the pastor's defense. He then told his flock, "I am going to give you an opportunity," reminding them of what most already knew, that a long protracted trial and defense would require "a great deal of money."

He told the crowd that helping him financially was part of "this fight between the powers of darkness and hell on the one side, and Jesus Christ on the other, and you can either pay it now or later." He then instructed the ushers to pass out some envelopes and cards. The envelopes were for checks or cash; the cards were for those who could not give at the time, but would pledge to do so very soon, within sixty or ninety days. The preacher asked for some to "put down $500 or $1,000 as your contribution." In fact, Norris said, "I am glad to make a contribution of $1,000 or more myself." As people put money in the envelopes and filled out the cards, Pastor Norris reiterated there was a "diabolical plot" against him and he promised his followers: "Before this thing is done, we are going to take the lid off and go down to the deepest, darkest, abysmal depths. It will cost a little money, a good deal. We don't care. In this war between heaven and hell there is but one issue."

To reinforce the conspiracy idea, Norris informed his congregants, while ushers walked through the room collecting contributions and pledge cards, that someone had tampered with their radio station during the previous Sunday-night broadcast of his message, "The Menace of Roman Catholicism." He told them that his sermon would be rebroadcast that night, and that "these hindrances are not going to get anywhere"; that "indications are that the air may be a little warm this week." This kind of language was "Norris-speak" meaning he was going on the attack once again. Responding to the pastor's personal and emotional appeal, "members showered over $25,000" on Norris for his defense and what they certainly saw as the greater cause.

CHAPTER TWENTY-EIGHT

"The Rulers of the Darkness of This World"

THAT NEXT FRIDAY, a front-page announcement in the *Searchlight* advertised Norris's topic for the meeting in the "Open Air Tabernacle" for Sunday night, August 8. Before the sermon, he would give "a list of witnesses" who would testify "on visits and threats of certain Roman Catholics and Knights of Columbus." The paper also told the readers: "A letter will be given out, written from San Francisco to Fort Worth by a certain gentleman who used to live in Fort Worth, who flaunted his big bronze Knights of Columbus emblem on his watch charm as he walked the streets of Fort Worth. He wrote a letter from San Francisco giving instructions on 'What to do with Norris.' That letter arrived in Fort Worth at 11 AM August 3 and by 9 PM that very day that selfsame letter was on the desk of the editor of this paper — the letter gives specific instructions on 'how to take care of our cause, the Roman Catholic Church.'" In Norris's view, it was okay to defend his church from attack, but somehow inappropriate, even sinister, for Catholics to do the same.

The notice in the *Searchlight* also indicated that Norris would talk about the recent election when he addressed the Sunday throng. An interview with Jim Ferguson, the former governor and husband of the sitting governor, was mentioned, one in which Ferguson seemingly blamed his wife's primary loss on Norris and his campaign against Roman Catholicism.

Also in the *Searchlight* that week, J.M. Gilliam wrote an item announcing the publication of a special volume of sermons on what he called "the present menace to American institutions of the powerful ecclesiasticism of Rome."

"Dr. J. Frank Norris for several years has been preaching a series of messages on Roman Catholicism delivered in whole or in part in the principal cities of America." Offering the complete volume to *Searchlight* readers for $1.50 or to be "sent free as a premium for three cash subscriptions," the faithful were guaranteed the "real truth" and background needed to understand the great Catholic "conspiracy" the way Norris did. The premium offer was just another way, wrote Gilliam, to encourage "all the friends who love the Fundamentals of our Christian faith" to help increase the circulation of the *Searchlight*.

J.M. Gilliam's name had been appearing regularly in the *Searchlight* for less than a year. Norris had met him during a visit to New York City's Calvary Baptist Church, where Gilliam served as a deacon and chairman of the finance committee. The New Yorker was a moderately successful businessman who had developed a unique writing instrument called the Dubel-Servis pen and pencil. As a member of the famous Baptist church on West Fifty-seventh Street, he was tapped for the high-trust positions of deacon and chair of the finance committee.

He impressed Norris, who lured him to Fort Worth. By the late spring of 1926, readers of the *Searchlight* no longer saw the name of L.M. Aldridge in the paper; Gilliam had taken his place as business manager. Norris was a hard man to work for, and virtually impossible to work with, and so turn-over among his staff was not uncommon.

Gilliam's flare for the entrepreneurial resonated with Dr. Norris. Norris was convinced that the *Searchlight* had the potential to become a widely read national periodical, and Gilliam embraced the dream.

As advertised, J. Frank Norris used his Sunday sermon to educate his audience about an effort by the Knights of Columbus in Dallas to raise a "Special Fund for the Fort Worth case." He read aloud from newspapers in Austin and San Antonio, quoting Jim Ferguson talking about the recent Democratic gubernatorial primary race lost by his wife, Miriam. "Pa" credited her loss "to certain causes" including the fact "that Norris broadcast a sermon against the Catholic Church." Of course, the preacher relished the idea of being seen as either kingmaker or spoiler. Norris also read from a letter purportedly distributed by a committee of the "Catholic Truth Society" of Fort Worth that said: "Catholic Citizen and Friend: Evil and Malicious influences are at work to abridge and destroy your rights and privileges, your citizenship is challenged, and it is your duty to know these influences the better to combat them. Do your duty and do it now!"

Norris aimed to reinforce with his flock the idea of a vast "deep laid conspiracy" against him. Never mind that he had inspired said "conspiracy" by attacking the Catholic citizens of Fort Worth, who mobilized in response. Norris was using a self-fulfilling prophecy to confuse the minds of local citizens, particularly those who might be in the jury pool. The nearly two-hour sermon — and the one that evening at the lot on Hemphill Street, with "20,000 reported at all services" — yielded First Baptist Church seventy-two new members and J. Frank Norris more recruits for his personal army.

Sunday morning, August 15, the topic of Norris's sermon was "The Rulers of the Darkness of This World." To further bolster his case that the "Romanists" were out to get everybody, the preacher made a point that the Catholics even sought to control the health care industry in town.

He asked rhetorically, "How many undertakers are there in this city? Six or Eight?" He continued, "I want to call this five thousand people to witness, you phone Spellman or Sloan or Harveson or the Fort Worth Undertaking Company or Shannon or any of them and here is what will happen every time. That Roman Catholic ambulance will be on the scene whether you call them or not. Yes sir, we have got proof, after proof of where that is so, and what do they do? Every time they will take the patient to St. Joseph Hospital." He told of a boy who had fallen off a roof, breaking both legs, asking to be taken to the Baptist hospital, only to be told no while en route to St. Joseph's. Of course, St. Joseph's was where the ambulance had taken D.E. Chipps after Norris shot him and where the lumberman was pronounced dead. If even Fort Worth's ambulance drivers were part of the "conspiracy," the crafty demagogue was suggesting, one has to wonder: Who else?

AS THE END OF August approached, Texas voters were asked to go to the polls once more, this time for the runoff between the highest vote-getters in the earlier primary. Though Dan Moody had bested Governor Ma Ferguson by more than 126,000 votes, he had of course fallen a few thousand votes short of what was needed for outright victory.

His preferred candidate, Lynch Davidson, having run a distant third, J. Frank Norris now found himself, somewhat reluctantly, supporting Moody. Anyone was better than the pro-Catholic, anti-Prohibition

Fergusons. He accepted a full-page advertisement for the *Searchlight* from the "friends of Dan Moody," indicating the preacher's tacit backing. The notice ran in the final two issues in August and said: "Vote for Dan Moody and Clean Government on Saturday, August 28th." It included an essay written by the "Fort Worth Friends of Dan Moody" asking local citizens to "redeem Texas from the blight of Fergusonism" by voting for Moody, calling him "a man of conscientious courage and a courageous conscience."

Mrs. Ferguson made a desperate attempt to connect Moody with the Ku Klux Klan, despite the fact that as attorney general he had sent several of the hooded nuts to the penitentiary. Battling a hay-fever cough, she thundered, "If Mr. Moody should be elected the governor all his crowd would be invisible and he would be responsible more to the Ku Klux Klan than to the Democrats of Texas." But the voters weren't persuaded. Dan Moody thumped the incumbent governor 495,723 votes to 270,595.

CHAPTER TWENTY-NINE

"A Matchup Between Polar Opposites"

FRIDAY, SEPTEMBER 3, J. Frank Norris officiated as his daughter, Lillian Gaddie Norris, married Charles Blanchard Weaver, a native of Wheaton, Illinois, and Harvard University faculty member. The preacher, usually craving publicity, blocked newspaper coverage of the private ceremony, attended by a small group of close friends and family.

The trial's start date having been moved to the end of October in order to avoid September's still-summery heat, all sides seemed to be saving energy for the fierce battle to come. Norris did his best to get his mind off the coming trial, and his possible execution. He took a trip by himself back to Hill County to get away and think. It had now been more than twenty-five years since his mother died. He found that going back to this neck of the woods gave him a connection to her, the woman who had nurtured and believed in him and had done her best to protect him from his father's drunken abuse.

The preacher was finding it hard to sleep and eat. Close friends worried over his state of mind. But soon he emerged from whatever depression he had been experiencing and plunged back into the daily details of running his church ministry. He believed that the ultimate measure of his life was in the impact he had on people as an evangelist. And while the weather remained warm that September, and the days still relatively long, he resumed a practice that had once been central to his ministry — "house-to-house visitation."

Norris would locate a neighborhood and go door-to-door like a Fuller Brush salesman. Some doors slammed in his face as soon as he introduced himself: "I'm J. Frank Norris, pastor of the First Baptist Church. Where do you go to church?" Some people engaged him in conversation for the sheer curiosity value of talking to someone who had recently killed another man.

Later he recalled: "I would go out there and spend the day walking from house to house, and when noontime came, I would go to the grocery story and get a dime's worth of cheese and crackers, and a bottle of pop, and eat it and swell up and go on till night came." Reverting to methods he employed before he had a radio station and newspaper, when he was just a hungry young preacher, seemed to reinvigorate Norris and to settle his nerves. It was also highly effective. By the time of his scheduled trial, First Baptist Church would announce that more than six hundred new members had been added in the three months following the shooting of D.E. Chipps by its pastor in its buildings.

This sense of purpose and serenity was in evidence as J. Frank Norris marked his seventeenth anniversary as pastor of First Baptist Church with little fanfare. As he stood before his congregation on Sunday, September 18, before announcing his text and theme, Norris said: "Beloved, we begin today our eighteenth year together. I will not, as perhaps it is customary, as might be expected, review any achievements or account any successes. We will face the future and leave the past, as it is, in God's hands." His message was subdued, some even thought it devotional, certainly not the typical J. Frank Norris fare.

There was also a lull around the Fort Worth Club. Several of its influential members had left town on a specially chartered "Sante Fe train" to see Jack Dempsey defend his title against Gene Tunney. While Amon Carter and friends sat in their seats at Philadelphia's Sesquicentennial Stadium on Friday, September 23, the rest of the Fort Worth Club members tuned in by radio back home.

This particular boxing match had become bigger than a mere sporting event. It had captured the attention of the nation as "a morality play involving a handsome, clean-cut former Marine from the sidewalks of New York," who was also a classic boxer, up against Dempsey, "a no-holds barred roughneck with a menacing scowl and a deadly punch who had been labeled a slacker for accepting a deferment during the Great War."

At the Fort Worth Club the rooting, not to mention the wagering, was nonetheless for Dempsey. The bout was a matchup between polar opposites. The champion was "the slugger who fought out of crouch and stalked opponents relentlessly." The challenger, on the other hand, in a manner reminiscent of "Gentleman" Jim Corbett, was "the stand up, manufactured boxer." Gene Tunney took the title that night by unanimous decision. In the dressing room after the fight, Jack Dempsey sheepishly told his celebrity wife, Estelle: "Honey, I forgot to duck!"

That Sunday as the crowd gathered for the eleven o'clock service at First Baptist, there was much talk about how quiet things had been. Even the recent issues of the *Searchlight* were notably absent anti-Catholic vitriol. What was Norris up to? Was this a change of heart? His message for September 26 was titled simply "A Praying Church."

Norris was actually laying low at the strong and insistent advice of his attorneys, all of whom told him that he was talking way too much, both to the press and his own constituency. They told him, in effect, to shut up if he wanted to avoid the penitentiary, or worse: the electric chair.

Meanwhile, Mayor H.C. Meacham had returned to Fort Worth, having spent the better part of August and the early days of September on an extended vacation in California. The stress of the Norris controversy, as well as the grief he felt — perhaps even a measure of guilt — over the death of his friend Chipps had taken a toll on his already sensitive health. He battled chronic stomach problems, insomnia, as well as issues with his nerves — and even heart.

Upon his return to the city, Meacham looked after pressing store business and sought to attend to the correspondence waiting in his mayoral office in city hall. Behind the nameplate HENRY CLAY MEACHAM — MAYOR was an unusually large stack of mail. As he began to sort through the pile, Meacham realized that he had become a celebrity of sorts as a result of his name appearing in the papers all over the country in connection to the Norris case. He did not like the attention.

There were letters from people inquiring as to whether they might be related to the mayor. Others sought help with mundane matters. The majority of the correspondence, however, expressed opinions on the already famous case. A few letters were critical of Meacham. One or two were even threatening. But these were generally unsigned. Most of the communications were supportive.

Many had questions they hoped Meacham could answer. A minister in Toronto, for example — the Reverend A.J. Vining of the College Street Baptist Church — wrote: "You are probably aware of the fact that your notorious preacher, the Rev. Dr. Norris, has a great friend in this city by the name of Shields." There is no reason to believe that Meacham had any idea about T.T. Shields of Jarvis Street Baptist Church in the Canadian city, unless maybe he had noticed Shields's name in the *Searchlight,* where he was weekly identified as "Bible School Editor." At any rate, Vining continued, "He [Shields] has frequently visited Fort Worth and on his return has always boasted about the very great congregations. He speaks about an audience (if I remember correctly) of '6,000.' I would appreciate it very much if you would be good enough to give me the official seating capacity of the First Baptist Church of your city?"

Meacham wrote back: "I am informed by the secretary of the city Fire Marshall that the rated seating capacity of the First Baptist Church of this city is 5,000." Many others asked essentially the same question: "Is it actually true that so many people go week after week to hear J. Frank Norris?"

Yes, it was true, and that fact irked a lot of people, Meacham included. Meacham was paying good money for good lawyers to ensure the man's conviction, and he hoped they did their job.

CHAPTER THIRTY

"Trying to Influence the Course of Justice"

FRIDAY, OCTOBER 8, the Tarrant County District Attorney's Office finally announced the start date for the J. Frank Norris murder trial. It would begin Monday, November 1. Newspapers across the country carried the story, and as journalists prepared to descend on Fort Worth, city officials pondered how to handle the crowds and publicity. Newspapers in the Hearst syndicate saw the potential for a great public spectacle. Their readers were told, "Behind a heavy curtain of secrecy, scenes are being shifted for the southwest's greatest court drama since the trial of Clara Smith for the slaying of Jake Hamon at Ardmore, Oklahoma, five years ago . . . Sensational revelations at the trial are promised by both sides in the case, and both insist the trial will not be postponed, nor the case transferred to any other county, despite rumors to the contrary."

The date having been set, the First Baptist Church publicity machine started up on Norris's behalf. Writing in the October 15 *Searchlight*, J.M. Gilliam rallied the faithful: "If it had been a bootlegger or tin horn gambler in Dr. Norris' position, there never would have been an indictment returned." He confidently stated, "The affair of July 17 is not the issue to be tried, but every issue that Dr. Norris has championed will likely enter the trial." He mocked the lawyers hired to assist the district attorney: "The hired prosecution — and it is a very strange thing that certain well-known forces and organizations should hire prosecution — came out in the press and practically admitted it would be impossible to secure a jury. The enemies of Dr. Norris hope for but one thing, namely to get a 'sinker' or two on the jury, hoping thereby to besmirch his name before the world." Gilliam also used his appeal to raise funds: "The conspiracy has forced us to spend no small amount of money, and we thank our friends everywhere who have voluntarily sent in their contributions."

Also in mid-October, the First Baptist Church announced "a parade of the faithful" scheduled for Sunday, October 31, on the eve of the trial. Church officials, presumably Norris among them, and likely a driving force behind the idea, estimated that "10,000" would march through the streets of downtown Fort Worth in support of their embattled pastor. Certainly this would be an unprecedented, not to mention somewhat crude, thing to do in relationship to a trial where one man was accused of murdering another.

The church's board of trustees, led by its chairman, attorney B.F. Bouldin, wrote to Mayor Meacham applying for a permit for the planned parade. The letter was delivered to Meacham at city hall by a personal messenger named Lee Joyce. Joyce was a Norris supporter and a former deputy sheriff who had recently lost his electoral bid for county sheriff. Meacham read it, paused, and crumpled it while replying for all nearby to hear, "No answer." When Joyce reported back to the Norris camp, all involved saw the mayor's curt two-word reply as an outright denial of the permit by the city. Making the most of the slight, the church then issued a statement describing Meacham's response somewhat hyperbolically, trying to create the image of persecution, with a powerful politician denying a church a simple permit because of his prejudice against a preacher.

However, as this statement was making its way around town, a notice arrived at First Baptist Church that the city had in fact granted them a permit for the parade. Apparently Meacham, or those around him, sensed that he had given Norris another public relations gift, just as he had with the firing of department store employees. Church leaders, however, decided not to let Meacham take it back. Speaking for the church, Norris attorney Chester Collins, who had recently joined the growing defense team, said: "It's a closed issue. We consider that the mayor objected to the parade when he refused to immediately give us an answer. There'll be no parade."

News of the now-scuttled parade plans was published in papers across the country.

The idea of a parade for a man charged with murder struck a nerve with many Americans. Some wrote to the mayor of Fort Worth expressing their outrage at the audacity of such a thing. The clerk of the office of commissioners in Xenia, Ohio, George Stokes, wrote to the mayor: "Hope you will be able to stand firm on not allowing a parade. My father was a minister of the Gospel but no murderer and if he had been he would not have stood for such a sympathy racket as that." Even legal scholars weighed in on the matter. An article in the *Ohio State Journal* titled "Influencing Justice" said:

> We hold no particular brief for the Mayor of Fort Worth, but it seems to us that the petition of the church board might legitimately have been refused on ground of public expediency. The parade obviously was intended as a demonstration on behalf of a minister who in a few hours thereafter would stand trial for murder. Such a demonstration could not but have its effect upon the prospective jurors, upon the community and even upon the court itself. No good end ever is served by trying to influence the course of justice. Such an attempt immediately casts suspicion upon those who are back of it and, as a rule, makes converts for the opposite side of many who otherwise would be neutral. Regardless of the fact that he wears the cloth and however large may be the measure of popular sympathy for him, the Fort Worth minister should go to trial strictly upon the merits of the charge for which he is indicted. Any attempt, however well intentioned, to stir up sympathy for him or to show how numerous and how strong his friends are can only react against him in the long run.

A.L. Van Hise of Columbus, Ohio, mailed a clipping of the *Journal* article to Mayor Meacham. "It is not a pleasant situation for you and being a long way from you about all I can do is to send my sympathy, but believe me it is real and sincere," he wrote in a letter accompanying the clipping. Meacham's appreciative reply confirmed that he was becoming wise to the manipulative ways of J. Frank Norris: "Upon advice from the lawyers for the prosecution, the same day in writing I gave them permission to parade. But they had no thought of parading. Their only idea was to get me to refuse so that they might have something to holler about."

As the end of October approached, representatives of the national press were pouring into the city. Nearly every arrival at the Texas & Pacific Rail Station in Fort Worth contained a reporter or two or three. Hotel reservations were being wired in daily. The trial was already being described far and wide as "the greatest drama in the history of Fort Worth."

Both sides in the case anticipated a trial lasting several weeks, maybe even a month. It was estimated that telegraph toll charges run up by journalists would exceed "$300 a day," and "the total expense to newspapers for handling the Norris trial story in all its details is estimated at a minimum of $1,000 a day" — an unheard-of sum in those days. Dozens of extra tables were installed in the courtroom to accommodate correspondents "from every section of the country." Extra telegraph wires were strung and extra machines installed. The plan was to provide nearly real-time reports. "Within a few minutes after the testimony is given from the witness stand it will be typed out by machine in hundreds of cities. Two or three telegraph operators with instruments will be at the building."

Special provisions were even being made to help attorneys, judges, and other court personnel gain access to the besieged courtroom. Many would "enter and leave the courtroom through a window and by a ladder to the ground."

One of the reporters who traveled to Fort Worth in the days leading up to the trial was a young lady from San Antonio named Bess Carroll. Sam Woolford, publisher of the San Antonio *Light,* had hired her as a cub reporter in 1923. The two would eventually marry and become quite the power couple in the city of the Alamo. A gifted writer, she would one day craft broadcasts to Nazi Germany for the *Voice of America* during World War II. Miss Carroll had decided to try to interview both the wife of J. Frank Norris and the widow of D.E. Chipps, knowing that this would be of great interest to her paper's readers. She hoped to "read the hearts" of the two women in telling their "great human story."

Mae Chipps had been monitoring developments from the background. She was publicity-shy and could easily become emotional when talking about the case, not to mention her dead husband. But Bess put her at ease when she telephoned, asking the widow if they could talk on the record, assuring Mrs. Chipps that she was interested in things more from the heart than the nuts and bolts of the case that others were writing about.

Finding her way to the Chipps bungalow on Lipscomb Street, she was invited inside. Young "freckle-faced" Dexter Jr. made his way to another room as the two ladies sat down in the kitchen. Over several cups of coffee they talked about what had happened and what it meant to the widow and her son. It was just Bess talking to Mae before long, and the widow wept as she shared memories and hopes she once had for the future.

The reporter asked if there had been talk of reconciliation between her and Dexter. The widow surprised Bess: "Yes, we would have probably remarried. My boy needed a father. You know it's so hard to rear a son, a precarious job for a woman alone. I feel that my son lost his father just when he needed him most." Mae told Bess of her love for Dexter, the breakup of their marriage notwithstanding. D.E. Chipps was "her dearest friend." She described their divorce as "unusual," assuring her guest, "Whenever I wanted anything, I called on him and my wish was always granted. Mr. Chipps was the most dependable man I ever knew."

Their separation was not tainted with the bitterness often present in most divorce situations. She knew that "the little cloud" that had arisen between them "could be easily brushed aside." Both parents "adored the same idol — the 14-year old boy, who was once their toddling baby," and "saw the sun of their lives rise and set on him."

When Bess Carroll wrote her article based on the interview with Mae Chipps, she said: "It was a great glowing thing that lighted commonplace existence for them, the love they shared for a tall freckled boy. It was a beacon showing them the way to future years." The journalist sentimentally began and ended her piece with the words, "It might have been!"

While taking great pains to present the widow of the slain lumberman as a sympathetic and sentimental figure, Bess Carroll approached Mrs. J. Frank Norris differently. She first observed the wife of the controversialist from a distance, attending her Sunday-morning Bible class. Presenting Mrs. Norris to her readers as "Spartan" and "unshaken," the reporter never actually arranged a personal interview. Describing the pastor's wife as "the assistant pastor of First Baptist Church" (something that certainly raised more than a few Southern Baptist eyebrows in those days), she emphasized Mrs. Norris as every bit as strong as her husband, minus the flamboyance and outspokenness. The reporter, having researched Lillian Norris's background, wrote about her childhood and being raised by a "hell-fire and brimstone" preacher. While the article that appeared in the paper was factual, it lacked the warmth and sympathy the reporter had felt for Mrs. Chipps.

In advance of the trial proceedings, the prosecutor confirmed that his office would seek the ultimate penalty upon a conviction of J. Frank Norris for murder. "The state will demand the death penalty." The stakes were as high as they get, and the nation waited to see if the pastor of the largest Protestant church in the country would die in the electric chair.

FIVE HUNDRED POTENTIAL jurors were summoned, and it was predicted that the trial would involve testimony from possibly one hundred witnesses from both sides. *The New York Times* informed its readers, "Not one week has elapsed since the killing that some sensation regarding the Norris case has not developed." One example illustrated the sense of determination, even desperation, already being exhibited by both the prosecution and defense. It emerged that the fourteen-year-old boy, Carl Glaze, reported to be a mystery witness during the July grand jury probe but never actually called to testify, was himself the subject of a drama. Initially Glaze had bragged to friends that he had seen J. Frank Norris shoot D.E. Chipps, having stopped by the office at just that moment. If so, he would be the only person other than Norris and L.H. Nutt to have actually witnessed the killing.

At first, the District Attorney's Office was elated about Glaze's potential testimony, because it reportedly varied from the story told by Norris and Nutt. But before the boy could testify, Robert Hangar removed his name from the witness list, indicating that Glaze's testimony was not necessary for an indictment.

Now on the eve of the trial, some behind-the-scenes maneuvers came to light. It seems that, fearing Glaze's testimony would be damaging to Pastor Norris, "friends and employees of the First Baptist Church locked Carl Glaze, 14, in the home of Mrs. Bessie Williams." He had been taken there to try to persuade, maybe even manipulate, him away from any account that might reflect badly on Norris or cast any shadow of doubt on his version of events.

Mrs. Williams, "a Methodist evangelist" who worked for the *Searchlight,* was also "the head of the Women's Ku Klux Klan organization" in Fort Worth. Mrs. Williams and the other "friends of Norris" pressured young

Glaze to repudiate his statements desired by the district attorney and modify his testimony to fit the Norris line.

Yet no charges of witness tampering were brought. For whatever reason, there appeared to be a willingness by the prosecution to tread lightly. Were they a bit fearful of J. Frank Norris, and the infamous eleventh commandment in Fort Worth, "Thou shalt not mess with J. Frank Norris"?

Visitors to the church offices on Saturday, October 30, were struck by the calm, even business-as-usual demeanor of Norris and his staff. One observed that "about twenty young men and women" occupied themselves with the business of Norris's ministry empire. The atmosphere was friendly and even at times filled with humor. People spoke in normal tones, only occasionally interrupted by "the crisp, magnetic voice of Dr. Norris dictating letters and giving instructions to his workers." The only unusual thing was the presence of a large amount of flowers, apparently sent to J. Frank Norris with best wishes as he went on trial for killing a man.

Sunday morning, October 31, 1926, a few minutes before eleven o'clock, Throckmorton Street between Third and Fourth in downtown Fort Worth was overrun with people. As the various Sunday school classes operated by First Baptist Church dismissed, congregants of all ages made their way toward the main doors of the sanctuary. The church orchestra, led by Brooks Morris, had begun to play upbeat hymns as the audience filed into the spacious room. Across the street from the office building containing Pastor Norris's study, the young people who had been meeting in the upper floors of the church-owned building flowed out to the sidewalk and past the J.C. Penney store on the street-level part of the same building. On this day more than two thousand young people were making their way from Sunday school classrooms to the main church service.

After the preliminaries of music and general announcements, Dr. Norris faced his congregation. He had a determined look on his face, and vibrancy had returned to his voice. The night before, his attorneys had reminded him to stay the same low-key course. Just preach a good sermon, no fighting, no fuss. But he sensed his flock needed a glimpse of passion on this day. Maybe he couldn't name names and talk about the "deep laid conspiracy," but he could remind people he was a master in the pulpit.

Dr. Norris chose as his subject the benign and most basic of all Baptist doctrines: baptism. But as he warmed to his theme, congregants soon became aware that the subject, though vital to all of them, was incidental to what was really happening. The service would not be about the message, but rather the messenger. J. Frank Norris would communicate with his followers in heartfelt code, and they would understand. There were some things he certainly couldn't say right then, but it was only temporary, only a matter of time. Meanwhile, he reminded them why they followed and loved him: He was their preacher!

Those in the crowd that day would acknowledge, "Never was there a Sunday in the history of the church when we needed a mountain-top, transfiguration experience." Even though "there were thirty news correspondents present," representing "all the great news agencies," the service would be an unapologetic "old time shouting" experience. National attention would not temper or inhibit them. Norris shouted, begged, pleaded, thundered, persuaded, and orated. It was church kicked up a notch, and the people were glad to have their pastor back.

Norris preached for an hour and then some, but the faithful didn't budge, and the press had no choice but to sit there and take it. Norris took the audience from scripture to scripture. With machine-gun-like delivery, he talked about the great truths of the Bible. He told stories that made his audience cry, others that made them laugh, and at every turn he pointed to the kind of commitment it would take to win the great battles of life. Described by one reporter in the crowd that day as "lithe, black-clad and eloquent," Norris reaffirmed his belief in the "literal interpretation of the Bible." And as he preached, the audience began to talk back to him, first with "Amen," then with "Glory." As the preacher talked passionately about heaven, a woman in the balcony began to shout loud enough to be heard by all. As she screamed her approval and agreement with the preacher, "at least 100 pairs of hands applauded." Acknowledging his emotional congregant, Norris told the church, "As long as we have members like this, the devil in his bottomless pit had better let this church alone."

Norris, as a speaker, did not like to wind down his sermons. Never would you hear him start to soften or slow down as he came close to his conclusion. He would follow the old African-American method, "Start low — Go slow; Rise higher — Catch fire!"

And as his voice rose higher and higher, his words swelling and thunderous, the preacher finally came to the crucial moment. It was time for the invitation. "Without a song, without a word, without standing, who will be the first to rise in the presence of this great audience and come?" he asked. While members of the press scattered throughout the massive room watched, a middle-aged man got up, then a young man made a move, and before long a throng of people was making its way to Norris from every corner of the auditorium. More than one hundred were baptized at First Baptist Church that day. The preacher said, "Here they come, praise the Lord!"

CHAPTER THIRTY-ONE

"Moses Versus Wild Bill"

AS THE CITIZENS OF Fort Worth began their day on Monday, November 1, they read in their newspapers details of what to expect as the Norris murder trial got started. They also read about the death of the famous escape artist and illusionist Harry Houdini the night before in Detroit. Would the Reverend Norris, who had wriggled out of many a mess before, including three criminal indictments fifteen years earlier, as well as two sensational trials, be able to escape conviction for murder and death in the electric chair?

Two hours before the scheduled starting time of nine o'clock, a crowd was gathered at the Tarrant County Criminal Courts Building. It included the same newspaper reporters who had sat through Norris's sermon the day before, and many, many more. For someone who had craved and courted publicity throughout his career, this was an extraordinary day. One of the reporters, Mr. Frank Baldwin of the *Austin American,* noted, "It is doubtful if ever a stage was set at a Texas murder trial to provide the world with facts on the Norris trial than what was arranged" that morning.

Baldwin described the scene as including "thirty-two seats, conveniently arranged at the front of the court room for newspaper representatives." They were arranged in four rows and spread out half the width of the room. They were all filled. Beyond that, telegraph wires were "conspicuous in the press gathering." He concluded, "If anybody at 9:25 o'clock this morning throughout the United States did not know who, when, what, and where about J. Frank Norris, it was their own fault by today noon."

Each of the wide-armed chairs bore the name of its owner and paper. The big services, the Associated Press, the United Press, and Hearst International (Universal), were given priority access to the telegraph lines. As the proceedings went forward, for example, the AP representative, W.C. Grant, would punch out copy on his special "noiseless typewriter." He then handed the pages to a telegraph operator, who would send the words around the country right from the courtroom. Others, like the Hearst representative, Roger Busfield, known as "competent and swift," would write the story in longhand, handing the finished pages to "pretty, long-lashed Bess Carroll." Phillip Kinsley, who worked for the *Chicago Tribune,* was there. He had been to Dayton, Tennessee, to report the Scopes trial and relished the idea of another big media circus trial. And newspapers from all over Texas were represented.

As Judge George E. Hosey took his place "within the enclosure furnished in dark walnut," he scanned the courtroom, noting the unusual, but expected, capacity crowd. To his right stood the clerk of the court. To his left was the witness box. He made eye contact with the attorneys. Sitting at the defense table were Marvin Simpson and Dayton Moses, a late entry and well-known courtroom star. Many saw humor in a man named Moses — a "big majestic man . . . broad, massive, formidable . . . gray haired, well groomed, and with a hint of twinkle in his eye" — defending a man of God.

Courthouse observers looked forward to witnessing a legal battle between Moses and "Wild Bill" McLean, "one of the best known and most invincible lawyers in Texas." McLean tended to be "wary" where Moses was "aggressive." To make it all even more interesting, they were reversing their usual roles in this particular trial. Moses had more experience as a prosecutor, whereas "Wild Bill" was best known for his exploits as a defense attorney.

Judge Hosey gaveled the proceedings to order, quieting the crowd, and inquired whether both parties were ready to begin. The first order of business, one that could take many days, would be the selection of a jury from the five hundred men who had been summoned. The courtroom was taken by surprise when Marvin Simpson asked the judge for a short recess. Defense attorney Chester B. Collins, Simpson claimed, was ill, and they wanted to prepare a formal motion for a continuance. Hosey granted the request, giving them fifteen minutes. During the recess, as all but the defense team and Norris remained in the crowded courtroom, many wondered if the move were a delaying tactic.

In fact, something else was going on.

At 9:40 AM Norris and his team reentered the room, making their way through the crowd and back to the defense table. Hosey again asked if all parties were ready. This time Dayton Moses spoke for the defense and, begging the court's indulgence, announced the defense's motion asking for a change of venue in the case.

Speaking for the prosecution, District Attorney Bob Hangar angrily asserted, "The State would controvert the motion." Then the court recessed again, this time so the prosecution could prepare a response. It soon became clear that the defense's motion had been planned for some time, as it "announced itself prepared with 71 witnesses to substantiate its claims" in support of the need for a change of venue. One observer described the gist of their petition, "a lengthy and double-barreled document," to be: "1. That there existed in Tarrant County so great a prejudice against Dr. Norris that he could not obtain a fair and impartial trial. 2. That there was a dangerous combination against him instigated by influential persons to prevent his obtaining a fair trial in Tarrant County."

The balance of the written motion expanded on the two points, while rehashing all aspects of the story leading up to July 17, 1926, including Norris's battle with the city over its decision to pay $152,000 for the St. Ignatius property and the firing of First Baptist Church members from Meacham's Department Store. The mayor was also the source of many "vindictive personal comments."

When court resumed during the ten o'clock hour, the prosecution vigorously and vehemently denied Norris's version of reality, saying over and over again, "If there were a few citizens prejudiced against him [Norris], their prejudice was the result of his own unwarranted attacks against them." As the lawyers wrangled over the issues, J. Frank Norris sat watching "with at least a flicker of a smile upon on his face, which at times broke into a broad smile — almost a grin."

The rest of the morning was occupied with the defense making its argument for the venue change. Mayor Meacham, O.E. Carr, and others heard their names mentioned again and again by Dayton Moses. It was alleged that "Meacham had contributed $5,000" and "O.E. Carr $1,500, and other people various amounts 'secretly' to the payment of the fee of the private prosecutors." Also cited by the defense was the charge that City Manager Carr had been quoted in the Fort Worth newspapers as saying he would pay "to any person $1,000 who would prove that Dr. Norris did not murder D.E. Chipps in cold blood, and who would prove that Chipps was armed at the time."

One feature of the defense's presentation that morning that took everyone by surprise was brought in as "Exhibit A":

> This defendant would further represent and show to Your Honor that as further activities on the part of said dangerous combination of persons against him instigated by influential persons aforesaid, there has been published and circulated throughout Tarrant County, Texas, for the purpose of fomenting and creating prejudice against this defendant, thousands of copies of the *Haldeman-Julius Magazine,* an infidel publication, whose chief business is to attack the Christian religion, published at Girard, Kansas, in the September, 1926, issue; and thousands of copies of *Pitchfork Smith's Magazine,* published in the city of Dallas, Texas, each of said magazines carrying what was purported to be by said magazines the true facts relative to the circumstances leading up to, surrounding, and taking place at the time of the tragedy for which this defendant is to be tried, but in truth and in fact distorting the truth thereof and published for nothing but the propaganda for the prosecution and containing plain, licentious lies for the purpose of distorting the truth, misleading and molding the public mind against this defendant in order to prevent and prohibit this defendant from obtaining a fair and impartial trial, a copy of said publications being attached hereto and made a part hereof.

Marcet Haldeman-Julius, who had interviewed Norris at length a few days after the shooting and written the piece that was now part of the official court record titled, "J. Frank Norris — Shooting Salvationist," was not in the courtroom that morning. She was on her way to Fort Worth but had wrongly assumed that Monday's proceedings would be mainly about "dilatory pleas" and the mundane process of jury selection. When she heard about the mention of her magazine and article in court that Monday, her first response was that the connection between what she had written and a "mythical conspiracy was of course too absurd for comment." She also noted, "All the copies of the September, 1926, issue sent there [Tarrant County] went as usual to our regular subscribers and to the newsstands."

As the time for the lunch break drew near, Dayton Moses pointed out that just a little more than a week earlier, on October 21, to be exact, his team had asked the judge for a copy of the list of potential jurors, requesting that one be sent to the prosecutors as well. The judge agreed to this, largely as a concession to the "prominence of all concerned and the intensity of feeling." This action was designed, presumably, to give both sides time to do sufficient background work, a tactic that would ultimately save time in court. The prosecution had agreed to the idea of the list being given out but indicated that it should only be done a couple of days before the trial.

The fact was that Norris's team wanted to conduct a fishing expedition to find evidence of the "deep laid conspiracy" they talked so much about. The prosecutors were fearful — likely with good reason — that the defense would attempt to manipulate jurors. In the end, the judge thought better of it and defaulted to prevailing practice: "The list of venire men should be furnished one day before the trial begins." Now the defense argued that by deciding to conduct things business-as-usual and not grant the defense request for the early release of the list, the judge was contributing to "the prejudice" against Norris.

Around noon, Hosey announced the break for lunch. Norris, who had been virtually muzzled by his attorneys in recent weeks, seemed pleased with the events of the morning. He also clearly wanted to talk. Striking up a conversation with one of the reporters heading out to lunch, he said, "What do I think of the trial so far? Well, all the big guns were sprung in the request for a change of venue. We will probably bring up some smaller ones for a little more firing later on, however."

That afternoon, the prosecution dealt with the various arguments specifically and thoroughly. District Attorney Hangar spoke, first reading a hastily written statement. The main points of it were that, though the special prosecutors were being paid, only Mrs. D.E. Chipps and H.C. Meacham had contributed to the fee. Furthermore, any controversy that became the fuel for Norris's attacks on the city leaders "grew out of the fact that in their official capacities they were endeavoring to force Dr. Norris to pay taxes to the city of Fort Worth, and water rent, in compliance with the law."

As to the matter of the city's purchase of the Catholic-owned property, something J. Frank Norris regularly referred to in conspiratorial terms, Hangar declared the transaction had been approved without any interference by O.E. Carr, and with no vote on the mayor's part. This seemed to take the teeth out of Norris's claim that it was all a manipulation on the part of Carr and Meacham to benefit the mayor's business enterprise.

Regarding "Exhibit A," the mention of the *Haldeman-Julius Magazine,* Mr. Hangar suggested that if the statements attributed to Norris by Marcet Haldeman-Julius were untrue, he had recourse via the civil court mechanisms. He added, though, that "certainly no prejudice could be created about which he might complain, by reference to his own statements as to the facts surrounding the homicide."

Their statement and oral arguments complete, the defense began to call witnesses. H.C. Meacham was the first invited to the stand by Marvin Simpson. All in the courtroom, having grown a bit weary of the chronic lawyer talk, were suddenly alert and anticipating the first real potential drama since the announcement of the motion for venue change. Meacham was asked about his role in hiring the special prosecutors — the subject of rumors and accusations since July. The mayor testified that he had, in fact, hired the lawyers "for a fee of $15,000, of which he had already paid $6,500." When asked when he had done this, he replied: "I first talked to them on Sunday morning following the Saturday on which Chipps was murdered."

Simpson pressed Meacham, "Why do you say 'murdered' — were you present?"

"Why, I thought he [Norris] admitted it."

"Didn't you tell that to someone," Simpson probed. "Didn't you tell a man by the name of Richie that Norris ought to be shot through the belly?"

"I did not!"

The mayor denied he had made that remark in front of his store after reading Norris's attack on him in the *Searchlight.* He also denied that he had fired several of his store employees because they were members of First Baptist Church. In a tortured attempt to explain why he did what he did, he told Simpson that the employees were discharged not simply because of their affiliation with the church, but because they had indicated they believed what Norris was saying about him. Simpson then asked Meacham about a reported meeting of "certain Fort Worth citizens" in early July at the Fort Worth Club — a meeting called purportedly to discuss what to do about J. Frank Norris. "Didn't you make the statement that you were going to get rid of Norris?" Simpson asked the mayor. Meacham replied that he did not recall making such a statement. He also denied that he had sought the US attorney's advice on stopping circulation of Norris's paper through the mails.

"Didn't one of the men at the meeting say there were only two ways to end the mayor's controversy with Norris, one to ignore him and the other to take a shotgun to him and didn't you say you'd be damned if you'd ignore him?" Simpson challenged.

Meacham said he didn't recall hearing anything like that.

When Simpson asked the next question, about Meacham's "personal feelings" toward J. Frank Norris, DA Hangar objected. Hearing a revised form of the same question, the mayor replied, "My feelings are mixed. I am in doubt whether Norris is perfectly sane." The mayor then told of a visit to Norris's office when Meacham was running for office. He said that there had been a telephone campaign attacking him, and he was sure Norris was behind it. Meacham told the court that the preacher assured him that he had nothing to do with the calls.

Special prosecutor McLean handled the cross-examination and drew out that the reason Meacham had conducted the meeting at the Fort Worth Club in July was "to discuss a proposed tax valuation survey and that the discussion of Norris came up afterward." Meacham was adamant that he "did not have Norris in mind" when he called that meeting. "Why did you employ special counsel at $15,000 to prosecute this case?" McLean asked. Meacham replied, "Because Chipps was my friend and I thought it my duty and right to defend him, and that I thought Chipps would do the same for me."

At the end of his testimony, H.C. Meacham left the stand and walked toward the door in the rear of the courtroom. For a brief but intense moment his eyes met those of J. Frank Norris. Then he looked away and quickly left the room.

CHAPTER THIRTY-TWO

"There Is No Opposition to a Graveyard"

BY THE TIME Mayor Meacham had gotten halfway or so through his testimony, it was already clear to most observers that a change of venue was virtually inevitable. Norris's team had been very effective and the case against the preacher getting a fair trial was compelling, even overwhelming. The witnesses coming after Meacham were almost superfluous. Three more were called that afternoon before the court recessed shortly after 5:30 PM.

When Judge Hosey called the court back to order the next morning around nine fifteen, the first witness called was a man named Mr. Back from the town of Mansfield. He said: "People are so prejudiced that it would be dangerous to try him in this county; there are people who dislike him so much that they would hang him if he were innocent, while there are others that would clear him if he were guilty. I believe his friends would qualify for jury duty as would those who are prejudiced." W.E. Connell, president of Fort Worth's First National Bank and "a tall, elderly, dignified man," took the stand. He had a hard time hearing and had to lean forward and ask again and again for questions to be repeated. He reinforced the notion that most of the intelligent people in town had long ago formed definite opinions about Norris. P.M. Dean, a faithful member of First Baptist Church, testified that he doubted his pastor could get a fair shake from local citizens. "Wild Bill" McLean asked him: "How much did you contribute to the lawyer's fund?"

"Not a dime!" — the witness thinking he was being asked if he had contribute to the fee of the prosecutors.

"Well, to the Defense Fund?"

"I put in some extra money — but it went through the regular budget."

Another Norris loyalist, Mr. Newcome, acknowledged that he had given $250 to the Defense Fund, adding that he was also sure the pastor could not get a fair trial in Tarrant County. It was the same with Clay Cook and

A.F. Plunkett, who also testified that they had been part of the group of three hundred or so men who went over the names of potential jurors the previous Sunday. The mayor of nearby Grapevine, Texas, and several others gave virtually identical testimony.

Finally Judge Hosey met with about three hundred men who had been summoned as potential jurors in the case. He asked how many of them had formed opinions on the Norris case. About 90 percent of them raised their hands. After this the judge, almost with a look of relief, announced that he was granting the defense's motion for the change of venue. But where could the case be tried?

The court recessed, and Hosey admonished the two sides to meet and come up with a suitable venue for the trial. Clearly he hoped this could be decided quickly and amicably. He was wrong. When the parties did not return to the courtroom in a few minutes, most assumed that it was going to be a while before any announcement was made.

People caucused in small groups talking about the case. Marcet Haldeman-Julius noticed from across the room that J. Frank Norris was surrounded by a small throng of men, many of them journalists, so she made her way over to them. Most of the questions being put to Norris were from D.L. Hartley, a young-looking veteran of the Great War working for *The Kansas City Star*. Norris seemed at ease and quite pleased with what had transpired. He dominated the conversation, not seeming to grasp that this was what the reporters wanted. The more he talked, the more they could write. He waxed confident, telling those around him that he knew how to read people and how to discern character. He could figure out who was a poker player, who was a womanizer, and other traits just by conversation, describing himself as an expert in human behavior. He told a feeble joke or two trying to create rapport with the reporters. There were stories from his revival preaching around the country, anecdotes that usually brought a lot of laughs, but this group only smiled enough to keep the pastor talking.

Shifting gears, Norris assured the journalists, "All newspaper men are my friends. Some of them don't like me. There is one certain man, he's dead now and I hope he's in heaven" — another attempt at humor. One reporter seized the moment and countered, "You mean if there is a heaven?"

"Well, there is a heaven and you know it, too."

At that another reporter injected, "That calls for a column interview."

Norris, ignoring the request for a sort of exclusive, told a story about speaking in a certain city where he and a columnist locked horns. "He kept taking a crack at me in his columns, and unjustly. So I asked my audience to ask him how long it takes a man dressed in blue pajamas to go down a hotel fire escape in below zero weather when a husband unexpectedly arrives in town." The journalist, so said Norris, "left town until after my meeting was over." He told the reporters gathered 'round that any venue would be fine with him, though he seemed to rule out Waco, the home of his alma mater, Baylor College. Presumably, the preacher's highly public criticisms of the school in recent years would make it hard to find untainted jurors there.

Hartley asked, "Do you feel that your aggressive ministry has built up your church?"

"Absolutely! What else? There is no opposition to a graveyard. We have had six hundred additions since this trouble — we have broken all records!"

"In spite of it?"

"In spite of it!"

Norris continued, quoting from the first chapter of Philippians: "You don't know the scriptures, 'the things which happened unto me have fallen out rather unto the furtherance of the gospel.'" He then told the journalists of his church members' loyalty to him. "They know that I have put everything I have into the church, that I have no money — nothing except my home; that I could have gone to other places. I could have gone to Boston if I wished. If I'd go to Kansas City tomorrow," he said, looking Hartley in the eye, "and announce I was going to preach in Convention Hall — it would be full."

Another reporter asked Norris, "Do you really believe in this conspiracy?"

"If it weren't true, I wouldn't have said it, and if it weren't true, they would have demanded proof."

"How old are you, Doctor?"

"Forty-eight and married to the same wife I started with," Norris said, using one of his punch lines that always worked in the pulpit. No one laughed. He talked about the future of the church, surprising the group when he said, "I want one auditorium that will seat ten thousand people on one floor." He mentioned that he had followers as far away as Florida and Canada because of his radio broadcasts. He waxed philosophical: "Sorrow and laughter come from the same thing in you. Take your work but not yourself seriously. I have reached the point where 'none of these things move me.'"

As he talked to them about the difference between killing and murder, directing them to the Sermon on the Mount for help with the distinction, the courtroom doors opened and the lawyers returned, having come to a decision about where the important trial would take place.

It came out that the defense rejected out of hand Dallas, San Antonio, and Houston, due to large Catholic populations and/or the fact that Norris was well known and notorious in those cities. The only city the two sides could agree on was the Texas capital — Austin. This, they told Judge Hosey, was where the trial should be heard. But Hosey did not immediately agree. He did not think Austin was a large enough place to handle the auxiliary factors in such a case — its attendant crowds and media circus.

A twenty-minute discussion followed of everything from hotels to restaurants in Austin. Finally Judge Hosey conceded, ruling a little after 4:30 PM on Tuesday, November 2, 1926, that Austin would be the site of Texas's most celebrated murder trial ever. J. Frank Norris would face the death penalty the following January, not in the city on the Trinity, but rather in the Texas capital located on the banks of the Colorado River.

Norris talked with reporters once again after adjournment, his lawyers having given up trying to muzzle the pastor. He said: "It's all over now since the change of venue has been granted." Savoring the moment and the publicity, he added, "They thought they were going to try me. But it looks like they tried someone else." The reporters took down every word, even though the pompous preacher's meaning wasn't always entirely clear.

"The purpose of our filing the application for venue change was not because we did not want the case tried in Tarrant County," Norris declared. He saw the disbelief on the faces of the journalists and continued, "I would have been acquitted here or in any other county." They weren't convinced, but they continued to write as the preacher talked. "We filed the motion to show that there was a conspiracy against me. Of course, the state will say that we did not prove it, but we alleged it in open court. It's a matter of public record and it was not denied by witnesses — it's just a matter of time until I am acquitted," Norris beamed.

That evening more details began to circulate around the city, and it became known that Travis County Criminal District judge James R. Hamilton would preside.

James Robert Hamilton was a well-known jurist, tough-minded, intellectually brilliant, and a great orator. He had been one of the first barristers in Texas willing to go toe-to-toe with the Ku Klux Klan a few years before, demonstrating fierce courage in the process. Many saw this as bad news for Norris, speculating that Hamilton would be tough on the preacher. He might have been better off taking his chances in Fort Worth after all.

That very same day, Texas voters elected Dan "The Man" Moody as their new governor, the youngest person ever elected to that office. He would be inaugurated in January, also in Austin. Interestingly, with all the talk about the capacity of the Texas capital as a venue for this major trial, no one in the courtroom that day seemed to realize the possibility of a conflict with such a major, even historic, political event.

The stage was now set for two big happenings to converge on Austin at the same time. A new chief executive would be sworn in, and one of the state's most prominent citizens would face trial and the death penalty. The two events would take place within one hundred yards of each other.

CHAPTER THIRTY-THREE

"A Plea Against Hate and Factionalism"

H.C. MEACHAM, still somewhat shaken by the ordeal of giving his testimony in the change-of-venue trial, not to mention just having to be in the same room with J. Frank Norris, went to his department store office that Wednesday morning to catch up on work and correspondence. He had been answering letters and queries from around the country since his friend Chipps had been killed in July. Meacham hated seeing his name in stories covering the shooting and trial and wished all the publicity could just go away. He was a bundle of nerves, not sleeping well or eating right.

The first letter he read that morning was written to him by a local attorney and fellow Fort Worth Club member named W.M. Odell. It seemed to express what so many in the city were feeling about the Norris case. Odell wrote:

> Every good citizen of Fort Worth should regret that the prize of
> unselfish public service should be abuse, slander, and tragedy. It
> must be comforting to you, however, to know that the attitude of
> most of the good people of this community is reflected in the fact
> that the man mainly responsible for the conditions mentioned
> should find it necessary to boast of the fact that he had succeeded
> in establishing in court that his conduct had so aroused public
> sentiment against him that he could not secure a fair trial in the
> community which knows him best. I believe that that sentiment
> is due more to the unjust attacks upon you and your official asso-
> ciates than to the tragedy which those attacks brought about.

Meacham, refreshed somewhat by Odell's thoughts and those of so many others, wrote back expressing his appreciation, adding, "If it be a fact that Norris could not get a fair trial in this county, he has only himself to thank for this situation." He also told Odell, "Personally, I am glad that it has been sent to Austin. I hope and believe that a jury can be found there which will try the case on the law and the evidence."

Mr. William Price of El Paso wrote to Meacham, sharing his perspective as a Roman Catholic, someone presumably by virtue of that affiliation alone likely to be seen by Norris and his followers as a part of the "deep laid conspiracy." He abhorred the idea of a minister of the gospel preaching and behaving as Norris did, only to claim self-defense when faced with the consequences of his own reckless words and actions. The mayor wrote back briefly, "You may be assured that most of the decent minded people in this community quite agree with you in your estimate of this character." To another correspondent, Meacham said that the change of venue had "been asked by the defendant upon the grounds that he could not get a fair trial in this, the community which knows him best."

A.T. McDaniel of Memphis, Tennessee, inquired of the mayor as to whether or not J. Frank Norris was a member of the Masonic lodge. Meacham replied: "Without making any investigation, I would give it as my opinion that it would be highly improbable that this man who has been indicted and tried for arson and perjury and is now on trial for murder, and who has been involved in many other crimes and scandals would have a membership in good standing of any fraternal organization worthwhile."

J. Frank Norris was also at his desk in his office that morning, working with his team to put out an expanded edition of the *Searchlight* that following Friday. The tabloid would have several extra pages and feature a banner headline claiming, "A Great Moral Victory." Norris published the defense motion for change of venue word for word, as well as a complete transcript of Mayor Meacham's testimony, in his paper. As a rule, he seldom bothered trying to hide bad news or criticism, knowing that most people would hear it anyway, so he frequently published verbatim material even if it contained negative information or insinuations about him. This practice tended to impress his followers, who saw it as transparent. It also had the potential to create sympathy.

The lead for the Meacham testimony printed in the tabloid bore the words, "Transcript of Evidence of Mr. H.C. Meacham Which Shows the Famous $15,000 Fee." The preacher hoped his readers would see this as further evidence of the "deep laid conspiracy" he had been talking about for so long. And never one to let a good crisis go unexploited, he described what he had talked about to the reporters in the courthouse: a vision for a new building. Possibly concerned that he had gone public with his dream without first talking to the staff and members of the church about it, he ran an article in the *Searchlight* titled "That 10,000 Seat Auditorium."

"It is no longer a guess," Norris wrote, "but an inspired prophecy that will be fulfilled, and that at no distant date. How wonderful to have an auditorium that will seat 10,000 on one floor; an auditorium large enough to take care of the multitudes of all ages both near and far. How heart breaking on last Sunday night to witness the great crowds that were traveling long distance to be present in the services. With the rapid increase in value of property at the present location it will be an easy thing to make the necessary deals that will give the First Baptist Church a huge auditorium with a capacity of 10,000 on one floor.

"There are increasing thousands who know the real issues, the inside facts," Norris said, assuring his readers that more and more people were developing "a just indignation over and against the dark, foul conspiracies that are now coming to light against the First Baptist Church and its work."

Norris then wrote about the impact the radio station was having on the growth of the church. "Because of the very large publicity given to the work of the First Baptist Church and ministry, a radio expert, a man who has had many years experience, estimates that our radio audience is above ten million." This was quite a claim, and in those early days of the medium there existed no real way to track listener patterns. But there is no doubt that Norris had a substantial radio following.

On Sunday, November 7, fresh from his victory on the change-of-venue motion, Pastor Norris spoke to another capacity crowd at First Baptist Church on the rather curious (for him) theme, "A Plea Against Hate and Factionalism." In the sermon he spent a great deal of time talking about all the wonderful features of Fort Worth, and how unfair it would be to judge the entire city on the basis of a few — in other words, the "conspirators" out to get him. Finally, after nearly an hour, he turned to "how to prevent factionalism." The preacher said emphatically, "I want to say this with all kindness. If you want factionalism to end in this city, don't do the thing that will cause factions to arise. That is the answer to that, yes sir!" The audience broke into thunderous applause, apparently missing the obvious irony of hearing such an admonition from someone who had turned instigation into an art form.

But if J. Frank had any illusions that his appeal would yield peaceable fruit, he was jolted back to reality the next day, when he was served papers in a civil suit filed by Mrs. D.E. Chipps on behalf of her fourteen-year-old son, Dexter Elliott Chipps Jr. The suit alleged that Norris, "on the 17th day of July, 1926 did shoot and kill, in Tarrant County, Texas, D.E. Chipps, the father of the plaintiff, and did thereby take the life of the said D.E. Chipps unlawfully, willfully and negligently and intentionally to plaintiff's damage in the sum of $150,000.00 as herein above alleged." Mrs. Chipps had engaged the firm of McLean, Scott, and Sayers, the same attorneys who had been hired as "special prosecutors" in the criminal case.

Responding to the suit, Norris's attorneys wrote in the *Searchlight,* "It has become evident to all fair-minded people that the case against Dr. Norris is not a case of prosecution but one of persecution." They characterized all the actions of the prosecution, those of the district attorney as well as the "special prosecutors," as part of "a systematic and persistent campaign with the evident purpose of harassing Dr. Norris with the hope of breaking him down or destroying his influence." They insisted, though, that "the reverse will be the results." Calling the action by Mrs. Chipps "a confession and an admission that there is nothing in the other case now pending," Norris's attorneys insisted the civil suit did not surprise them. And as always, they did their best to turn the issue around, declaring, "Where there is large money back of the prosecution — as has now been admitted — it is not surprising that any schemes or plot may be hatched and brought to light."

The new lawsuit wasn't J. Frank Norris's only new problem that November. Likely as a result of all the publicity given his case around the country, and the specific testimony given during the change-of-venue proceedings, his various ministry activities faced more intense scrutiny. The *Searchlight* came under investigation. On Monday, November 15, attorneys for the office of the Texas secretary of state showed up at the tabloid's offices with a notice denying their business permit. The basis of the order had to do with a rule "which bars foreign corporations making their principal headquarters in Texas." The *Searchlight,* it was charged, was organized as a Delaware corporation. The attorneys demanded access to records there on the spot and J.M. Gilliam and the staff complied, allowing the state representatives to go through their files.

The investigators spent the full day in the *Searchlight* offices and soon were joined by inspectors from the Post Office who appeared to be looking for evidence to use in revoking the paper's mailing permit. But by the end of the day, all of the investigators determined that there had been no violation of the law or postal rules. It was clear that the *Searchlight* was based in Fort Worth, though with offices in New York and Chicago, and it fully qualified for the second-class postage permit it had used since March 1917.

Faithful readers were outraged by this intrusion, and it only served to reinforce to them the idea that the ministry was under siege by sinister forces. In the next edition of the paper, the "wild and mad efforts, backed by powerful wealth," were characterized yet again as "no longer prosecution, but persecution."

When it came to the other powerful arm of Norris's media empire, station KFQB, the preacher had anticipated the coming of radio's greater regulation. Quietly he had been scheming "officially" to disconnect the station from First Baptist Church. That same month, his office announced that KFQB had been sold to an outfit called Lone Star Broadcasting Company. In reality, this was a new company created by business manager J.M. Gilliam specifically to buy the station. There was an arrangement in the terms of sale guaranteeing the church access to programming and the ability to air its services for decades to come. Gilliam soon moved the station's broadcast studios to a basement room at the nearby Westbrook Hotel, though the transmitter and towers remained where they were.

So while the Commerce Department, led by Secretary Herbert Hoover, prepared the Radio Act of 1927 — forerunner to the Federal Communications Commission (FCC) — Norris did an end run around the pending legislation. He was well aware that his ranting over the radio that had stirred up controversy and set the stage for the July 17 shooting had inspired many citizens to complain that "there ought to be a law" governing such behavior. It was just a matter of time before he would be muzzled, so he found a way to protect his important radio ministry. Broadcasting gave him access to the masses — more than a local church or weekly tabloid *ever* could.

In a letter to Congressman Fritz G. Lanham, who represented the district including Tarrant County in Washington, DC, Meacham indicated that he had heard that the issue of radio regulation was going to be discussed in the House of Representatives soon and suggested that there "should be some Federal Legislation that make it a criminal offense for anyone to utter libelous things about a person or company over the radio and it should be made possible to recover damages in the Federal Courts on such libelous things." No doubt J. Frank Norris's weekly ritual, the broadcasting of his Sunday sermons, was forefront in his mind.

The mayor continued, "We have had several instances showing the necessity for such legislation here in Fort Worth recently. If you have been keeping up with the news from Fort Worth, it will not be necessary for me to sight [*sic*] any of these instances. But, for fear you were not here last Sunday night, I will mention that it was put on the air a statement to the effect that our city manager, Mr. Carr, has lost $50,000.00 through gambling in cotton futures, and the implication was very clear that this was the city's money that had been lost and that Mr. Carr was a thief and a gambler." Meacham told Lanham, "This broadcasting is calculated to impair Mr. Carr's usefulness, both at home and abroad."

Norris had, in fact, thundered against the "imported city manager" that previous Sunday night, carefully choosing, yet carelessly using, his words for maximum effect. He called O.E. Carr a "tax embezzler" for risking city money on a "$50,000.00 gambling deal." He was dealing in half-truth and innuendo. But it was more than enough evidence to further convince his followers of the corruption of city officials who wanted to get rid of their pastor. The fact Norris had killed an unarmed man in his office got somehow lost in his equation.

And Norris was connecting with an audience. On Sunday, November 21, 1926, the day he was preaching his gospel of attack on civic leaders, seventy-six new members joined First Baptist Church.

CHAPTER THIRTY-FOUR

"A Civil Action"

IN THE CLOSING weeks of 1926, Pastor Norris concentrated on his work with the church. He had announced a goal of seeing a thousand new members joining between the time of the shooting of D.E. Chipps and the start of his trial early in the new year.

When he had a particularly notable conversion or "testimony," he would always trumpet the news to his congregation, his radio audience, and readers of the *Searchlight*. For example, when a woman named Irene Gillman from Wichita Falls, Texas, wrote a letter to an Austin newspaper, Norris got a copy and published it. Gillman wrote:

> I went into a house of ill fame there at the age of sixteen and I conducted one in the tenderloin district there many years, also one quietly in another part of the city after public ones were closed, and now at the age of forty-two I am going to try to educate myself and work harder for Jesus than I did for Satan, and I have a baby boy and a baby girl that I am working and sacrificing for, hoping to rear them WORKERS for JESUS, and if they can do a hundredth part as well as I believe Frank Norris has for God and the right living for men and women and boys and girls, I will be thankful and satisfied and I also am praying for Frank Norris.

Testimonials such as this reminded readers of J. Frank Norris the crusader, who had attacked vice in Hell's Half Acre in Fort Worth and in similar enclaves in other cities. They also, by inference, suggested that Norris, because of his efforts, would be attacked and opposed by the "dark forces" behind the immoral enterprises.

Adding further pressure, at the end of November the City of Fort Worth filed a suit in district court against the First Baptist Church for "delinquent taxes," the issue that had started all the trouble in the first place. Surprisingly, and largely unnoticed up to this point, Norris's church was not the only house of worship with a tax problem. Also sued that day was the First Christian Church, located just a couple of blocks away from First Baptist. The city alleged that together the churches owed the municipality $82,500 "for back taxes on property which the churches rent to business concerns, which the city maintains does not come under the classification of 'for religious purposes.'" Ironically, the largest part of this sum was *not* owed by First Baptist, but rather by the neighboring church. But clearly, the mayor and city manager were not giving up on the issue.

In early December, J. Frank Norris proudly announced that the subscriber list for his paper had grown to 71,148. He told his readers, "The record growth of the *Searchlight* from nothing to this stupendous high water mark is the phenomenon in the newspaper world. Think of it — reaching this high level without capital." And he reminded them of exciting things to come: "The greatest issues are to be discussed in these columns in the near future. The inside history of certain well-known events, courthouse experiences, and other things will be printed in these columns, real inside information that will not be given in the daily press or any other publication."

And before the month was out, the preacher would excitedly proclaim, "The 1,000 Mark Passed," meaning that many people had joined First Baptist Church since the day he shot D.E. Chipps.

Meanwhile, on December 6, Norris's attorneys filed a demurrer in the civil suit against the preacher, hoping to avoid the suit altogether, or at least having to deal with it until after his criminal trial. There was concern that "on the record" testimony might find its way into court in Austin; he wanted the judge overseeing the case to dismiss the suit on the grounds that the underlying facts did not sustain Mrs. Chipps's claims.

The lengthy brief attached to Norris's filing revealed an aggressive line of attack on the dead lumberman, a likely preview of the defense's criminal trial strategy. Mrs. Chipps, on behalf of her son, was seeking compensation to replace the support lost when her husband died. She indicated that she and her son had been regularly receiving a thousand dollars per month since their divorce.

Norris's lawyers denied this and charged that Chipps: "Spent and dissipated said earnings in orgies, gambling, and for the use of intoxicating liquors, and in his associations with people of the underworld." Their motion went on to add "that the estate of the said D.E. Chipps at the time it is alleged that the said D.E. Chipps was killed by this defendant . . . was wholly insolvent, in that the said D.E. Chipps had spent all of his earnings up to said time in a wild, riotous and profligate living, and in the habitual use of intoxicating liquors and in his association with a great many people of immoral and disreputable character until the time of the alleged death of the said D.E. Chipps."

The preacher who had built his following by "naming names" and attacking the reputations of his enemies, was clearly prepared to demonize the man he had shot in an effort to gain an acquittal.

But the preacher had another card up his sleeve that he had hoped to reveal during the criminal trial. Norris had tasked several people, first volunteers and then members of his paid legal team, with fully investigating the life of Mr. Chipps, digging up whatever dirt they could find.

So in his filing in response to her civil suit, he delivered devastating information to the widow of Dexter Elliott Chipps. By the time she'd met her ex-husband, he was in business for himself and doing fairly well. He had swept her off her feet, but he behaved differently when drinking and she finally decided she didn't want to take it anymore. She was granted a divorce on October 15, 1925.

Mae never knew about the *first* Mrs. Chipps. And she never knew that there was another boy, now a grown man, who had been fathered by D.E. Chipps, who was named Daugherty Elliott Lynn Chipps. She also never knew that her ex-husband, the man she loved, had deserted his first wife and son. Norris had copies of the various legal documents about Chipps's marriage to one Bessie W. Chipps, as well as the papers granting her a divorce from Dexter on the grounds of desertion back in 1902.

Bill McLean and Sam Sayers, themselves surprised by the revelations, had the sad and difficult duty of breaking the news to their client. Mae Chipps broke down and cried, but in the end the shocking news did not dissuade her from fighting Norris.

Judge H.O. Gossett, virtually ignoring the Norris filing, notified all parties that depositions for the civil suit would begin just after Christmas on Monday, December 27, in his Fort Worth courtroom.

Until then, all parties would spend the Christmas holiday with their families. The preacher, however, found it hard to relax. Some who had been supportive of him were starting to waver. A few preachers in the fundamentalist world were beginning to break rank.

In Wilmore, Kansas, a group called the Fundamentalist Association of the World gathered in convention. Speaking to the group, Dr. G.W. Ridoul, a professor of pastoral theology at Ashbury College, said, "a fanatical, denouncing, fire-eating abusive fundamentalist can never advance the cause of truth." He added, "I think it is not too much for fundamentalists to demand that any man whose hands have blood on them had best be retired from the platform and pulpit." Hearing this from a man who was vice president of an important fundamentalist group, J. Frank had to wonder if this was the beginning of a larger abandonment by the faithful he so very much wanted to lead.

A rare Fort Worth snow fell on Christmas Saturday, and the Norris family experienced a quiet day at home. Mae Chipps and her son ate dinner with the Meacham family at their beautiful home on Elizabeth Boulevard.

Meanwhile the newspapers in town, along with many others around the country, published an interesting interview with Judge George E. Hosey, the man who had recently ruled to change the venue of the Norris trial. The subject was the state of the law in Texas, but Norris watchers read something else between the lines. Though Hosey never specifically mentioned Norris by name, what he had to say was on point.

The judge opined that because Texas was a relatively young state compared with its neighbors, its laws and practices were not yet strong enough to effectively deal with violent crime, particularly murder. He was hopeful that it all was changing with the "natural process of its evolution" but still saw real justice as something in the distant future. He admitted that "much of the state's criminal procedure and its handling of crime is archaic," with the violator having "too many chances to go scot-free."

In words that seemed to speak directly to the Norris case, he continued, "Under the existing laws of Texas, murder may be committed without fear of punishment, provided the murderer has slightly more than average

intelligence." Hosey bemoaned the fact that in the past two years Tarrant
County had seen seventy murders, with only a few criminals ever going
to the penitentiary. He blamed a lot of this on lax rules of investigation,
comparing Texas with neighboring Arkansas. There, the judge said, "the
homicide squad surrounds the scene of a killing as soon as notified. All
others are kept from the scene. All material evidence and clues are picked
up. All witnesses found are bundled into cars and taken before the grand
jury." Certainly that scenario was very different from the confusing events
in and around the First Baptist Church offices on July 17, 1926.

Judge Hosey spoke, almost admiringly, of how things were done in
England. There, he said, "a murderer is tried and sent to the gallows within
three weeks after the killing," noting that in Texas it could be months even
before a trial. He told reporters that, in his opinion, trial judges should have
"wider powers in ruling on motions for continuance and other matters that
cause delay." He further indicated, "Power to suspend sentence should be
vested in the judge, the district attorney and sheriff, rather than in the
jury, as at present." He longed for a time when there would be "stability of
the law and certainty of punishment under it."

Reading Hosey's analysis of the odds of beating a murder charge in
Texas surely must have made Norris smile. Later on Christmas Day, the
telephone rang in the Norris household, and Norris agreed to meet with
the caller that very day.

Soon Larry L. Sisk, representing Hearst's International News Service,
appeared at the Norrises' front door. Greeting Mrs. Norris and the others, he
was asked if he would like something to eat. He smiled and indicated that he
was actually quite hungry. Lillian went to the kitchen to prepare a plate for
him from the leftovers that had just been put away. While all others left the
living room, J. Frank Norris invited Sisk to a seat on the sofa and retreated
to his favorite chair. The reporter began with a question about how he felt
about the upcoming Austin trial. Norris, without hesitating, boasted that he
was sure of his ultimate vindication. "I'm as good as acquitted right now."

The pastor continued, "I haven't any fears as to the outcome when my
case comes up at Austin. Austin is a small enough place to insure an unbiased jury, as the smaller places are not plastered with sensational newspapers trying the case even before it is called." The irony of the editor of

the weekly *Searchlight* tabloid taking a dig at sensational journalistic practices in an interview with a reporter who worked for William Randolph
Hearst was apparently lost on both men.

Norris told his guest that he was sure the change-of-venue proceedings had established the existence of a conspiracy, and that was the reason
the judge ruled in his favor on the matter. After describing once again, in
familiar detail, the whole "deep laid conspiracy" against him, Norris told
Sisk, "We can prove that Chipps made several threats against my life, even
before he came to my office." The reporter instantly recognized this as new
territory. Was the preacher suggesting that he knew about Chipps's threats
before the lumberman came to his office? What would this mean to his
defense and prosecution?

Norris, seeming to catch himself, maybe having tipped his hand too
much to the reporter, quickly interrupted his own thought, "Even if threats
had not been made previously, the fact that he was in my office threatening
me, gave me the perfect right to defend myself when I thought that my life
was in danger. I maintain that a minister of the gospel has the same right
to defend himself in his own study as a bootlegger has to defend himself in
his bootlegging den."

As worshippers gathered in the auditorium of First Baptist Church the
next day — the last Sunday of that fateful year — the congregants enjoyed
a children's program featuring more than five hundred youngsters, led by
Miss Kathryn Jackson. Though it was a bitterly cold and snowy day on a
holiday weekend, a large crowd turned out. Workers in the church office
had been hearing from radio listeners about plans for a Christmas weekend
convergence on their church by supporters from around the region. People
from more than forty towns and cities, some from Texas, others from
places as far as Nashville, Tennessee, and Baton Rouge, Louisiana, occupied "the center tier" of the balcony, a section that seated one thousand.

J. Frank Norris had a severe cold and was tempted to cut his sermon
short, but hearing of so many who had traveled so far to hear him, he
pushed himself and delivered a sermon based on Luke 13 titled "Lessons
from a Triple Tragedy — A Call to Repentance." He felt no better and was
in a foul mood as he preached later that Sunday night. During that sermon
he became very angry and made public a sensational charge. He told his

congregation that in the previous two weeks, the safe at the offices where several of his attorneys worked had been "tampered" with no less than four times. Someone apparently was trying to break in and steal documents "relating to the defense plan" for the upcoming trial.

Pastor Norris stayed home the next morning nursing his cold. He had not planned to attend the deposition session in Judge Gossett's court, anyway, unless called by his attorneys. He saw this civil action as a nuisance and an excuse on the part of the prosecution to dig at him.

CHAPTER THIRTY-FIVE

"Perhaps I Should Withdraw That Remark"

HENRY O. GOSSETT had served as a county court judge dealing with civil matters in Fort Worth since 1922. Born in Camden, Arkansas, in 1877, he studied law at the Fort Worth Night School of Law. He spent his early career in the towns of Odessa and Longview before coming back to Fort Worth in 1919. He had handled his share of cases, but none could compare to the civil proceedings related to the J. Frank Norris murder case.

The first person called to give deposition testimony on Monday, December 27, 1926, was the widow Mae Chipps. As she took the stand, Norris's attorney Marvin Simpson approached to question her. In response to his questions, Mrs. Chipps talked about how she had married Dexter in Shreveport, Louisiana, back in 1908. Speaking "in a low voice and direct manner," she acknowledged to Simpson that she did not know Chipps had a former wife, adding, "I didn't think he had a son and I don't know it now."

When asked why she had divorced D.E. Chipps, the widow immediately blamed his drinking. When he was sober, her husband was attentive, tender, affectionate, and a good father. But when he drank alcohol he was different. "I objected to Mr. Chipps drinking, and outside of that we had no trouble."

"Did he ever get drunk?"

"I really don't know. I never observed drunk men. He didn't drink in front of me. He used some profane language and directed some of it toward me on some occasions," Mae Chipps expanded. In her divorce filing she had cited drinking and profane language, and she had also accused her husband of being "cruel" to her.

"Sort of a mental cruelty," she told Simpson.

"As a matter of fact he drank and got drunk all the time?" he pressed.

"No sir, he did not."

The next witness to be deposed was Mayor Meacham, who was clearly not in good health. He approached the witness stand with the help of a cane. Simpson began his interview of the mayor with a pointed question: "You are interested in seeing Dr. Norris found guilty, aren't you?

"Surely," Meacham replied.

"You have obligated yourself to pay $18,500 for that purpose?"

"Yes sir."

"Would you pay more?"

"Yes, if necessary."

"Would you pay $50,000?"

"Yes sir."

"$100,000?"

"I don't think I could stand that much," the mayor replied. "But I would give a hundred thousand dollars if I had it."

The most sensational exchange of the day, one that would make the front pages of newspapers across the country, came during the testimony of Fort Worth city manager O.E. Carr. As Carr answered Simpson's questions, all rather routine, he wandered a bit with one answer. Not knowing where the witness was going, Simpson decided to let him talk. Carr told a story about something that had apparently happened a few months before. Most in the room were hearing the story for the first time.

Carr told of a man coming to see Mayor Meacham and offering to "kill J. Frank Norris" for five thousand dollars. The mayor, sensing a trap, told his visitor that he would not listen and that, in fact, he'd pay "an equal amount to save the pastor's life," and instructed the man to leave. Meacham immediately called Carr and told him what had happened.

Everyone was stunned. This was big. Did someone want to kill the preacher for hire? Was someone trying to catch the mayor of Fort Worth in a trap? Marvin Simpson measured the witness and asked the question that had instantly popped into everyone's mind: "Why didn't you have the fellow arrested?"

O.E. Carr paused, then turned to Judge Gossett while pointing at his questioner: "Because I thought Simpson sent him." He was indicating that both he and the mayor saw the offer to kill Norris as a trick being played by Norris and his attorneys, particularly Marvin Simpson. This was quite an interesting charge and sounded ironically like the kind of "conspiracy" talk regularly used by the defense.

Simpson was livid. Here he was in open court and a witness under oath was accusing him of trying to entrap a city official. He exploded and lunged toward Carr, saying, "If you think that, you're just a liar!" But he quickly caught himself and calmed down, somehow finding the composure to finish questioning the witness he now utterly despised.

After Carr stepped down and made his way from the stand, Simpson probed, "Do you still believe it?" — meaning the idea of him sending a would-be fake assassin. Carr said, "Sure do."

At that, Marvin Simpson, attorney-at-law, "struck Carr with a staggering blow." The city manager had already put his overcoat on but tried to fight back until others in the room separated them. While associates led Simpson from the room, Carr, clearly rattled by what had happened, told defense team member Dayton Moses, "Perhaps I should withdraw that remark."

Following Carr's testimony and the subsequent tussle, Judge Gossett decided he had seen and heard enough for now. He determined it might be better to take testimony on the civil matter after the criminal trial was over. He abruptly suspended proceedings until further notice.

The next morning the news was on America's doorstep. *The New York Times* lead said: "Lawyer for Norris Strikes a Witness — Fight in Court Comes in Taking Deposition in Suit of Son of Slain Man."

As a fitting end to a year in which so many bizarre things had happened in Fort Worth, O.E. Carr, perhaps motivated by countrywide news reports suggesting he had failed to hold his own against Marvin Simpson, called a few reporters to his city hall office to issue a public challenge to Simpson. In the courtroom he'd had on his overcoat and been taken by surprise, and he wanted a rematch, a fair fight, with the gloves on. They could box at the next local Elks Council event and sell tickets, with all proceeds going to charity.

But Simpson refused.

The last issue of the *Searchlight* for 1926 hit subscribers' mailboxes on the last day of the year. In it, J. Frank Norris told his readers that "instead of $100,000 worth of hate" — a reference to Mayor Meacham's deposition testimony that he would be willing to pay that much to see Pastor Norris go to the electric chair if he had the money — "he will plead for the largest and abounding peace and good will for the year 1927." The preacher piously proclaimed, "Life is too short and eternity is too long to spend time, energy, brains, reputation, character, and money in order to get even with somebody else." The preacher then announced that the first services of the year at First Baptist Church of Fort Worth would feature a great choir of "500 voices" and addresses by attorneys Dayton Moses and Marvin Simpson. Norris wanted to make sure his congregation was prepared for the trial to come, both in the courtroom in Austin and the court of public opinion. "These attorneys will say some things Sunday that will be exceedingly interesting." He also announced that, in expectation of a great crowd, claiming the church had to turn away "over 2,000" the Sunday before, "Arrangements have been made for an overflow meeting in the auditorium across the street," right above the J.C. Penney store.

This edition of the *Searchlight* featured an ad from the Chicago-based Moody Bible Institute. This was not unusual; the institute had advertised in the tabloid many times before. But the ad's content, given the circumstances surrounding the tabloid's editor, was intriguing. The notice read:

> Whatsoever ye do, do all to the glory of God.
> — I Corinthians 10:31
>
> If each Christian would adopt the above verse as his or her watchword for the year 1927, what a change would be noted before the close of the year. How often we do things for our own glory or for our own advancement is only too well known by each of us.

CHAPTER THIRTY-SIX

"Apparent Danger"

AS JANUARY BEGAN, Austin readied itself for an unprecedented convergence of people and attention. The new governor, Dan Moody, would be inaugurated at midmonth, and before that the old courthouse near the capitol would host the biggest trial in the city's history, and perhaps the biggest spectacle the state had ever seen. The eyes of Texas and the nation would be on Austin. In 1927 the central Texas city located on the banks of the Colorado River was home to not quite fifty thousand people.

Jury selection was scheduled to start on January 10, but pre-trial maneuvering was already well under way. The "special prosecutors" who had worked with the Tarrant County District Attorney's Office in the wake of the shooting and through the indictment and change-of-venue processes would now team up with attorneys from the Travis County prosecutor's office. J.D. Moore was district attorney, Irish-born and with the thick brogue to prove it. Though officially in charge of the case, he was clearly overshadowed, if not a little intimidated, by the high-powered legal talent at his prosecution table. Also, with the passing of 1926, a young attorney named Jesse Martin replaced Robert Hangar as the Tarrant County DA. And H.C. Meacham had hired an Austin-based law firm, Shelton and Shelton, to help as additional "special prosecutors."

So J. Frank Norris, pastor of America's largest Protestant church and facing the electric chair if convicted, would be prosecuted by the largest and most storied group of lawyers ever to work together on such a case in Texas.

He did have impressive mouthpieces of his own. Dayton Moses, "Marvelous" Marvin Simpson, and a host of other old courthouse hands were seasoned and savvy. But would they be enough?

The decade had already seen the Clara Smith Hamon trial, one in Chicago involving thrill killers Leopold and Loeb, and the Scopes trial in

Tennessee. But the trial of a preacher killing an unarmed man could be even bigger. Dan Moody's young-political-star-in-a-hurry story always ran a distant second in the papers and conversation.

On Tuesday, January 4, the Travis County District Attorney's Office announced that among those being subpoenaed to appear at the trial were members of "previous grand juries." Presumably the use of the plural implied the calling of not only those on the recent grand jury in Tarrant County, but also certain members of the bodies that indicted Norris for arson and perjury back in 1912. Norris's legal team, still working in Fort Worth, was appalled at this. Simpson called it a clear attempt on the part of the prosecution "to get before the public that Rev. Mr. Norris had been indicted previously. Those attorneys know that such testimony is not admissible." One reporter asked Simpson a follow-up question, not about the case itself, but rather about his recent courtroom fisticuffs with O.E. Carr. The lawyer, annoyed at the question and questioner, curtly called it "a closed incident unless he wants to reopen it."

Asked if he was aware of Carr's challenge from the week before, the idea of putting the gloves on for charity, Simpson, growing even more bothered, said, "I am not trying to be a prize fighter. I don't care to entertain the Elks Club, or suppose they want me to. Carr threw out his 'prize fight challenge' to make a joke out of a serious proposition."

Within a few days, all the principals in the case would begin making the trek to the Lone Star state capital. Norris made it public that he planned to preach somewhere in Austin on Sunday, January 9. Summerlike weather had briefly and unseasonably moved in, and one reporter suggested that the warm temperature and growing sense of excitement in town "gave to this peace-loving city the air of going through a lull before a storm."

Norris would be a no-show, however. He came down with an attack of tonsillitis and would be unable to speak anywhere that Sunday.

A "venire of 500" men was turned over to the defense and prosecution. From this unprecedented large number, twelve men would emerge as a jury to sit in judgment of the preacher. The defense was reportedly scrutinizing the list to identify Roman Catholics, while the prosecution was on the lookout for any Klan members or fellow travelers. Many thought the proceedings would "bring back the dark clouds of religious controversy," with the Klan pitted against the Catholic Church. There were abundant rumors, attributed to "the camp of the defense," that the Invisible Empire would be "playing a strong undercover part to the case."

Alex Philquist, the longtime district clerk, made it public that security would be tight. All those entering the courtroom would be searched for weapons, and "no disturbance of any kind would be allowed." He also announced that telegraph instruments would be barred from the courtroom itself, a decision that did not sit well with the national news services or the Fort Worth papers. He had apparently studied the brief, but intense, scene in Fort Worth the previous November and was determined to manage the media circus.

M.R. Toomer's *Fort Worth Press,* working with the United Press news service, sent a team of reporters to camp out in Austin for the duration, boasting that readers "will not be disappointed in the coverage of the trial." Jack Gordon was going. He was a local favorite with a knack for digging up interesting details and tidbits. Then there was Hal Faust, who was on loan to the paper from the *Houston Press*. He had a lot of "big trial" experience. Glen Pricer would be in Austin, having followed and written about J. Frank Norris for many years.

The work of these wordsmiths would be augmented by the presence of Sidney Van Ulm, a gifted sketch artist. His drawings dispatched back to Cowtown from the capital would capture the imagination of readers across the country. Toomer would be there, too.

J. Frank Norris, though still ill with a cough and respiratory ailments, traveled to Austin via Pullman car late that Saturday. Passengers on the train said that the preacher's cough "broke the silence of the car." Mrs. Norris stayed home to teach her Bible class on Sunday and visit some sick church members on Monday. She indicated that she'd catch up with her husband later that week.

Norris had booked a room at Austin's prestigious Driskill Hotel. Built in 1886, it was located on Sixth Street in the heart of downtown, a short walk from the courthouse. The preacher loved to walk, so it was a perfect fit for him. He stayed in room 78 on the hotel's third floor all that Sunday, not even venturing out to church, hoping the rest would help him recover.

On Monday he woke up early feeling somewhat better and met Dayton

Moses, who was quickly emerging as the real star on his defense team, for breakfast in the hotel's dining room. Moses told Norris there was no need for him to be in court later that morning. The defense was having a hard time rounding up some of the witnesses and would likely ask for another day to locate them.

One of the witnesses in question was Norris's secretary, Miss Jane Hartwell. Since she had been at the scene when the shooting took place, her testimony would be important to the trial. But she had recently checked herself into the Harris Sanitarium in Fort Worth. Her physician, Dr. O.R. Grogan, said she was suffering "from almost a complete nervous breakdown and several other things" and that "every effort is being made to restore Miss Hartwell to a condition that will warrant her making the trip to Austin the last of the week."

After breakfast, the preacher went out for a stroll to enjoy the unusually warm and sunny weather. As he walked, he was keenly aware of people looking at him. If they hadn't known what the controversial preacher looked like before, his nearly full-page, full-body picture in many morning newspapers, arms crossed with a firm facial expression, rendered him instantly recognizable.

By the time Norris returned to his room, lawyer Moses had left word for him that the judge had given them the extra day, but jury selection work was going forward. Norris tried to rest but couldn't, so he made his way to the courthouse around 9:30 AM and spent his time there writing letters at the defense table. For much of the time he seemed oblivious to what was going on around him.

Judge James R. Hamilton slammed his gavel down calling for order around 10 AM. His first action was to clear the courtroom of everyone except the lawyers, witnesses, and venire men. He then swore in the potential jurors: "You and each of you, solemnly swear that you will make true answers to such questions as may be propounded to you by the court, so help you God?"

There was a roar of "Ayes!" from 351 potential jurors — all men.

The judge then began asking questions to see if there were any health or other reasons for exemption. Some were excused because they weren't qualified voters in the state, a few because they weren't actually citizens of

the United States, and others because they could not read or write. Soon
Norris put his pen and paper away and started to watch what was happening. He looked around the courtroom and noticed a man standing in the
back, James W. Swayne, the former district judge from Fort Worth who
had presided over the preacher's 1912 perjury trial. Now he worked in
Austin as a member of the state industrial accident board. Norris nodded
to him, wondering what Judge Swayne was doing in the courtroom.

Looking away from Swayne, for a brief moment Norris's eyes met those
of Mae Chipps, the widow of the man he was now charged with murdering.
She was dressed in black as if for mourning with "a long string of heavy
black beads about her neck." Next to her was her son, Dexter Jr. Norris was
seeing him in person for the first time. The Chipps boy was approximately
the same age Norris had been when he lunged with a knife at the man who
had shot his father, taking three bullets, injuries that would lead to a two-
year convalescence. Mrs. Chipps instantly and nervously looked away,
and Norris fixed his attention toward the front of the room. He watched as
Hamilton listened to dozens of potential jurors give excuses as to why they
couldn't serve. Some reasons were accepted; most were not.

There were questions about religious affiliations, both sides wanting to
avoid jurors who leaned too much for or against Norris's fierce version of
Baptist Protestantism. They were asked if they had formed any firm opinions about the case. Did they have a problem with the death penalty? Had
they received or read the *Searchlight*?

The Reverend Norris had arranged for nearly ten thousand extra copies
of the *Searchlight* to be circulated around the capital city. The tabloid had
become a conspicuous and unavoidable presence in town during the days
before his trial, creating something of a problem for the prosecution.

The defense's first preemptory challenge was to W.R. Stowers, a father
of six who was not a member of any church. His wife, though, was a Baptist.
Dayton Moses asked Stowers if he was opposed to the death penalty. He
answered in the negative. He would also convict a preacher just as easily as
any other man if he were guilty. The state loved him. Not the defense. And
so it went.

Early on in the process, it was noted how easy it was to keep off the
Norris jury. One writer for the *Star-Telegram* suggested, "Say you are an

ardent evolutionist, say you admire Clarence Darrow for his beliefs. There will be a lifting of eyebrows and 'huddling' together of heads among the lawyers. You haven't got a chance."

Better yet, "Say you don't believe in *'apparent danger.'*"

Apparent danger had already become the "most famous expression contributed by the trial." And it was the most vital question each juror faced from the defense attorneys. The term related to a crucial legal argument — a doctrine of sorts — that Norris's team clearly planned to emphasize in the trial.

> Apparent Danger: You can believe your life is in danger by reason of actions of an adversary and kill him, only to discover afterward you were laboring under a misapprehension; yet the homicide you have committed is justified in the eyes of the law.

If the defense could prove that J. Frank Norris "thought" he was in danger, even if there was no actual evidence found afterward to support his belief, he would go free.

By the time Hamilton adjourned court for the day at about 2:30 PM, around one hundred potential jurors had been excused. There was more of the same in court on Tuesday, and by Wednesday only 5 jurors had been selected from the 173 left in the pool. Early on in the process, "a number of negroes" were sent home, and it was widely reported that "following the custom in this state they will be excused by agreement of attorneys."

Over the next several days, the jury began to take shape. Many were rejected because they had heard Norris on the radio or read the *Searchlight*. It was a frustrating and tedious process. Each morning Norris would meet with his legal team in the coffee shop of the Driskill Hotel. Then he would walk the six blocks to the courthouse.

The first man to make the cut was W.D. Miller, a former sheriff of Travis County, accepted by the prosecution and defense after only five minutes of interview. After a handful more were rejected, Mr. C.J. Brown, a forty-seven-year-old machinist who attended the Baptist Church sporadically, made the cut. Then O.D. Moore, a "peddler" who preferred the Pentecostal church, became part of the jury.

Walter Johnson, a twenty-seven-year-old Lutheran, and Will J. Dill, nearly seventy years old and a retired fireman who did not regularly attend church, but who had once been a member of the Knights of Columbus, joined the panel, followed by C.A. Galbreath, a butcher who had no church affiliation, but who was a Mason.

They were halfway there.

The Reverend J. Frank Norris had built a religious empire by the mid-1920s, including the nation's largest protestant church, a successful tabloid newspaper, and a radio network.

The new First Baptist Church building c. 1913. With additions over the next few years, it would eventually cover an entire city block. The previous building was destroyed in a mysterious fire early in 1912. This building would itself burn down in 1929.

Norris was indicted several times after his church building burned in 1912. These twelve men served on the jury at Norris's arson trial in 1914. (University of Texas at Arlington Special Collections)

Pastor Norris dictating to his long-time secretary, "Miss" Jane Hartwell. Many referred to Hartwell as the "generalissimo." (Corbis UK, Ltd.)

Dexter Elliott Chipps was shot and killed by Norris in the church office on July 17, 1926. (P&A Photos/Corbis UK ltd.)

D.E. Chipps owned a lumber company with offices in Fort Worth's Wheat Building.

(Chipps Family Collection)

D. ELLIOTT CHIPPS

D. E. CHIPPS LUMBER CO.
FORT WORTH, TEXAS

PLAIN AND QUARTER SAWED
RED AND WHITE OAK, ASH,
COTTONWOOD AND GUM LUMBER
OAK TIES, CAR TIMBERS

LONG AND SHORT LEAF
YELLOW PINE
TIES, TIMBERS AND LUMBER
CAR MATERIAL

D. E. CHIPPS LUMBER COMPANY

MANUFACTURERS AND WHOLESALERS OF

HARDWOOD AND YELLOW PINE LUMBER

FORT WORTH, TEXAS

Saturday 15 15

Dear Son

Was sure glad to get your
letters thought you had forgotten me
Glad to hear you are having a good time
would have written to you sooner but
Your old Dad has been awfully busy
I think you are a great ball
player You must be showing them how
Kraft played the game
Be real good and give them all
my regards Lots of love
Yours
Dad

ALL QUOTATIONS MADE AND ORDERS ACCEPTED ON BASIS OF PRESENT FREIGHT RATES, AND ALL AGREEMENTS ARE CONTINGENT UPON STRIKES, ACCIDENTS, DELAYS OF CARRIERS OR OTHER CAUSES BEYOND OUR CONTROL

A letter D.E. Chipps wrote to his son, Dexter Jr., shortly before his death. (Chipps Family Collection)

The Fort Worth Club's new building, opened in March of 1926. (University of Texas at Arlington Special Collections)

Members of the first Fort Worth City Council under the city's new charter in 1925. Mayor Henry Clay "H.C." Meacham is second from the left. (University of Texas at Arlington Special Collections)

A late edition of a Fort Worth newspaper on Saturday, July 17, 1926. By the next morning, nearly every newspaper in America would be following the story.

Amon G. Carter, founder and publisher of the *Fort Worth Star-Telegram* and president of the Fort Worth Club. (University of Texas at Arlington Special Collections)

J. Frank Norris at his desk in November of 1926. The sign on his desk reads: "Life aint in holding a good hand, but in playing a poor hand well." A portrait of Norris's hero, William Jennings Bryan, hangs above the desk.

Pastor and Mrs. Norris at the change-of-venue hearing in Fort Worth, November 1926. Norris's attorney, Dayton Moses, is speaking.

Mrs. Mae Chipps and her son Dexter Jr. as the Austin, Texas, trial is about to begin in January 1927.
(Corbis UK Ltd.)

Norris walks to the Travis County Courthouse, January 1927, with his attorney, Dayton Moses. (Corbis UK Ltd.)

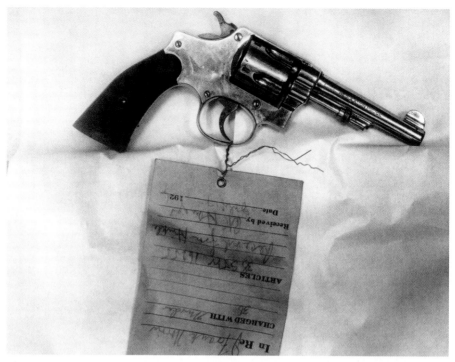

The "Night Watchman's Gun"—a .38-caliber Smith & Wesson—used by J. Frank Norris to kill D.E. Chipps. (Corbis UK Ltd.)

Prosecution attorneys Sam Sayers and W.P. "Wild Bill" McLean, courtroom scene from Austin, Texas, trial, January 1927.

W.P. "Wild Bill" McLean was one of the most celebrated Texas lawyers of the 1920s. Already famous for helping win acquittal for Clara Smith Hamon, he joined the prosecution because he despised J. Frank Norris. (Chipps Family Collection)

J. Frank Norris seated behind his lawyers, Marvin Simpson and Dayton Moses. (University of Texas at Arlington Special Collections)

First Baptist Church Sunday School teacher, L.H. Nutt, testifies. He was sitting in Norris's office at the moment of the shooting. (University of Texas at Arlington Special Collections)

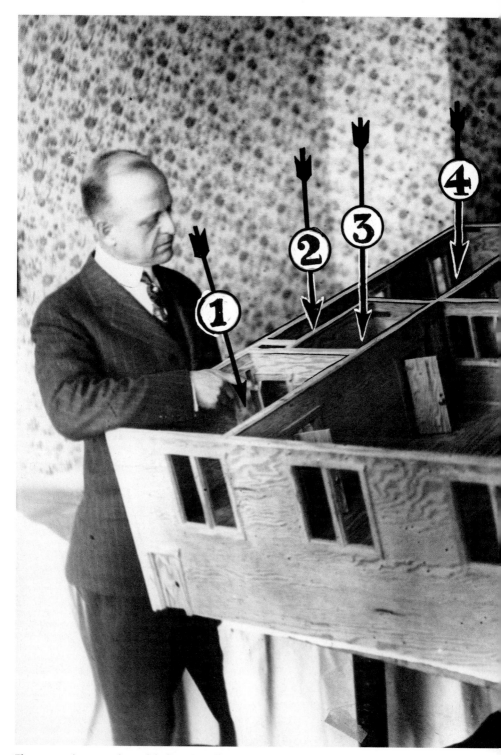

The prosecution created a model of Norris's office area, referred to in newspapers across America by reporter Bess Carroll as a "doll house." (University of Texas at Arlington Special Collections)

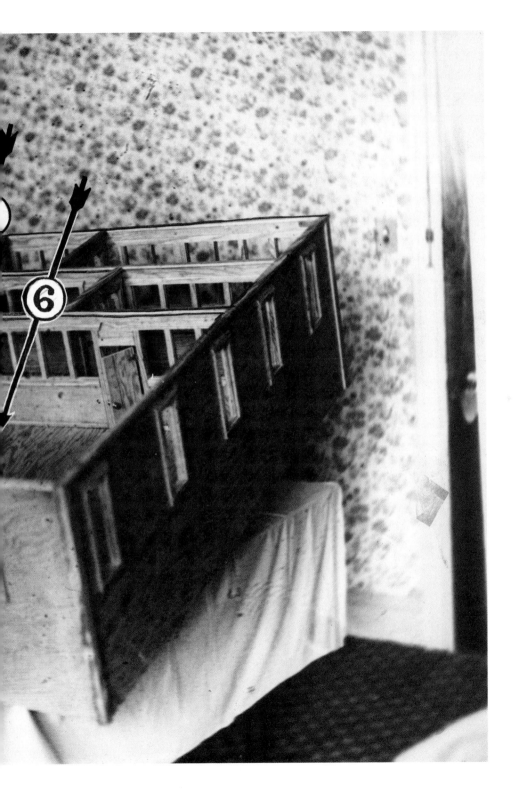

Fred Holland, a former Fort Worth police officer, testified in the Austin trial that he had warned J. Frank Norris about D.E. Chipps the day before the shooting. (University of Texas at Arlington Special Collections)

J. Frank Norris
testifying at his
murder trial on
January 21, 1927

(Corbis UK Ltd.)

CHAPTER THIRTY-SEVEN

"There Is Hate Written All Over the State's Case"

AS THE WEEK rolled on, lawyers for both sides, though focused mainly on the jury selection process, managed to keep the charges and countercharges circulating in the papers. This was not hard, as reporters were swarming the courthouse, hotel lobbies, and restaurants.

"Wild Bill" McLean, who loved the limelight almost as much as the man he was prosecuting, responded to a group of journalists that it would be "the death penalty or nothing at all" when told that Norris was confident of "complete vindication" and desired nothing short of that. When pressed as to why the prosecution was so adamant about pressing for the ultimate penalty, McLean asserted that he had come to that conclusion "only after a long and careful deliberation of the evidence at hand."

When J. Frank Norris, in turn, heard about McLean's comments, he flashed a fiery-eyed stare and retorted, "I can't believe it. There is hate written all over the state's case . . . And hate you know, defeats its own purpose. Hate undermines the nerves; it gives one a bad heart; it clouds one's memory; it blurs the vision; it is like the stinging snake, when it has nothing else to strike, it turns and fastens its fangs in its own quivering flesh. Oh, there isn't anything that it will not strike down. We are prepared."

The reporters wrote down every word, wondering how much of the sound bite was a set piece from one of the preacher's sermons.

While jury selection was under way, the defense was also busy filing a motion asking Judge Hamilton to ban "questions concerning any previous indictments on a felony charge against J. Frank Norris." Hamilton did not rule on it, saying he "presumed the attorneys themselves knew such questions were inadmissible and they would not ask them."

Though Marvin Simpson had been the first among equals on the defense team up to this point, in the days leading up to the trial the newspapers treated Dayton Moses as its star. Reporters loved to find an angle, one that would capture the imagination of the public, and they thought they had it by puffing the standoff between Moses for the defense and McLean for the prosecution.

"Nowhere in Texas," one journalist wrote, "are there two lawyers exceeding in reputation in criminal practice than Bill McLean prosecuting Norris, and Dayton Moses defending him."

"The fight of McLean versus Moses then, will be intensely contested" and "long remembered in Texas," the newspaper said. "To the victor, too, will go as spoils a reputation for ability not to be dimmed for many a day."

Dayton Moses, a popular figure in Fort Worth, was also well known and well liked in Austin, having put himself through night law school in that city while working days in the "land office." "Fresh from a ranch" in Burnett County, where he had been born, the attorney had come of age in the capital and clearly was comfortable working the press and public around the corridors of law and power. In fact, Dayton Moses, District Attorney J.D. Moore, and Judge James Hamilton were "old-time friends," which contributed to anticipation that the trial would be a great show.

But for the jurors the trial would be a burden. There was the pressure of having a man's life in their hands, and the temporary relinquishing of their own freedom. Once selected to be on the jury, each man was led to a room on the third floor of the courthouse. There he could play dominoes, the popular game of the day, but there wasn't much else to do.

Judge Hamilton told one prospective juror that a member of such a panel "in a murder case is virtually under arrest. He cannot talk to others, he cannot read newspapers, and is constantly in custody of an officer of the court until the jury is discharged."

The first six men selected took their dinner that Wednesday night at a nearby boardinghouse and made a request for supplies: "some kindling and wood, a shaving outfit, and a pair of socks." Juror Miller had spent other nights confined in jury rooms, but it was always as a sheriff who had the key to the door. The men settled in for what looked to be a "confinement of several days."

Over the next couple of days, they would be joined by the other half of their team: W.T. King, blacksmith; G.V. Potter, machinist; J.T. Cunningham, farmer; T.H. Tumey, who had just days before resigned as a member of the Ku Klux Klan; Lee Caldwell, auto salesman, and also former Klan member; and Andrew McAngus, an Austin grocery merchant. The jury was complete at 5:15 PM, and the trial would begin the next day — Friday, January 14.

With the jury impaneled, word spread around the courthouse about the potential for a "surprise" witness or two, both to be presented by the state. One was a woman. There was talk that she had been near Norris's office when the shooting occurred and had possibly even heard some of the words exchanged between the preacher and the doomed lumberman.

A fierce storm of wind and rain drove out the mild air, and the day before the trial was clear and cold. Several people noticed men carefully carrying a large object into the building. It was a miniature reproduction of Norris's office area at the First Baptist Church. Built under the direction of the prosecution and brought in pieces from Fort Worth, it had been reassembled in a large room at a nearby hotel before the trip over to the courthouse. It would serve as a visual aid while the state presented its case.

A southbound Katy (the nickname of trains affiliated with the Missouri–Kansas–Texas Railroad) was making its way through the Texas countryside on its 185-mile trek from Fort Worth to the capital city the evening before the trial. The passenger list was a who's who of names associated with the shooting and trial. L.H. Nutt, the bank auditor and Norris church deacon who was in the study the moment Chipps was shot, was on board, as was Miss Jane Hartwell, looking pale, but feeling well enough to make the trip she knew she couldn't avoid.

City Manager O.E. Carr was on board, too, his spirits no doubt buoyed by a ringing endorsement of the city manager form of government from an eminent world leader carried by one of the Fort Worth papers: "Government, to be good, must be efficient. It must achieve the greatest net result with the minimum of lost effort. There must be unity of policy, unity of responsibility and unity of direction. Without these, government becomes a slipshod, haphazard, hit or miss business, able to continue only because it can demand tribute from the entire nation."

Specifically addressing the job Mr. Carr held in Fort Worth, one that had been the center of much controversy since the day he came to town, the article continued, "American municipalities are recognizing the needs of centralization of the administrative powers and of the fixing of their responsibility in their adoption of the city manager plan." The efficiency expert and man of the future behind the words was none other than Benito Mussolini.

Pullman Car 180, however, was the focus of attention for other passengers on the train, particularly the journalists. Resting just a few berths apart were Mayor H.C. Meacham and Mrs. J. Frank Norris. They had come face-to-face earlier when Meacham left the smoking car, passing each other in the aisle in what was described as "a tense and embarrassing moment for each."

Back in the smoker, Carr told reporters, "It doesn't make any difference" that Norris's family was on the train. He also told them that, though he didn't mind making the trip, he wondered why he had been subpoenaed by the defense, "I don't see what they want with me down there." Someone observed, "Maybe Simpson wants you down there for a little excitement." Everyone in the car laughed. Carr just rubbed his chin and grinned, slouching in his seat. About 11 PM he headed off to his berth to get some sleep. Along the way, he saw L.H. Nutt, whose "face turned red, and a broad grin spread over his face after the manager had passed."

The older Norris boy, J. Frank Jr., was traveling with his mother, but ten-year-old George Norris had to stay home, at least for now. Seeing his mother and brother off at the station in Fort Worth, the younger son told those around him, "I am Dr. Norris' boy. My father may be back Sunday, or it may be longer. If he is not back by next Friday, I am going to Austin with my brother," the yet younger sibling, Jim Gaddie Norris.

It was now just a matter of hours before J. Frank Norris would go on trial in one of the most celebrated courtroom dramas of its day.

CHAPTER THIRTY-EIGHT

"I Have Killed Me a Man"

J. FRANK NORRIS met again with his legal team in the Driskill dining room early that Friday before donning his overcoat for the brisk walk over to the courthouse. Entering the room where his future would be decided, he made his way to the defense table, removing his coat and folding it under his chair. Along the route from hotel to courthouse, he had picked up a copy of that morning's *Austin American*. The preacher sat down and perused it.

He was observed to be "as calm as was Gene Tunney at the battle of the Sesquicentennial. He has the most magnetic personality," wrote Gene Fowler, friend and protégé of the famous writer Damon Runyon. Fowler was covering the trial for the Universal News Service. "He chews gum with all the vigor, but a trifle less noisily, of Will Rogers." Continuing to compare Norris with the country's favorite cowboy, Fowler went on: "Indeed, he has the drawl, the shrewd viewpoint and all but the burlesque instinct of Will."

Another reporter approached Norris, attempting to engage him in small talk and possibly glean a quote or two. He asked the preacher if he had been aware that one of the spectators the previous day was a woman who had shot her intoxicated husband to death and was later acquitted of all charges. The preacher, who knew the fear and misery inflicted on his mother by his own drunkard father, replied: "I wish I had been on that jury. Ninety-nine per cent of the women who are in trouble are right. Usually it is some man who is the cause. I think men who beat women deserve any punishment."

He was asked if he had any comment on the report that certain "bookies" in Dallas were giving odds on whether or not he would be convicted and that many were placing bets. The well-known foe of gambling and catalyst in the legislature's ban on racetrack betting in Texas back in 1908 said, "I'm sorry that I am on trial for my life and regret that my friends and my enemies would bet on a matter so serious."

The preacher talked about the future and about his plans for an even bigger church "as soon as this storm passes over." He hinted, "We have had several attractive offers for our present site and probably will accept one of them in the near future." Then, scanning the room and motioning for a few other journalists to join them, Norris handed out several copies of a "written statement" he wanted them to have before the trial began. At the top of the page were the words, "By Dr. J. Frank Norris." The statement began, "To my multitude of friends who have wired and written their love and sympathy in this hour of sorrow to me and my family, I will say I am glad the whole conspiracy is soon to come to light. Read Psalm 27." The verses of the psalm were printed on the page. Several papers ran his statement in full on page one later that day.

H.C. Meacham left his room at the Stephen F. Austin Hotel and walked toward the courthouse. As he entered the building, he was immediately peppered by reporters' questions. Indicating that he would be willing to talk a bit before going into the courtroom, he told the journalists, "I feel it is my duty. I don't mind coming here a bit. I feel it is my duty as mayor to be here."

"Don't you feel like you are a sort of martyr in this case?"

"Why no." The mayor nervously laughed. "I don't think anything of the kind. I am here to go through whatever they wish, and I am here willingly." He continued, "I can't conceive of the pastor being acquitted. I know the facts and I am sure he will be convicted."

At 9:25 AM Judge James Hamilton entered the courtroom and took his place on the bench. A man in his midsixties, the judge wore a bow tie and a stiff-collared white shirt that offset his dark robe. He was balding but sported a full mustache. The Teddy Roosevelt pince-nez glasses, the kind held on the face by a spring gripping the nose, gave him the look of a stern schoolmaster.

His bench was made of walnut and decoratively ornate. Behind him rose a backdrop, also of walnut, that gave his perch something of the feel of the pulpit in an elegant Gothic church. The wings to the backdrop flanked the judge on both sides. The walnut tower rose to a height of about twenty feet, topped off by a handsome Star of Texas. A single light hung down from a cord, stopping about eighteen inches above the magistrate, illuminating his entire desk.

Hamilton banged his gavel, and the trial was officially under way. Nearly six months to the day had passed since the death of D.E. Chipps.

The indictment was read, and J. Frank Norris answered emphatically: "I am not guilty!"

"Call your first witness."

"The State calls Mr. Joe P. Langston to the stand."

The mention of the completely unfamiliar name led to whispers and speculation that maybe this was one of the surprise witnesses. But instead he was the contractor who had developed the miniature model of Norris's office area that sat prominently at the front of the courtroom. It had been placed on a table and was tilted at an angle so the layout could be seen from the front without the viewer having to stand right over it. The incredibly detailed replica of the First Baptist Church Sunday School Building, home to the offices of the pastor and the *Searchlight,* even had tiny doorknobs on its doors.

"How do you enter the building?" Bill McLean asked Langston.

"You enter from a door on Throckmorton Street."

For about an hour Langston answered McLean's questions, all designed to give the jury a good sense of the layout of the scene of the crime. At times the witness stepped down from the stand to point out certain features of his model. Judge Hamilton was given a long pointer to use if he had any questions.

Norris noticed that the jury was very interested in testimony he thought to be tedious and overdone. The twelve men leaned and twisted so as to see and hear better. Hearing would be a problem throughout the trial, as the courtroom's high ceiling absorbed and muddled sound. On cross-examination, Marvin Simpson asked a few clarifying questions, but by and large the testimony of the contractor, though put on by the state, did not concern the defense.

Bess Carroll, who had written about Mrs. Norris and Mrs. Chipps, was watching for a new angle to her next story. She hoped to file something with Universal that day. Staring for a while at the scale model of Norris's office in the front of the courtroom, she soon thought: "Doll house!" She began to make some notes and put thoughts together. "This miniature house, product of weeks of painstaking work, would delight the heart of any girl," she scribbled on her notepad. "Yet it may decide the fate of J. Frank Norris. For on the floor of this tiny model, a dead man walks again, as witness after witness brings back the ghost of D.E. Chipps. It is a strange battleground, for Texas — this doll's house. Blood stains its floor again, as that lurid scene is brought back from its grave through the medium of memory." Numerous papers pulled her story from the wire service and ran it.

NEXT THE PROSECUTION called O.W. Phillips, the undertaker who had prepared D.E. Chipps's body for burial. McLean began, "For what concern were you working on or about the seventeenth day of July last year?"

"Robertson & Mueller Undertakers."

"Did you know D.E. Chipps during his lifetime?"

"Yes sir."

"Where was the first place you saw the body of D.E. Chipps?"

"In the morgue."

"Who drove it there?"

"I drove it there."

Phillips went on to describe the wounds on Chipps's body, "There was one bullet four inches below the breast, on the left side."

"Did you probe that?"

"Yes sir."

"Where did it go?"

"It ranged upward to the heart."

"Did it stop at the heart or go on through the heart?"

During a pause before Phillips's answer, sobbing could be heard. Mae Chipps, sitting not more than six feet from the man who had killed her son's father, was overwhelmed emotionally as she heard the wounds that killed her ex-husband described in graphic detail. Her son, with a stoic look on his face, put his arm around his mother.

Phillips continued, "I couldn't say that it went all the way through it. I probed into the heart."

"That is one. Where were the others?"

"There were two on the right side about an inch and a half or two inches below the collarbone, on the right side."

"How far were the bullet holes apart from each other?"

"About five inches."

When McLean was finished with the undertaker, he turned to Simpson and said, "Your witness." But Norris's attorney replied: "We have no questions at this time to ask the witness." Someone noticed J. Frank Norris yawning at this moment.

Next up was the ambulance driver, F.W. Spreen, who corroborated the previous testimony and described the scene as he arrived at Fourth and Throckmorton.

"Was Chipps dead when you got there?"

"No sir; as I picked him up and laid him on the stretcher, he took his last breath."

More audible sobs came from the back of the room.

The state was moving its case along, thus far, at a brisk pace. McLean would next question City Detective C.D. Bush. When he came to giving a description of Chipps's body as it was lying on the floor, Marvin Simpson stood and objected: "Well, if the court please, we don't think that it is necessary for him to describe the condition of the body. We object to that as being prejudicial and unnecessary, about that part of it. The location we have no objection to."

Hamilton countered firmly, "The objection is overruled."

Simpson said, "Note an exception, for the reason that the testimony is — "

McLean interrupted and instructed the witness, "Go ahead and describe."

Simpson was livid. "Just a minute. For the reason that this testimony is calculated to inflame the minds of the jury and prejudice the jury against the defendant; the testimony with reference to any blood coming from his mouth wouldn't serve to illustrate or explain any issue in this case."

But Simpson's complaint was in vain. The line of question and answer would continue in great detail.

McLean then shifted attention from the blood issue and asked Bush about the examination of Chipps's body and what was found on his person when he died. The witness replied, "Well, there was a pocketbook and in it two one dollar bills, an envelope, I believe, a piece of paper of some kind, and a cigarette holder, and in his hip pocket there was tobacco — a Prince Albert tobacco can because we had a time getting it out of his pocket."

"Now, let's have this cigarette case described. It may become material later on with some other witnesses," McLean pressed.

"It was just a small cigarette holder."

"Well, now have you stated everything that was found? What about pistols and knives and knucks?"

"Didn't find no pistols, no knives, and no knucks; didn't see anything else on Mr. Chipps."

A few minutes later it became clear where the prosecution had been going earlier, as McLean, returning to the blood issue, asked Bush: "Now did you notice yourself any blood other than that you have described about Chipps in that room?"

"Yes, I did."

"Well, let's have that."

"After the body had gone out and we left the room, looked around and didn't find anything and went out and in the other room, I seen a small clot of blood — oh, probably as big as a dollar, or something like that, in the other room — that is, the first room you get in."

"That is the little anteroom?"

"Yes sir."

The state was trying to make an important point: If that small spot had been blood — Chipps's blood — it would raise the possibility that the lumberman had been shot in the anteroom and his body moved by someone back to Norris's office. This would also indicate that the preacher would have likely shot Chipps from a distance and possibly as he was leaving the office, not as the man charged him, as had been Norris's story all along.

But for now the state just left the issue there.

Marvin Simpson began to cross-examine the detective. "Now, Mr. Bush, this spot of blood that you described there, I believe you say, was about the size of a dollar?"

"Yes sir. About that size."

"Now, tell the jury whether or not that was, from your observation of it, all blood or blood and something else?"

"Well, I didn't pay that much attention to it. I could not say. It looked like a bunch of tobacco spit at first to me."

"Have you or not testified about that matter before?"

"Yes, before the grand jury."

"Now, what did you tell the grand jury it was?"

"Just a spot of blood."

"Did you not tell them, Mr. Bush, that it looked like a spot of blood?"

"Yes, it was damp. I told them it was damp."

"Did you or not tell the grand jury it was spit or blood?"

"I don't remember whether I did or not, but it was damp and just looked like — "

"Well, just a minute. You were before the grand jury a few days or shortly after this, weren't you?"

"Yes sir."

"And you don't remember whether you told them it was — it looked like to you, spit or blood?"

And so it began. Soon, having painted a picture for the jury, establishing the details of what happened in Norris's office on July 17 — that D.E. Chipps had been unarmed and that he had died less than ten minutes after J. Frank shot him — the state called one of the rumored "surprise" witnesses.

His name was H.H. Rains, "a sporty young man of medium height, dark haired and dark eyed." At the time of the killing he was an employee of the Moore Rubber Company, which rented the space directly below Norris's offices from First Baptist Church. His job was to make out the work order tickets and "oversee the colored men who waited upon customers, changing their tires for them."

After a few preliminary questions and answers, and in response to Bill McLean's query about what he had heard that fateful day, Rains said: "I heard shots. I worked on the service floor directing darkies out there — " McLean cautioned the clearly nervous and excited witness to calm down and speak slowly.

"After I heard the shots — in about three minutes I was up there. When I got to the stairway, I heard Dr. Norris say — " McLean interrupted the witness, wanting to make sure the next words achieved maximum effect. Rains sat quietly for a moment and took a deep breath. Then he gave the line that would become the trial's first resonant quote and would make headline writing quite easy for many editors that day.

"Dr. Norris said, 'I have killed me a man.' I turned around. A Negro was there. The dead man was laying there. Some other fellow was there."

"I have killed me a man."

The phrase dripped with the kind of cynical emotion that seemed very unclergy-like. Is that what J. Frank Norris really said? Marvin Simpson was champing at the bit to cross-examine this so-called surprise witness. Rains's testimony was important and potentially damaging to Norris, but Simpson noticed what many in the courtroom had also seen: The man's demeanor was nervous, even quirky.

When McLean indicated that he had no more questions for him, Rains thought he was done and started to step down. Simpson bolted out of his chair and, almost sneering, barked: "I'd like to ask you a few questions, if you aren't in a hurry."

McLean took exception to how Simpson was talking to the state's witness.

Norris's attorney took some time to question Rains on his life experience. The defense had done their homework, and even though this witness was billed as a surprise they'd known he was coming and were prepared. Simpson's questions and Rains's answers conjured up the image of a misfit, someone who bounced from town to town and had difficulty holding a job.

Simpson spent the better part of the next hour going after Rains from every angle, microanalyzing every detail, every syllable, every vocal inflection, trying to neutralize the phrase, *I have killed me a man.* And along the way, Rains grew more and more frustrated with his questioner.

At one point Rains lost his cool and screamed, "When I came down — do you hear me? — I told them a man had been killed up there, and J. Frank Norris had killed him a man!"

"What are you getting so mad about?" Simpson asked. McLean muttered to the judge, barely audibly: "Watch the conduct of the lawyer, and see who is getting mad. A witness has rights in this courtroom, Your Honor."

Hamilton rapped his gavel several times for order.

Simpson then asked Rains about what happened after he went back downstairs where he worked. "Did you tell Mr. Moore that night that Dr. Norris said: 'I have killed me a man'?"

Rains, still visibly upset, guardedly replied, "Yes. What do you want?"

"I'm getting to that," Simpson snapped back.

Rains barked back, "Well, let's have it!"

Gesturing angrily, the lawyer moved his finger toward the face of the witness and said, "You are going to have it!"

The sharp crack of the judge's gavel interrupted the angry exchange. Simpson then inquired as to whether or not Rains had ever used "abusive language" when talking about J. Frank Norris. The witness said that he had not.

As he neared the end of his examination, Simpson knew that the defense would have its moment. When it came time to call their witnesses, they already planned to bring forward several who would cast some doubt that Rains really heard Dr. Norris speak so coldly and callously.

His testimony over, "the stocky, somewhat handsome young man" stepped down, to the disappointment of several of the women in the room, who "appeared to be enjoying his testimony greatly." He would be the last witness of the morning; it was well after noon and time for a break. Rains stood by the courtroom door for a short while, glaring angrily at Marvin Simpson.

Marcet Haldeman-Julius, who was watching with great interest and planning to publish her own account of the happenings, observed: "My own impression is that the young man really heard the shots and really did go up to see what had caused them, that he saw Norris and got a quick glimpse of Chipps, but I doubt very much whether he actually heard Norris say anything." She found herself somewhat repelled by Rains, describing him as "one of these 'know-it-all' kind," and as "decidedly too smartly up-and-coming to inspire one with undue confidence in his assertions. Nor did he seem to have a clear natural memory."

CHAPTER THIRTY-NINE

"I'll Come Back"

JOURNALIST GENE FOWLER filed a piece, telegraphed across the country via his wire service, that said, "The prosecution got off to a stumbling start." He told his readers that he had the impression, based solely on the trial's opening morning session, that they might "limp into port with a leaky hull, broken propeller shafts, and a heavy list to port."

And he was not alone in feeling this way. Possibly, some thought, Bill McLean was having trouble finding his rhythm as a prosecutor. He'd built his reputation as a defense attorney, the kind Norris might have wanted on his team, if the lawyer hadn't hated the preacher so much.

At precisely 3 PM Judge Hamilton, sending a clear signal this first day that he planned to oversee punctual proceedings, took his place on the bench and slammed the gavel down, demanding order. Looking at the prosecution table, he said: "Call your next witness." At that, Jesse Martin, the new DA for Tarrant County, stood and told the court, "The State calls Mrs. Parker."

The courtroom door opened and, while people squirmed and half stood to see who was coming in, "a mild-mannered little woman" seventy-six years of age — though most observers agreed that she looked "much younger" — made her way gracefully and deliberately down the room's center aisle toward the witness stand. She was "a slender, trim woman of genteel bearing" with a "motherly face." She was wearing a black silk dress and a fur-trimmed coat. Rounding out her ensemble was a hat that was described diplomatically as "unfashionable, but substantial." As she passed the defense table her "eyes were fastened fearlessly on J. Frank Norris." He did not look in her direction but rather leaned back in his chair, locking his fingers behind his neck, as he often did.

The lady's presence created quite a stir in the room, tempting Hamilton to use his gavel again. As she took off her coat and hat and raised her right hand, it was clear that she was the other surprise witness for the prosecution. But what would she have to say?

Bill McLean walked toward the witness stand. Reporter Jack Gordon described him that day as "the sort of lawyer the flappers would call cute." He was aggressive and effective, but not polished, regularly struggling with his syntax. But he was ready to demonstrate that he was more than up to the task of his uncommon role as prosecutor.

The witness, in soft voice with a southern lilt, gave her name as "Mrs. Roxie E. Parker," the widow of Texas judge W.R. Parker. Her "golden brown hair" was accented by spots of gray and parted in the middle, being brought down "to a soft knot at the back of her neck." She wore "gold-bowed spectacles," and on her "small, aristocratic hands" were "gray-kid gloves." She kept the gloves on for the entire hour she spent on the stand.

By the time McLean, smiling and clearly proud of his team for keeping this witness out of the public eye before now, began to question Mrs. Parker, the room was silent and rapt with attention.

"Do you know the defendant Norris?"

"Yes, I have seen him twice," the genteel witness answered.

"Mrs. Parker, were you in his office at any time previous to the killing of Mr. Chipps?"

"Yes, I was in his office once."

"Did you go with anyone up to his office, or how come you to go up there the first time?"

The witness told her story. Mr. John Homan, who ran the downtown Fort Worth garage where she serviced her Nash automobile, had suggested that the folks over at First Baptist might be interested in acquiring her eighty-acre property, located twenty miles or so from Fort Worth near the town of Grapevine, for a summer camp for kids. She had been trying to sell the place for a while after the death of her husband and then that of her son.

McLean asked, "What is the character of your home out there? What kind of place is it?"

"I have a beautiful country place. I have a spring lake, lots of springs, and I have a two-story, aeroplane bungalow with eight rooms and bath, and out buildings, and it is in a wonderful grove of big oaks."

The late judge and his wife had named their place "A Thousand Oaks."

She had gone to see Norris about the property, and the preacher had an office girl write down some details about it. He assured Mrs. Parker that he would get out to see it soon. She recalled that conversation as taking place in June 1926.

Norris never came.

Not one to give up easily, Mrs. Parker decided that if she had any chance of selling her country home and acreage to Norris's church, she needed to go and see him again. "One has to follow up on these things," she declared. So on Saturday, July 17, Roxie and her daughter drove to town to run a series of errands. They planned their last stop before heading home to be the offices of First Baptist Church. They took some clothes to the laundry and visited some friends and "discussed various ailments." This brought mild laughter from those in the room who were enthralled by the lady and her story thus far. Even Judge Hamilton smiled briefly.

"Now Mrs. Parker," McLean continued, "what day was it that you started to his office with reference to the death of Chipps, the day of the week, if you know?"

"It was on Saturday afternoon."

"Now, who drove you up there?"

"My daughter; she drives my car all the time."

"All right. Is your daughter married?"

"She is a widow."

"She is a widow. Does she have any children?"

"Yes sir."

"All right. Now, when you got to where the office of the defendant was, where was the car stopped?"

"It was on that street south of the church, the street running between Throckmorton, and I believe Taylor is back of it, isn't it?"

"I don't know."

"Anyway, it was facing east, facing Throckmorton and toward the east."

"You mean the car was facing Throckmorton?"

"Yes, east."

"East. All right. Anyone else in the car with you and your daughter?"

"No."

"Well, what did you do when the car was stopped?"

"I got out and started up to Dr. Norris' office."

"Where did your daughter stay, if any place?"

"She sat in the car. I went up the stairway."

"All right. Mrs. Parker, show the jury what street you came in on. What street was it you came in on? This don't show the street." McLean directed her attention to the scale model of Norris's office area.

Mrs. Parker stepped down from the stand and walked over to the display.

"I came on the street facing Throckmorton; then I crossed over to Throckmorton side of the church."

"Now explain to the jury how you got up to his office, so they can see it. Now don't get between the jurors." With that, the lawyer gently guided the witness to a spot where the jurors could clearly see what she was doing.

She continued, pointing with her gloved finger as she testified, "I come up the steps and went in this door."

"Now, push it open, just show them how you went."

Though the effectiveness of the scale model, the so-called dollhouse, may have been questioned after the morning session, the prosecution was demonstrating its worth now.

Mrs. Parker said, "The door was open. This open" — indicating the main entrance to the office area from the stairs. "When I went in, I started in, I just got inside when the opposite door opened — "

"What a minute," McLean interrupted. "You are talking about an opposite door. Just show these gentlemen what opposite door it was that opened."

Mrs. Parker pointed and said, "Here. That is the little room I was in. Isn't it?"

"I don't know."

"Isn't this," the witness pointing, "the little anteroom? This is where the bench is. That is where I first went in. I went inside here: when I got inside this door, this one opened." She was pointing across at another door, though still seeming a bit unsure of exactly what she was looking at. "It just seemed — "

Again McLean spoke, trying to be gentle and not make his witness uncomfortable. "Take your finger and show the jury how it opened. Now they have got a lot to see, if you can turn a little more this way." The attorney demonstrated. McLean looked over at Sam Sayers, his longtime friend and law partner, who was sitting at the prosecution table. Sam had a look on his face that "Wild Bill" read with ease. They should have found a way, before today, to get this particular witness in a room with this scale model. Not doing so was a big oversight.

However, it really didn't seem like the jurors were put off by Mrs. Parker's mild uncertainty about some of these details. After all, she was seventy-six years old, and it had all happened six months before. The looks on their faces told the story. The twelve men saw her as a very compelling witness.

Still standing near the scale model, Mrs. Parker continued her answer. "Well, it opened, this door — " She pointed to the model of Norris's office door. " — opened that way, and a man came out in this position." At this the witness illustrated the man standing with his hand on the edge of the door. "As well as I could tell, as well as I would know, he had the door in his hand, I don't think he had the door knob."

"Put your hand on the door just like you say the man had his."

She did and then continued with her story. "He was facing just as I am standing, pulling this door this way [indicating], but didn't shut it; while it was coming to, it opened back. Dr. Norris appeared in the door and the man, as the door went back, says, he put his hand up like this." Mrs. Parker raised her hand to about the level of her chin, in a manner as if to indicate a wave or farewell gesture. "It was all done in an instant; he says, 'I will come back,' and he turned as he said it, facing back toward the open door."

Reporters had turned into stenographers about this time, trying to take down every word spoken by this unlikely star. She continued, "When the man said that, he was shot, he staggered a little bit around this way" — illustrating with her body how the man had turned — "back facing opposite way he was at first.

"Just as he was doing that I left, and I heard some more shots. Oh, I don't know how many, it seemed to me it was two or three."

"All right, now Mrs. Parker, just have your seat," McLean suggested, pointing her back to the stand. Waiting a moment for her to get settled, he then pressed, "Did you know D.E. Chipps during his lifetime?"

"No."

"Are you related to anybody that is related to D.E. Chipps so far as you know?"

"I never heard of it."

"Now, Mrs. Parker, when the man was closing the door, when it flashed open, how long was it before the shot was fired?"

"It seems to me that it was instantly, while he was almost there. He staggered out; it threw him around further, with his back; as he was staggering around I turned."

"Now, what did you do when you turned?"

"I went downstairs."

"Mrs. Parker, who did that shooting?"

"Dr. Norris."

"This gentleman sitting over here?" McLean moved in the preacher's direction, pointing at him.

"Yes," affirmed Mrs. Roxie E. Parker.

All eyes were on J. Frank Norris as he turned and whispered something to Dayton Moses, almost as if to ignore the witness.

"Did you see or notice anybody else there as the shots were being fired, or just after they were fired?"

"I didn't see anybody in front of me at all."

"Now state what, if anything, happened when you turned to go down the steps."

"As I got to the head of the steps, there was a boy passed me."

"Now, about what size boy was it, if you can get at it?"

"Well, he looked to be about 13 — 13 or 14 — maybe 15."

"What did you do then?"

"I got in the car. I crossed the street."

"Now, what, if anything, occurred in the street after you left the scene of this killing to go to your car? What happened before you got to your car?"

"I liked to have been run over!"

"What happened?"

"The man threw his brakes on, screeched the car, made a noise like — the man threw his brakes quick, and said something, but I don't know what he said. I went on across the street."

She finished her time with prosecutor McLean describing how she then got in her car and went home. "Wild Bill" thanked Mrs. Parker, smiled and looked over at Norris, then said to Marvin Simpson, "Take the witness."

Mr. Simpson, "who had been flushed with his early success" just a while before, rose slowly from his chair, running his hand through his reddish and tousled hair. The lady's testimony had caught him and his team by surprise. Newspapers across the country would describe it almost universally as his having been "caught flatfooted," like an overconfident boxer who, feeling good about his performance in the first round, gets knocked on his keister in the second. The defense had, of course, known of Mrs. Parker. Her name was on the witness list, and they had made preparations to counter her testimony. But they had not anticipated the prosecution featuring Parker so prominently in its case.

Pausing before his first question and taking his first measure of Mrs. Parker up close, Marvin Simpson looked into her "steady brown eyes" that were "far from dim although they look through tortoise shell rims." He began, "Let us see now, Mrs. Parker. How long did you say you have lived out where you are now living?"

"It is two years last October."

"Where did you move from to the place?"

"Fort Worth."

"How long had you lived in Fort Worth at the time of your marriage to Judge Parker?"

"I never lived in Fort Worth before I married him."

"Where did you live before that time?"

"Oklahoma City."

"Had you been married before?"

Simpson dug out that both she and the judge had been divorced before marrying each other. Possibly, he thought this "revelation" might shake the sympathetic image of the witness. Moving on through questions about her first meeting of Norris, Simpson tripped Parker up. "Now, what time of the month was this that you had this first conversation with Mr. Homan, when you say he suggested that you go to Norris?"

"I don't know."

"About what date?"

"I don't know. It was in the summer. I don't know. It was June or July."

"Was it the same day that you went up to see Dr. Norris the first time?"

"Yes sir."

"That is the first time you had ever talked to Mr. Homan about the matter when Dr. Norris' name was connected with it?"

"Yes."

"That is the same day you went up to see Dr. Norris the first time?"

"Yes."

McLean and Sayers, sitting at the prosecution table, cringed as she answered Simpson's question, knowing that their star witness was getting confused and falling into a trap; her time line was wrong, but there was nothing to which they could object.

Simpson soon, though, shifted gears and invited the witness to come back to the scale model. Showing her where he wanted her to stand, the lawyer continued, "As I understand it from you, you came up and found this door open. That boy that passed or met was along here someplace?" McLean pointed to a place in the anteroom near the wall connected to the stairwell.

"Well, my recollection is, as I went out of this door here, it seems to me the boy was right there," she said, pointing out the locations. "And I either kinder run into him or he into me, I don't know which."

Simpson spent the better part of the next fifteen minutes trying to put a hole in Parker's testimony about what she saw. But though she was fuzzy on the dates of things, she never wavered on the specific details about what she saw. And Norris's lawyer knew, as did Norris himself, that Roxie E. Parker's testimony placed D.E. Chipps in the anteroom, not the preacher's office, at the moment of the shooting, leaving the impression that the body had been moved, not to mention that Chipps might not have been charging toward Norris at the fateful moment.

Under intense questioning from the defense attorney, Mrs. Parker said "the man" was "four, maybe five" feet from Norris when the shooting started.

"Now, Mrs. Parker, after that one shot — was it one shot at first?"

"Yes sir."

"Then there was a pause in the shooting?"

"I don't think so; I think as I turned my back they kept on."

"Take this rod, if you will, and give us the measure of the shots, as you remember the reports of them."

"I can't do that, for I don't know."

"Try it."

"I don't know," she said, clearly flustered. She looked at Hamilton, "Judge, I was so amazed, or excited, I was almost paralyzed."

"How far had you gotten into that anteroom office before that door opened?" Simpson asked.

"I just stepped in the door."

"And you think you got maybe to the head of the stairway, going back, before the last shot was fired?"

"I don't know," the witness answered, now beginning to look quite weary.

"Mrs. Parker, who did you first tell this to?"

"To my daughter."

"When?"

"Immediately."

"Who else did you tell it to?"

"A man named Dr. Hall."

"Where does he live?"

"In Dallas."

"How long after this occurrence was it before you told Dr. Hall of it?"

"It was several months."

"Who did you next tell it to?"

"To Judge McLean."

"How come you to tell it to Judge McLean? Do you mean this gentleman here, Mr. McLean?"

"Yes."

When asked why she told Bill McLean, Mrs. Parker launched into a rather lengthy monologue describing a conversation with the afore-mentioned Dr. Hall. They had been discussing some real estate he had purchased and the improvements he wanted to make. In the course of the conversation at his place, she saw a newspaper on the table and a picture of J. Frank Norris. "A terrible thing," Hall told her, and Mrs. Parker told the doctor what she had seen. He told her that she needed to talk to someone. This all had taken place shortly after the case had been transferred from Tarrant County to Travis County.

Marvin Simpson rubbed the back of his neck, as if in pain, and continued with an obvious question: "Now you know, of course, that the grand jury was investigating this matter at the time?"

"Yes."

"And you did not go before the grand jury?"

"No sir."

"And you did not tell any official?"

"I told nobody but my daughter, until I told Dr. Hall."

Her work done, Roxie Parker left the stand and exited the courtroom.

On the way out, Marcet Haldeman-Julius shook her hand and asked if they might talk soon.

Her testimony had directly challenged J. Frank Norris's version of events in subtle but important ways. The scene she described showed Chipps outside of the preacher's office and with hand raised in an apparent farewell gesture. She saw him leaving the office when he was shot, not aggressively reentering it. He had said, "I'll come back" — not some of the other words Norris and the defense had been putting in Mr. Chipps's mouth the past six months since the lumberman's death.

If her story were true, the case for self-defense, and its image of a drunken lumberman lunging toward the pastor in a threatening way, was not. The defense-driven idea that Chipps had made the classic "hip pocket move," as if going for a gun, would also be inconsistent with what Mrs. Roxie E. Parker had told the world.

As the woman who had captured the imagination of all in the room went out the door, "Wild Bill" McLean rose to his feet and uttered a phrase no one anticipated, at least not right then.

"The State rests!"

CHAPTER FORTY

"It's a Frame Up!"

EVERYONE IN THE courtroom was stunned. The prosecution had called only six witnesses, occupying a mere five hours of the court's time in making its case. What about all the other witnesses who had been subpoenaed? How could such a serious trial about such a sensational crime, with such a controversial defendant, warrant less than a day to argue? The court of public opinion had been dissecting and discussing every detail for months. How could the state claim they had done their job in only three hundred minutes?

But McLean was adamant that his team had made the right move. "We had an unimpeachable witness in that old lady. She told enough, and to call anymore would be just bl-a-a-ah," he said.

As he walked along the courthouse corridor at the end of the day, he strongly hinted that the short presentation of the state's case was part of a larger strategy. "It is forecast, however," he said, "that the state intends an elaborate rebuttal." The state would let the defense put up witness after witness, day after day, and then chisel away at their case employing the skills and instincts of the masterful defense attorney that McLean was.

The announcement of the end of the state's case caught Norris's attorneys unprepared. They had not planned to begin presenting their case on that very first day. But prepared or not, they began and called Mr. John E. Homan as their first witness. The owner of the local Nash automobile dealership was certainly not the first witness Norris's lawyers had planned to call, but it was now important to challenge at least some details of Roxie Parker's testimony while it was fresh in everyone's mind.

"Are you acquainted with Mrs. Roxie Parker?" Marvin Simpson asked the first witness for the defense.

"Yes sir."

"How long have you known her?"

"Two years."

"What was the occasion of your acquaintance with her?"

"I sold her an automobile."

"Did you sell the automobile to her for cash or terms?"

"On terms."

"Tell the jury whether or not you had any conversation with Mrs. Parker at any time in reference to her selling any property to Dr. Frank Norris, the defendant, first, with regard to any indebtedness that she owed you?"

"As near as I can remember, it was some time last winter."

"You mean of 1926?"

"About a year ago this month, as near as I can recall, about this time in 1926."

"All right, Mr. Homan was that in connection with that conversation — did you have any conversation with her with reference to her selling to Dr. Norris or attempting to sell to him any property?"

"Yes."

Simpson paused for effect then said, "Now, then, I will ask you to state to the jury what it was."

Homan cleared his throat, then explained: "Mrs. Parker owed me a note that was quite a bit past due, and she was unable to meet it, and she came into my office one day and asked me if I would call up Mr. Norris and make an engagement for her to meet him in his study, with a view of her selling him this property. She had a farm about twenty miles from Fort Worth at Grapevine. It was a farm she had fixed up as a kind of show place, and she told me at the time that she could not meet the note unless she sold this farm, and she was under the impression that Norris might be induced to buy it for his church, as a camp, and asked me to make this appointment, and I don't recall whether I did or not. I remember the conversation, and remember she came later, however."

As Homan testified, he appeared indifferent, almost disinterested. It was infuriating to him to be in this spot. He despised J. Frank Norris and had ever since the preacher had, in his mind, ruined the great First Baptist Church with his antics. John Homan had been a member of the church when Pastor Norris was called in 1909. He had even voted for the guy. But when the building burned and the congregation became so divided, he saw it all as a result of Norris's methods. He still regretted having to testify at one of Norris's trials back in 1912. He had been brought to the stand as part of the ill-fated change-of-venue motion back then, telling the court that he didn't think Norris could get a fair trial in Fort Worth. He was sure the preacher was capable of murder, just as he was sure Norris had set the fire in 1912 and then lied under oath. So the very idea of helping Norris's defense made him ill.

But he was a man of his word and took his civic responsibility seriously. So he told about how Mrs. Parker had come back about "a week or 10 days" later, because "I was pressing her pretty hard for the money."

"Now, do you know whether that was before the month of March, 1926?"

"Yes sir."

"How do you know that?"

"Because she paid her note off in March of 1926," the witness replied, further claiming that he hadn't seen her since. The testimony directly contradicted the time line Mrs. Parker had described. If she had been several months off in her memory about her meeting with Homan, could she be wrong on the other parts of her testimony? This was the question Simpson was trying to suggest to the minds of the jurors.

When McLean cross-examined Homan, he asked the automobile dealer if he recalled Mrs. Parker bringing her car in for repairs and asking her while she was there whether she had been able to connect with Norris. Homan insisted that wasn't the case. But as McLean pressed, he seemed to doubt himself. Increasingly, as McLean demonstrated his counterpunching skills, the witness gave answers such as "I can't be positive, I don't remember."

Finally, when McLean swarmed him with a barrage of questions asking if he could swear to the fact that Mrs. Parker *hadn't* talked with him in June or July (as she had testified), he burst out an exclamation: "No sir; no sir. I can't swear to that because I don't remember!"

Homan's testimony finished, Judge Hamilton announced an adjournment — court would resume, he said, at nine o'clock Saturday morning.

As the Reverend and Mrs. Norris walked back toward the Driskill Hotel, a reporter caught up with them and asked if the preacher had any comment about Mrs. Roxie E. Parker's testimony. Norris stopped briefly and tersely replied: "It's a frame up!" That was all any reporter would get from the usually talkative minister that evening. And everyone around J. Frank — friend or foe — saw his demeanor as indicative of someone "harboring a struggle within his heart."

There was much talk around the Texas capital that night about Roxie Parker. Some remarked that she looked a little like the famous portrait of Whistler's mother, though "rather extravagantly," one thought. Others dug out that she had been born and raised in Mississippi and that her uncle had been governor of that state. Gene Fowler told his readers that Mrs. Parker had been "as beautiful as Dresden china in her twenties," somehow quoting "old time beaux from the south."

Some talked about the country home she had been trying to sell to J. Frank Norris as an idyllic setting. "There are bubbling springs and she has built rustic seats and little glass houses for the painted buntings, fly catchers and orchard orioles." The consensus among veteran courtroom watchers was, "If un-refuted, Mrs. Parker's testimony was simply devastating." She had described a "big, irascible but warm-hearted Chipps shot down, as hand uplifted in warning and swaggering, but unmistakably farewell gesture, he was leaving the study." Her appearance was "the vivid picture of the day."

As Marcet Haldeman-Julius went over her notes about what she had seen and heard that Friday, she found herself — though clearly impressed with Bill McLean's lawyer skills — wondering why other witnesses weren't called to support Mrs. Parker's testimony. What about her daughter in the car? Where was the driver of the car that nearly ran her down? She finally decided that the prosecutors were planning "an elaborate rebuttal." That had to be it.

Several of the Fort Worth law enforcement crowd wound up at the same Austin restaurant for dinner that night and "shoved three or four tables together to have a real 'family dinner.'" Chief Lee sat at the head of the table, joined by Officers Rabb, Hinkle, Lewis, Ford, and Hamilton.

At another table nearby some of the trial "fans" — including a journalist or two — were raucously reenacting parts of that day's trial in silent-movie subtitle fashion: "He's lying now!" "He's trying to bully her!" "She's telling the truth!"

It was assumed, as everyone retired for the evening that Friday, that the defense would start out the next morning by calling L.H. Nutt to the stand — previously believed to be the only eyewitness to the shooting. It would be very interesting to see how his testimony would square with what the woman of the hour had said early that day.

CHAPTER FORTY-ONE

"I Will Kill You!"

IT WAS CLEAR long before the doors to the courtroom opened shortly after nine o'clock on Saturday morning, January 15, that more people — many more people — than the day before hoped to get a seat, or at least find a place to stand. Ultimately "hundreds were turned away," and the bailiff pushed the standing spectators as far back as he could before then actually locking the courtroom door. Some ambitious folks in the standing section eventually "sneaked forward" during the day, "until they were on the backs of the huddle of lawyers." They had never seen such a spectacle. The room was so full that some reporters literally had to crawl through a window throughout the day to get to the telegraph instruments that were now set up in the court clerk's office.

The first order of business for the defense was to try to cast doubt on the testimony of H.H. Rains. His claim that J. Frank Norris had coldly declared, "I have killed me a man" — though not as devastating as Roxie Parker's testimony — needed to be countered. Toward that end, Marvin Simpson and Dayton Moses would offer the testimony of a witness named H.M. Williams.

Dayton Moses would handle the examination of Mr. Williams. Journalist Jack Gordon observed that Moses, speaking first from his chair at the defense table, looked "for the world like John Chinaman's Buddha." Filled with nervous energy, Moses "twiddled his fingers in his lap" as he began.

"In what business or occupation are you engaged?"

"I am city salesman for the Moore Rubber Company."

"Mr. Williams, do you know a man by the name of H.H. Rains?"

"Yes sir. He worked for us up to and until January 12."

"How long have you known Mr. Rains?"

"I have known him about a year."

Moses got to his feet and was moving toward Mr. Williams.

"When did you first hear that there had been trouble upstairs in that building?"

Williams described the scene. He had just pulled up in his car, parking it in the small adjacent lot, when he noticed a lot of people clearly excited in the shop. He asked Rains, who was out of breath, what had happened, and he learned that someone had been shot in the church office.

"Who said that?"

"Rains."

"Now, when you first drove up on the vacant lot did you see Mr. Rains?"

"Yes, sir."

"Where was he?"

"He was kinder leaning against the building, right at the corner."

Dayton Moses, becoming animated and pointing his finger, challenged his witness: "Did Mr. Rains say at any time during the day in your presence that he had heard Dr. Norris say, 'I have killed me a man'?"

"No, sir."

"Do you remember the occasion of the setting in this case against Dr. Norris in the Criminal District Court of Tarrant County?"

"Yes, sir."

"Now, about that time did you have any conversation with Mr. Rains regarding the matter of whether he knew anything about the case? If so, where did that conversation take place, and what was said?"

"Well, that was some time after it had happened. That was long about the change of venue. I asked him what he knew, what he thought about it, what he really knew about it, and he said: 'I don't know a damn thing, Bill.' So that is all I said."

After excusing Williams, the defense recalled H.H. Rains and Moses went to work: "You testified on yesterday, did you not, that you had never used any abusive language regarding Dr. J. Frank Norris?"

"Yes, sir."

"Do you remember the occasion of Mr. Williams purchasing a radio last summer and talking to you about it?"

"I don't know anything about Mr. Williams' home affairs; no sir."

"I didn't ask you that. Please answer my question."

"I don't."

At this moment Judge Hamilton scolded Rains: "Mr. Witness, now you listen to what he says, and answer the question."

"All right, sir," Rains replied sheepishly.

Moses waved his finger at the witness and resumed his question: "I will ask you if it isn't true that on a Monday after the killing of D.E. Chipps, or shortly thereafter, or about that time, there at the place of business where you and he both worked."

"Yes, sir."

"If he didn't have a conversation with you in which he told you that he had heard a very good sermon last night over the radio, preached by Dr. Norris?"

"No, sir."

"And you replied in substance — "

Rains interrupted, "No, sir." This prompted another rebuke from the judge: "Wait until you hear the question."

"All right, sir." This time Rains's reply was a little sharper.

"And you replied in substance you didn't care to hear him — "

"No, sir. I didn't."

Once again, Judge Hamilton scolded Rains: "Will you wait until he gets through?" And again the witness answered, "All right, sir."

Moses pressed on, " — and referred to the defendant in this case, Dr. J. Frank Norris as a son of a bitch?"

"No, sir. I didn't."

"Now, I will ask you if on numerous occasions there around that place of business if you haven't frequently and contentiously referred to Dr. Norris and expressed your ill will about him?"

"I have nothing against him, no sir."

Dayton Moses glared at Rains for a moment and then turned to the judge. "We request the court to instruct him to answer the question."

Hamilton countered, "I thought he said — "

Moses interrupted the judge, "He said, 'no sir, I have nothing against him.'"

At this, Bill McLean sprang from his chair and said emphatically, "He answered as intelligently and clearly as any man can."

Moses, ignoring Wild Bill, pressed Rains, "All right. Now, then, didn't you on one occasion, talking in the presence of Mr. Williams, say in substance, that you didn't like Dr. Norris because of some things he had said about you at your wife's funeral?"

"At my wife's funeral?" This mention rattled H.H. Rains. The witness seemed for a moment lost in thought, unable to reply, mumbling, "I have nothing against him."

Moses was finished with Rains, and McLean indicated that he had no more questions. H.M. Williams was brought back to rebut Rains's testimony. He reinforced that he had indeed heard his tire shop coworker talk abusively about Norris, raising the possibility that Rains had not told the complete truth on the stand, and reducing the substance of the allegations against Norris to the question of whether one liked or disliked the preacher.

Having rebutted the state's star witnesses, the defense now called to the stand L.H. Nutt. The only witness whose testimony was more hotly anticipated was Norris himself.

It fell to Marvin Simpson to conduct the examination of Mr. Nutt. Simpson began by dispensing with Nutt's obligatory personal information: He worked at the Fort Worth National Bank as an auditor at the time of the shooting; he was still working for the bank, but it had since merged with another and his job description was a work in progress; and he had known J. Frank Norris for a dozen years.

"Do you remember about what time you left the bank, July 17?"

"Between 4:00 and 4:30 in the afternoon."

"What did you go to the church for?"

"I went by to see if we had teachers for our department for the next Sunday morning."

"Do you mean the following Sunday morning?"

"Yes; the following Sunday morning."

Then Marvin Simpson revealed that the defense had a dollhouse of its own. The courtroom door opened and two men entered carrying another scale model for display in front of the room. Simpson said: "Before we go any further with this witness we have a model that is constructed according to scale which these gentlemen, when they see it, will agree to and also it has the exact replica of the furniture that was situated there at the time, which we would like — we would like to have this model removed and the other one put in here in order that we may make some observations with reference to the furniture."

McLean countered, "Examine your witness. We don't want to make any agreement that the furniture there is like it was then. That is a matter of proof." Simpson, deciding not to make a point that the defense had accepted the prosecution's scale model unreservedly, said, "That is all right."

Simpson guided Nutt along in the telling of his movements that fateful Saturday. He described climbing the stairs to the second floor of the Sunday School Building and chatting briefly with Miss Jane Hartwell.

"Where did you first see the Doctor, Mr. Nutt, if you remember it?"

"Either at his desk or coming out into the main office or at the stenographer's desk."

"What were the first words, if you remember, that were spoken between you and Dr. Norris when you went in there?"

"Dr. Norris said: 'Do you know Chipps?'"

"What did you say?"

"Well, I hesitated and I says: 'I think that I do know him down at the bank — I think that he does business down at the bank."

"All right. Did you see Mr. Chipps there in the office there that afternoon after you said that to Dr. Norris?"

"Yes."

"Now, through which one of these doors entering that office you were in did Mr. Chipps enter?"

"The door in the west of Dr. Norris' office."

"Now, where were you sitting at the time Mr. Chipps entered?"

"The chair west of Dr. Norris' desk."

"Now, Mr. Chipps" — Simpson cringed and corrected himself — "Mr. Nutt, when Mr. Chipps entered the room did he knock before he came in?"

"No, sir."

"What were the first words spoken by him?"

"He said: 'I am Chipps' or 'This is Chipps' or 'My name is Chipps' or to that effect. He announced his name, I don't remember exactly the term that he used."

"All right, what else?"

"I raised up to my feet and says, 'I know this man; I know him down at the bank.' He addressed his remark to me; he said, 'Yes, I know you.' And he started over to the settee, and as he went over — "

Simpson slowed him down, "Just a minute. Where was the settee located?"

"In the northwest corner of Dr. Norris' office. And as he went over to take his seat he said, 'I am D.E. Chipps the lumberman.' He says, 'I sell lumber all over this country and lots of it.' And by that time he had seated himself on the east end of the settee. And following that immediately he says, 'I have got something to say and I will say it to you,' looking in my direction and then he turned his remarks in Dr. Norris' direction and he says, 'If you talk about my friends Meacham, Austin, and Roach any more,' he says, 'I am going to kill you.' And he had his fists clinched with a deter- mined, defiant, mean, angry look."

Nutt said Norris spoke up and told the lumberman that he wouldn't change his sermon, in fact inviting Chipps to come and hear it.

"What did Mr. Chipps say?"

"Well, he got up out of his seat and says: 'If you do I will kill you.'"

Mr. Nutt told the court that J. Frank Norris had then said, "'I don't want any trouble with you, but that is enough, there is the door.'" The witness indicated that Chipps refused to go, at which time Bill McLean objected that Nutt was making a conclusion. Legal wrangling went on for a couple of minutes, after which Judge Hamilton instructed the witness, "Just state what was said."

"Dr. Norris says, 'There is the door.'"

"Well, what did he do then?"

"Well, he remained standing there with his lips quivering."

"What direction was he looking?"

"Looking toward Dr. Norris."

"Where was Dr. Norris at that time?"

"Dr. Norris had gotten up and was standing right in front of him, facing him."

"Where were you?"

"I was over here in this chair." Nutt used his forefinger to point out exactly where in the scale model.

"How many times did you say Dr. Norris asked him to leave?"

"As many as two times."

"Then what did Chipps do?"

"He went out."

"What way did he go out, Mr. Nutt?"

"He walked out slowly."

"What took place, if anything, or what did you hear, if anything, after Mr. Chipps went through that door?"

"Dr. Norris says: 'I repeat what I have said.'"

"What did Mr. Chipps say?"

"He says: 'I will kill you!'"

"Now, where was Mr. Chipps, if you know, when he made this last statement you have described that, 'I will kill you'?"

"He had gone out into the anteroom."

"Where was Dr. Norris, if you know, when you heard Mr. Chipps say, 'I will kill you'?"

"He was pretty close to the door there, within two or three feet of the door in his office."

"Now, where did Dr. Norris go, if any place, from where he was there?"

"He walked back to his desk."

"What was the next thing you heard or saw, Mr. Nutt?"

"The next thing I saw was Mr. Chipps appeared in the door again."

At this moment, the defense asked for a short recess, which Hamilton granted, setting the stage for the dramatic description by Norris's most vital witness at shortly after eleven o'clock that morning. When court resumed, the judge banged his gavel and instructed Marvin Simpson, "Take the witness."

The lawyer faced L.H. Nutt and asked, "Now what did you hear, if anything, before you saw him there or at the time you saw him, either?"

"At the time he made his appearance he says, 'Let's go to it!'"

"Now where, if you know, was Dr. Norris at the time Mr. Chipps appeared in the door and said that?"

"He was back at his desk."

"Could you see Dr. Norris back there, see what he was doing?"

"I could have, but I didn't."

Nutt then described the scene as D.E. Chipps reentered Norris's office, and how the lumberman made a threatening move: "He made a motion with his right arm, and when making that motion his coat flopped back so that I could see his — this part of his chest or breast or his shirt and, at the same time he made some motion with his other hand up over his shoulder here — I can't tell you, I can't describe how it was or when it was, because I can't remember, but this other hand had some motion, and his attitude was — "

At this McLean said: "Well, now wait — " But Nutt countered, "I am trying to answer the question." Wild Bill decided not to press and motioned with his hand for the witness to continue. He would have his chance to dig through Nutt's testimony during cross-examination soon enough.

"The next thing happened, the shots rang out," Nutt said.

"Do you know where Dr. Norris was, with reference to where you was, when the shots rang out?"

"He was to my right and to my rear."

Nutt testified that he "didn't know" how many shots were fired but described the movements of D.E. Chipps immediately following them. "He backed back toward the outer door of the anteroom, and was kinder backing sideways, and backed back almost within two or three feet of the outer door, and was facing almost south, and he stooped to pick up something, and then walked back into Dr. Norris' office, through the same door, and walked over to the east end of that office and turned around and fell over, with his head toward the west, and began bleeding."

Simpson asked him to describe what Chipps had been attempting to pick up. "It looked like something in a brown case, possibly from four to six inches long. I don't know exactly what it looked like or what it was, but my recollection is it was a brown case."

After a few more questions to make sure Nutt's story had been thoroughly told, Simpson indicated that he was done. Hamilton pulled out his pocket watch and announced another short recess, after which the prosecution could begin cross-examination of the man.

L.H. Nutt's testimony featured two crucial parts of J. Frank Norris's defense. First, he shot D.E. Chipps as the lumberman was threatening him verbally while reentering the pastor's office after first leaving. And most important, he had made what came to be described by the newspapers as a threatening "hip pocket move" as if to reach for a gun. Additionally, the image of the wounded man staggering around, and then stooping to pick up a mysterious object, was clearly designed to make jurors wonder what the object, in fact, was. Could it have been a gun?

After about ten minutes, things were up and running again and Bill McLean was ready to start counterpunching. He approached the witness box casually with hands in his pockets, then pulled his left hand out and motioned toward Nutt while beginning to frame his first question.

"You say you did not hear Norris make the statement, 'I have killed me a man'?"

"I did not."

McLean quizzed Nutt on various details of his testimony and about his movements in the first moments after the shooting. The witness had difficulty describing where he went and how he got there, using the phrase "I don't remember" several times. It was clear that at least part of his inability to describe things with precision was that he had been in shock at that fateful moment the previous July.

McLean pressed Nutt, "Did you look to see whether or not he [Chipps] was armed?"

"No, sir."

"You have testified here a while ago that in your judgment he was going to inflict serious injury or kill Dr. Norris?"

"Yes."

"Then why didn't you look to see whether or not he had anything to kill him with?"

"That never occurred to me at all."

More questions about that day followed, about Nutt's trip to the courthouse to make his statement and about the ten-thousand-dollar bond many men had signed for Pastor Norris. McLean then came to a comment that, if true, certainly indicated that Norris may not have seen the whole thing as that big of a deal at the time.

"Isn't it a fact that when the bond was signed and he [Norris] walked out of the courtroom, he said in your presence and hearing: 'Boys, I'll preach tomorrow at the same old place'?"

"I don't remember."

For the next forty minutes or so as the lunch break approached, McLean took Nutt through his story, asking probing questions. The most telling moment came when the bank auditor said that he could not "swear" that Norris had shot Chipps because he was watching Chipps at the moment shots rang out and never noticed a gun in Norris's hand.

"Did Norris shoot Chipps?"

"I don't know."

"You were only six feet from both of them, don't you know Norris shot Chipps?"

"It would be a conclusion on my part; I couldn't swear to it."

It was an odd admission and seemed to reinforce the image of the defense's key witness as someone who was not all that sure of himself and his recollections. One observer noted that Nutt's face had become "expressionless as if all thought had been wiped from it by a sponge."

In the final minutes of that morning's session, just before Judge Hamilton called for the lunch recess, Bill McLean grilled Nutt about the specific words the banker had put in Chipps's mouth — "I will kill you." The prosecutor brought out Nutt's original statement from July 17, 1926, as well as his grand jury testimony, reminding the witness that in both cases the dramatic phrase had not been uttered in a stand-alone way, but rather as part of another statement. For instance, when Norris told Chipps that he was going to preach his sermon no matter what, the lumberman had said, "If you do, I will kill you."

The idea that Chipps uttered the phrase "I will kill you" while reentering the office was new ground and had never been attested to by Mr. Nutt before this trial. Why now? Why not back in July when, presumably, the events were fresher in his mind?

To some, as decent and nice as Nutt appeared to be, he seemed to be close to lying on the stand for J. Frank Norris. Such cynics saw him as a "rabbit-like sort of man who would be naturally squeamish about perjuring himself, but for Norris' sake he may have gathered the courage to stretch the truth on this supreme occasion."

Court adjourned for lunch shortly after noon that Saturday.

L.H. Nutt was back in his seat in the witness box at 2 PM as the trial resumed following a lunch break. He was passed back and forth between the defense and the prosecution, as the attorneys probed the smallest details of his testimony. Bill McLean pressed the witness about Chipps trying to pick something up in the anteroom while reeling from several gunshot wounds, asking: "Don't you know a man shot three times would have remained down if he stooped down?" Nutt replied that he did not feel qualified to make a judgment like that.

"Haven't you and Norris sat down and gone over your testimony?"

"Yes, we have talked it over some."

"Did Norris ever tell you that he killed Chipps?"

"I don't recall he ever did."

He was insistent that he never saw a woman — meaning Mrs. Roxie Parker — or anyone else in the anteroom or near its outer door at the time of the tragedy. But he also acknowledged that from where he was sitting at the time, he would have not been likely to see anyone.

Mr. Nutt allowed that it was possible that Dr. Norris had the gun in his pocket as he saw Chipps leave the room. This is, of course, the moment that Mrs. Parker had testified to seeing Norris fire the first shot. But Nutt testified that Norris went back to his desk and Chipps reentered the office, where Norris shot him.

"Did you go to his body and administer to his wounds?"

"No, sir."

"Did Norris?"

"No, sir."

The reporters in the room scribbled feverishly, trying to take down every word they could. Copy runners were nearby waiting for a signal, a nod, or a hand holding up a piece of paper, indicating their services were needed to get text to telegraph operators as quickly as possible.

By the end of Nutt's time on the witness stand — more than three hours for direct and cross-examination — the two divergent versions of events offered by the prosecution and defense had been fully established. The balance of the testimony over the next several days would be designed to reinforce both. Did J. Frank Norris shoot D.E. Chipps as the lumberman was leaving the office and saying, "I'll come back," as Roxie Parker had testified? Or did Chipps leave and then come back and say "I'll kill you" and "Let's go to it" as Norris's deacon L.H. Nutt had said?

As the defense called its next witness, however, it became clear that at the same time it sought to bolster its own version of events that day, it would also go on the attack against D.E. Chipps's reputation. Never mind that Chipps was not there to defend himself, or that his widow and their fourteen-year-old son were sitting in the courtroom. Norris's attorneys would do their best to raise him from the dead and show people what the "victim" was really like.

Mr. Fred Holland, a former police officer from Fort Worth, took the stand. Simpson got to the point: "Now, Mr. Holland, were you or were you not in Fort Worth on the sixteenth day of July, 1926?"

"I was."

"Were you there in Fort Worth on the fifteenth day of July, 1926?"

"I was not until late. I drove into Fort Worth something around 10 o'clock."

"All right. Did you or did you not see on that occasion — on the fifteenth — see D.E. Chipps anyplace?"

"I did. Standing in front of the Texas Hotel."

"Who was he with, if anyone?"

"Harry Conner."

"Who is Harry Conner?"

"He is City Detective for the city of Fort Worth."

"Did you or did you not hear any conversation between D.E. Chipps and Harry Conner on that occasion?"

"I did."

"Did it have reference to Dr. Norris?"

"It did."

"Tell the jury what it was?"

"Well, I heard D.E. Chipps say to Harry Conner that he was going to kill a goddamned preacher and Harry Conner asked him who he was going to kill, and he said, 'Frank Norris.' Harry Conner said, 'When?' and he said, 'Either tonight or tomorrow.'"

The courtroom became alive with murmuring conversation. This was new information being brought to public light for the first time. Judge Hamilton made quick and sharp use of his gavel, insisting on order.

"Now, Mr. Holland, tell the jury whether or not, if you know the condition of D.E. Chipps at the time he was making this statement, with reference to whether he was drunk or sober?'"

"My judgment, he was drunk."

Then Holland testified that he told J. Frank Norris in the pastor's office about all of this the next day — which was Friday, July 16 — meaning that the preacher had knowledge about Chipps and some threats the day before the shooting.

Holland described his conversation with Norris: "I asked him what was the matter with he and Chipps, what they were spatting about and he said: 'Why, I don't know. I don't even know the man. I have heard of him. What about him?' and I told him about what I had heard, and he asked me — he said: 'Who is Chipps?' and I said, 'Well, he is a wholesale lumber dealer, that is my understanding.'"

Holland told the court that Norris had then asked about what the police did with him the previous night — had the drunken man making threats been taken to jail? Holland told the preacher that he didn't know.

Then in the lengthiest single answer to a question in the trial thus far, Fred Holland testified to all that he did know about D.E. Chipps and had imparted to Norris the day before the lumberman made his fateful visit to the preacher's office. The former patrolman told of an encounter he'd had with Chipps back when he was still walking a police beat about two and a half years earlier. One morning about two o'clock, Chipps was wandering through the area, and Holland observed that, "He was feeling a good deal," implying the effects of alcohol. The police officer asked Chipps a question or two, and they got into an argument, the lumberman quickly becoming angry. Asked where he was going, Chipps replied: 'None of your goddamned business.'"

Fred Holland then testified about saying to Chipps: "If you don't want to tell me who you are or where your bed is, I will have to give you a bed." The policeman told Chipps that he was going to call "the wagon" for him. As Holland grabbed Chipps's right arm with his left hand, the lumberman exploded, "You or no other son of a bitch is going to lock me up!"

Bill McLean sat and listened to Holland's testimony, growing more upset with every word — this was all new to him. Finally, when he could stand it no more, and in an exercise void of lawyerly diplomacy, Wild Bill bolted from his chair and without even using the word *objection* interrupted the witness being questioned by defense counsel.

"Do you mean you told Norris all of this?" McLean asked Holland. The witness, taken by surprise by the highly irregular question from opposing counsel, as was everyone in the room, looked over at McLean and sheepishly said, "Sir?"

Marvin Simpson thought for a split second of challenging McLean's very right to ask a direct question of his witness this way during direct examination, but decided not to — instead letting a flustered Wild Bill have some rope. Maybe he would hang himself.

McLean repeated, "Do you mean you told Norris all of this?"

Holland, still unsure of the question and even as to whether or not he should respond directly to the other lawyer, said: "Did I tell Mr. Norris that?"

McLean said, "Yes."

Holland looked over at Simpson, who nodded approvingly. Then the witness told McLean, "Yes I did."

McLean had a frustrated — even confused — look on his face.

He waved a hand dismissively and sighed, "Well, go ahead." Then he took his seat.

Fred Holland continued his story with more details about Chipps's behavior. Chipps had taken a swing at the officer, who responded with a punch knocking the lumberman to the sidewalk. This, according to the witness, seemed to shake Chipps up, and soon he was begging the officer, "Pardner, I don't like to go to that jail, I don't want to be locked up. I have got a room at the Westbrook Hotel."

Holland told the court that the inebriated man identified himself as D.E. Chipps, pointing at the building they were standing near. "I have an office right up here in this building, in the Wheat Building; I am in the lumber business. If you will let me go to my room I will guarantee you I won't bother you any more." Holland told the court he had decided that night to let Chipps go.

The witness further testified that on Friday, July 16, he had told the Reverend Norris about the trouble Chipps had with the house detective at the Westbrook, a Mr. Stanley. Chipps, he told Norris, had also been in trouble at the Texas Hotel across the street from his office in the Wheat Building.

"Did you tell him what the details of that trouble at the Texas Hotel were, or any of them?"

"Yes, sir. I told him that he was barred from the Texas Hotel, that he couldn't go there and get a room on account of the way he acted." Once again, a flabbergasted Bill McLean was on his feet interrupting and Simpson stood aside like a bullfighter sidestepping a bull. "Well, did you tell Dr. Norris all of this you are now relating?" McLean asked.

"The best I remember."

Again, the special prosecutor sat down, while resignedly uttering, "All right. Go ahead."

The witness then told about Chipps causing trouble at a downtown Fort Worth gasoline filling station. They had called over a police officer known as "Pop Hinkle." That gas station incident also included a gun discharging as the officer was trying to take it away from Chipps.

Simpson wanted to make sure this part of the story was emphasized, "Now, right there — did you tell Dr. Norris if you knew what Chipps was trying to do with the gun at the time this man you say they call Pop Hinkle took it away from him?"

"No, I didn't tell him who, just — all I told him was that he had trouble with him over there with a gun." Simpson had Holland verify when he had met with J. Frank Norris in the very office where Chipps would die, and the witness testified that it was sometime between 10 AM and noon on Friday, July 16.

When it was finally time for Bill McLean to cross-examine Fred Holland, he tried to get the former police officer to offer a perspective about the difference in Chipps's behavior when he was sober versus drunk. The witness caused widespread laughter in the courtroom when he said that he had "never seen Chipps sober."

While McLean was questioning the witness, it was Dayton Moses's turn to interrupt — but his concern had nothing to do with the special prosecutor's questions. One of the spectators, as Moses described it, was "sitting there, looking at the jury and grinning like a monkey."

"A man is on trial for his life," Moses said, "and I say that such conduct is indecent and inhuman." McLean interrupted Moses, suggesting, "Such remarks made in the presence of the jury were highly improper and prejudicial to the rights of the State of Texas." Hamilton didn't bite, choosing to ignore the issue, and instructed McLean to proceed with his questions.

McLean pressed Fred Holland, "Didn't you read in the newspaper that Norris said he had never even heard of Chipps and then didn't you go and tell Norris he was the man you had told him about?"

"I read the statement, but did not tell Norris that."

When Holland's testimony was over, he was excused, both sides having felt they'd made some points. If Norris knew about Chipps's threats the day before, then his state of mind at the time of the lumberman's fateful visit to the church office would certainly have been one of something other than indifference. But if that were the case, then he certainly could not claim that he had never heard of Chipps before asking L.H. Nutt about him, right after D.E. Chipps called Norris from his room at the Westbrook Hotel.

Next up was a Fort Worth physician by the name of Dr. Webb Walker. Dayton Moses asked the doctor for a physical description of D. E. Chipps.

"He weighed about 200 pounds, possibly more. He was quite a physical man."

Moses asked him about Chipps's fondness for booze.

"I would say that I had seen Chipps under the influence of liquor. He was quarrelsome and unruly when he was drinking. He was sometimes abusive."

When McLean cross-examined the good doctor, he asked, "And when not drunk, he was a polite, kind gentleman?"

"Yes, sir."

"And when Chipps was sober, you have seen him apologize to people he had offended while drinking?"

"Yes, sir."

The final witness of the afternoon that Saturday was Sterling P. Clark, a former sheriff of Tarrant County.

Moses: "Mr. Clark, were you acquainted with the general reputation of D.E. Chipps in Fort Worth when under the influence of intoxicating liquor, as to whether he was a man of a kind and inoffensive disposition, or a man of overbearing, violent and dangerous character?"

Before Clark could answer, Judge Hamilton admonished him: "Answer 'yes' or 'no.'"

"Yes, sir."

Moses: "Was that reputation good or bad?"

"It was bad."

Conducting a quick cross-examination and noticing that the judge seemed to be quite ready to call it a day, Bill McLean asked the former sheriff: "How long have you been in the employ of Norris in this case?"

"I have never been in his employ in this case."

It was now well after 5 PM and Judge Hamilton announced an adjournment, with court to reconvene the following Monday morning.

N.A. Stedman, a staff correspondent for the *Fort Worth Star-Telegram*, observed that the "crowd that jammed itself into every nook of the Criminal District Courtroom here, crawled at snail's pace out of the scene of the Rev. J. Frank Norris murder trial toward sundown, Saturday." A few reporters lingered in the room as the crowd exited, putting finishing touches on their stories about the day. Frank Baldwin, editor of the *Waco News-Tribune*, chose to ignore Simpson's role almost entirely and wrote a descriptive piece about "two master artists" — one named McLean and the other named Moses. He said they "finished the rough of their canvas — the killing of Dexter Chipps — with the dusk of Saturday, each with a separate perspective on the easels which predominate Rev. J. Frank Norris, alleged murderer, as the central figure. The former had dabbed on red hue of murder, cold blooded, and intensified it with the crimson of provoked homicide. The latter, knowing freedom from penal servitude the stake, portrayed his a landscape of justification, and as court adjourned was calling upon brush after brush to intersperse the setting with 'bad, quarrelsome, and dangerous character.'"

Baldwin paused, reread what he had written, and summoned a copy boy. The lad took off for the court clerk's office, now the domain of the all-important telegraph operator.

CHAPTER FORTY-TWO

"A Worn, Thumbed Man"

AS THE FAITHFUL gathered in the mammoth auditorium at Fourth and Throckmorton Streets in downtown Fort Worth on Sunday morning, January 16, they knew that their pastor would not be in his own familiar pulpit. A Presbyterian preacher from Austin, Rev. J.H. Harrison was to tend J. Frank Norris's flock that day. The minister chose as his text for the occasion a scripture from the Book of Exodus, chapter 22: "If the thief be found breaking in, and be smitten so that he dieth, there shall be no blood-guiltiness for him."

He then preached for an hour about the virtue of self-defense.

Following the sermon, and before the smaller-than-usual crowd was dismissed, a letter from Norris to his church was read from the pulpit. "I am feeling fine," he wrote, "though a thousand things are preying on my soul." The preacher used words that were now very familiar to the congregants: "framed," "hired prosecutors," "deep laid conspiracy." At the conclusion of the reading, the congregation cheered.

Norris himself did not attend church that morning in Austin, but Mrs. Norris did — choosing that city's First Baptist Church for worship, before driving over to Lockhart, Texas, to visit where she had lived as a girl. The preacher, meanwhile, stayed in his room at the Driskill and listened to the service from Fort Worth on the radio.

He met with a few of his attorneys for lunch, then went back to his room. Lillian returned around 6 PM, and they decided to venture out for a Sunday night service at Austin's First Methodist Church, where the Reverend W.F. Bryan, a Norris acquaintance, was the pastor. Bryan had advertised a special message for that evening titled "Austin's Most Worthy Citizen — Some Lessons to Be Learned." There were rumors floating around that the Methodist cleric was "going to cut loose with some hot stuff" about the Norris case. And if he intended to draw a big crowd with that teaser of the sermon title, he succeeded. When he rose to preach the sermon, he faced "the biggest crowd which Austin has seen in one of its houses of worship in a blue moon." And in the crowd, up in the balcony and hardly noticed, sat Dr. J. Frank Norris and his wife.

In fact, Bryan talked little about Norris and the case, except for saying, "I would not choose the methods of Brother Norris to deal with Fort Worth. I am not built that way, although other notable men of the pulpit have used the Rev. Norris' methods." He did offer some frank talk about Fort Worth itself. "I've known Fort Worth for a long time — I was raised in Dallas, just 30 miles or so away — and as far back as I can recall the tough element has controlled Fort Worth."

Also in the crowd that night was *Fort Worth Press* reporter Jack Gordon. He had noticed Norris sitting up in the balcony and quickly caught up with him when the service dismissed. Norris invited Gordon up to his hotel room for a conversation.

As they sat down a few minutes later, Mr. Gordon looked around the room, a comfortable and elegant suite. There was "a heaping vase of carnations" on one table and a Bible open on the dresser.

The reporter thought Norris looked extremely tired. His first question was about the service they had just attended. "How did you feel? Didn't you itch to jump up and let loose from the platform yourself?" J. Frank Norris smiled — no laugh — just a simple smile. Gordon asked him about the "crack" Pastor Bryan had made about Norris's methods. "Don't be silly," Norris replied, still with a smile. "One of my dearest friends — a great man — the Rev. Bryan."

Mrs. Norris passed around "a sack of apples." Norris devoured his "with evident enjoyment," Gordon observed. Then he got up and grabbed another. Soon candy got handed around. The phone rang several times — "friends, friends, with good wishes," said Norris. Miss Jane Hartwell, the preacher's ever-present secretary-gatekeeper, stayed in the background fielding the calls, "Yes, Dr. Norris is in conference, thanks, thanks — "

The reporter found himself feeling "important."

Norris had already told Gordon that he couldn't, under advice of his lawyers, answer serious questions about the trial, so the reporter stuck with the human-interest stuff. He asked about Norris's Bible. "How long does a Bible last you?"

"I wear out an average of two Bibles a year. I don't read much else," Norris answered as his "voice betrayed a near physical exhaustion."

Deciding that he wasn't going to get any news out of the preacher, and in consideration of Norris's clear weariness, Jack Gordon wrapped things up quickly and excused himself.

Gordon left Norris with a copy of that day's paper from Fort Worth. And before he went to sleep that night he read about himself on its pages, as well as other news from home. There was also news from far away — his eye resting on a story about a politician in London, England, by the name of Winston Churchill, that nation's chancellor of the exchequer. The piece was titled "Churchill Can Talk," and it was about how Mr. Churchill was breaking all records with the sheer number of his words published in the *Parliamentary Gazette,* "more than 160,000 words in just the past few months."

There was another event getting ready to make news in Austin. Dan Moody would be inaugurated as Texas's new governor that Tuesday. His wife, Mildred, found herself resenting the fact that her husband's big moment was being overshadowed by Norris's murder trial. But she put on her best face. "It's going to be a great adventure," she told some friends. Mildred had only been Mrs. Moody for about a year. The gubernatorial campaign had been the couple's honeymoon, and the Texas governor's mansion would be their newlywed cottage. Absent the Norris trial, this political fairy tale would have been the talk of the town.

Many wondered how the area around the capitol building and court-house would be able to handle the crowds for a celebrated murder trial and such a large political ceremony. But that would all happen on Tuesday. What news would Monday's trial proceedings bring? Rumor had it the defense planned to call nearly twenty witnesses. Such a list would require several days, perhaps weeks, to work through.

The next morning, Monday, January 17, more than 150 people — "mostly ladies" — were lined up before eight o'clock waiting to get into the court-room, which would not open until nine o'clock. As Judge Hamilton walked into the courthouse, a reporter asked if he had any plans to adjourn the trial during Dan Moody's inaugural. He indicated that it was "not likely," adding: "I don't see how any attention can be paid to the inaugural with this expensive trial going on. This case is costing thousands of dollars a day. Witnesses are here waiting at heavy expense."

Dr. and Mrs. Norris walked through the Driskill lobby around eight thirty that morning, en route to the courthouse. Many watching them were struck by the irony. Norris had made a career out of being against a lot of things — "Sunday picture shows, corrupt city officials, monkeys" — but one thing he had never been "against" was publicity. Now the man who craved the limelight was enduring a personal hell in it.

The preacher and his wife passed the newsstand in the hotel lobby, stocked with a variety of local and out-of-town publications, most bearing Norris's name prominently in their headlines. Down Congress Avenue, there was more of the same. "Probably no thoroughfare in the world," wrote one reporter, "has more newsstands per block than Congress Avenue's promenade of the paper-devouring legislator." Norris walked with his gaze "straight ahead" and "his eyes seemingly in distant focus." He held Lillian's hand in one of his own and his Bible in the other. Though the sun was up, it was well hidden behind dark clouds. When Dr. and Mrs. Norris arrived at the courtroom they noticed that every light was burning, as was typical during the darkness of the evening.

The courtroom door opened a bit early that morning, and the room was quickly filled. Several people whispered about the unusual sight of "two patriarchal old men, with long flowing beards like that of Michelangelo's Moses," who were seated on the front row of the spectator area. Someone asked the bailiff about them and he replied, "Never saw them before here."

The thunder of Judge Hamilton's gavel interrupted the speculation. The defense called its first witness, Mr. C.C. Littleton. Dayton Moses was again questioner for the defense. Within a minute or two Littleton had testified that he had known D.E. Chipps and that his reputation was "bad."

All Bill McLean could glean of benefit during his cross-examination was that Littleton never knew Chipps to carry a gun.

Next the defense called Fort Worth City Detective Harry Conner — the man Fred Holland had overheard Chipps telling he planned to kill J. Frank Norris.

"Did you ever have any talk with D.E. Chipps with reference to Dr. Norris?" Moses asked Conner.

"Yes, sir."

"All right. Now, Mr. Conner, relate to the jury the conversation that you had with Mr. Chipps there."

"Well, we was out in front of the hotel there, waiting for a cab, and the question was brought up."

"Just tell what led up to the conversation then, the conversation you had there with him."

"I was trying to get a gun from him."

At this, a wave of murmurs washed over the courtroom, requiring a few sharp raps of Hamilton's gavel. "Tell what you said, what you were doing, and what was said between you and him," Moses continued.

"I asked him to give me the gun, and wasn't he afraid of getting in trouble with it, and he told me no, that he was going to kill him a goddamned preacher."

There was more crowd noise and another demonstration of the gavel.

"Tell the jury exactly what he said. Use the words that Mr. Chipps used there, the words you used and the words he used, as near as you can remember them."

"He said he was going to kill the goddamned preacher if he didn't let his friends alone and I asked him who and he said J. Frank Norris. I told him 'there is no use of a man getting into trouble.' I said, 'you can get in more trouble in one minute than you can get out of in nine years if you go up there messing around.' We talked on, and he got very rough, and in a few minutes the cab pulled up at the side door and I stepped to the corner and loaded him in the car and he said he was going home. We did not talk very long, five or ten minutes."

"Tell the jury whether or not he was under the influence of liquor."

"Yes, sir."

Moses turned and indicated to Bill McLean that he could begin cross-examination.

"Did he have a gun on him?"

"Yes, sir."

"Did you take the pistol off of him?"

"No, sir."

"You turned a drunk man loose on the streets with a pistol?"

"Yes, sir."

That's as far as McLean pressed Harry Conner. But O.E. Carr decided then and there that after the trial he would fire Harry Conner. And he did.

Next, the defense called A.B. Hamm, a livestock man, whose testimony reinforced the image the defense was painting of a man who morphed into a monster of sorts when he drank. The next witness, J.O. Hart, offered more of the same.

And the attack on the late Dexter Elliott Chipps was far from over.

The defense next called a man named J.T. Pemberton. Norris smiled and nodded at Pemberton as the witness made his way toward the front of the courtroom. Next to Mrs. Norris, no one in that room had known the preacher longer than good old J.T.

Jesse Thomas Pemberton had just two weeks before retired from his prominent Fort Worth banking position, having served as president of the Farmers & Mechanics Bank for many years. He was born in Missouri the year the Civil War ended and first moved to Texas when he was thirteen. Pemberton was a well-known Fort Worth citizen. In fact, he would later be eulogized in the *Star-Telegram* as having been "responsible for much of the development of Fort Worth in the early part of the century."

Mr. Pemberton was also one of the "boys of the club" — the Fort Worth Club, that is. He somehow managed to move in two very different worlds. He was a wealthy and quietly influential man of finance, but he was also a longtime member of First Baptist Church and loyal follower and friend of J. Frank Norris.

His part in the J. Frank Norris story began way back in 1909 when, already a very successful banker, he opposed calling J. Frank Norris to the pastorate of the First Baptist Church, trying to warn the congregation about the great change a Norris pastorate might bring.

Norris did get the call, of course, and it wasn't long before he was displeasing some of the very people who had heralded his coming. Ultimately, after the burning of the building and the preacher's earlier indictments for perjury and arson, six thousand of those who had been "pro-Norris" left the church in bitterness.

Pemberton, however, the man who had warned them, stayed. He had helped Norris financially over the subsequent years and never wavered in his faith in his pastor. The Norris-Pemberton relationship was a curious one to many of his friends in the city, and they sometimes questioned his judgment, though never to his face. They liked him. Everyone did. Now here he was ready to testify for his pastor in a murder trial. What would he have to say?

Pemberton and Norris had formed an unusual alliance. Of course, J.T. had no problem speaking his mind to and about J. Frank, but it never seemed to bother the preacher. Back in March 1924, the front page of the *Searchlight* featured the headline: "What Pemberton Thinks of J. Frank Norris." In it, the influential Fort Worth financier said:

> Norris has caused me more trouble than any other man that I ever saw. He makes me mad half the time, when I go to hear him preach. Sometimes when I go to hear him, I swear I will never hear him again. He disturbs my conscience. He seems to take special delight in preaching on the things that I do and I wish he would leave me alone. I can usually get along very well until I go to hear him preach one of his sermons where he goes into the private conduct of the members, and I don't know why, but it seems that he has a special hobby on preaching on the things that I do, but I have decided that if the Lord can get along as well as He does with Norris, that I can afford to get along with him, too.

Those courtroom observers and trial buffs who had done their home-work knew as soon as Pemberton's name was called that his testimony promised to be, at the very least, interesting. Here was a man who claimed both Dr. J. Frank Norris and Dexter Elliott Chipps as friends.

"Do you know Dr. J. Frank Norris?" Dayton Moses asked as his opening question.

"Yes, sir."

"Are you a member of his church?"

"Yes, sir."

"You are his friend — I say, you are Dr. Norris' friend?"

"Yes, sir."

"Did you know D.E. Chipps?"

"Yes, sir."

"How long did you know Mr. Chipps?"

"I think twelve or thirteen years."

"Mr. Pemberton, did you know the general reputation that Mr. Chipps here in Fort Worth when under the influence of liquor as to whether he was a man of kind and inoffensive disposition — or a man of overbearing violent and dangerous character? Do you know that reputation?"

"It was bad."

Dayton Moses yielded to Bill McLean for cross-examination. "Wild Bill" began with the question: "Do you mean by that that when he was drinking he was a quarrelsome man?"

"Yes, sir."

"And that is all you mean, isn't it?"

"No, I mean more than that."

"Huh?" Pemberton's return took McLean by surprise. But he moved on, ignoring the response.

"All right. Now, you have been intimately associated with him, haven't you?"

"Yes, sir."

"Played cards with him?"

"Yes."

Norris was adamantly opposed to "card playing" and in fact had those who served key roles in his church affirm that they did not use "playing cards."

Here was J.T. Pemberton, a deacon at First Baptist Church, testifying that he regularly played cards over the years with the man his pastor was charged with murdering.

"Drank liquor with him?"

"No, I don't think I ever did." The answer was not quite the resounding denial Pemberton's spiritual leader might have hoped for.

McLean sensed fear and weakness in the witness and pressed, "Well, did you see him drink when you didn't drink?"

"Yes, sir. I have seen him drink a good deal at the club, but I didn't drink with him. I don't think I ever took a drink with him."

Again McLean pitched the question, "Don't you think you ever took a drink with him?"

"No," said Pemberton, but his voice was soft.

"Well, you mean by that he was quarrelsome when he would be drinking or playing cards? Did he when some fellow beat a full house or a flush for him?"

"I never saw him play — "

"I understood you to say you played cards with him."

"I played pitch with him and rummy and things like that in the Fort Worth Club," Pemberton replied, perhaps hoping his pastor would make the distinction between gambling games and other card games.

Soon McLean shifted gears. "I will ask you this question: Are you the same Pemberton who carried the letter from Dr. Norris to the Baptist convention to try to get him in?"

This was a reference to J. Frank Norris's chronic issues with the Texas Baptist General Convention, in fact Southern Baptists everywhere. He had so polarized the denomination with his constant attacks on perceptions of modernism that he and his church had been shut out of the movement many times. Yet he would persist in trying to come back in order to be heard on this or that matter. Usually unsuccessful, he would then use the pages of the *Searchlight* to attack what he delighted in referring to as the "Baptist Machine." Of course, in Norris's eyes, the rejections stemmed from a big conspiracy against him and his church and were not the logical result of his own behavior.

Often when Norris wanted to petition for reentry and acceptance, he would use agents to carry his message. J.T. Pemberton was one of his "go to" guys when it came to Baptist politics.

Pemberton never got the chance to answer McLean's question on the matter, because Dayton Moses objected on the grounds that the question about Pemberton's role as a denominational emissary for J. Frank Norris was "irrelevant, immaterial, and prejudicial." Judge Hamilton agreed.

McLean went back to the issue of cards and drinking. "Now at the time you claim that you were playing bridge, pitch, whatever it was, with Mr. Chipps at the Fort Worth Club or any other place, were you an officer, a deacon in Norris' church at the same time?"

"Yes, sir."

"And you still are?"

"Yes, sir." Then, catching himself, Pemberton corrected what he'd said: "No, I believe I am a deacon, not an active deacon."

Puzzled as to the distinction, and not at all familiar with Baptist polity or the inner workings of Norris's mammoth church, McLean probed, "Do you know whether you are a deacon?"

"I have been a deacon in the church. I haven't been an active deacon for years. I have been a deacon for years and years of the church; I was ordained a deacon a long time ago."

Pemberton felt a sense of relief when McLean announced that he had nothing further for this witness and Dayton Moses had no redirect questions.

Throughout the morning witness after witness — a car dealer, a hotel detective, a state legislator, and others — testified as to the bad character of D.E. Chipps, especially when he had been drinking. He was "quarrelsome," he "drank much," he was "nice when not drinking," he was a "dangerous man," and so on.

And the impression was being deeply implanted in the minds of observers that Mr. Chipps pretty much drank all the time.

After lunch, a Fort Worth–based barbershop "quartet" — E.T. Jenkins, D.F. Park, R.E. Hancock, and H.G. Leath, who all worked as barbers in the popular Tonsor Barber Shop in downtown Fort Worth — would also testify that Chipps was a regular patron of their establishment, came in just about daily in fact, and had been drinking before noon on the day of the shooting.

He had a conversation with the man in the next chair — a conversation about J. Frank Norris. The other man was Kirk Van Zandt, the Fort Worth city secretary. The Van Zandts were the bluebloods of Cowtown.

Chipps asked Van Zandt if Norris had gotten his job yet, meaning presumably that Chipps saw the preacher as trying to get certain city leaders fired or run out of office. Mr. Van Zandt indicated that he was staying out of things and "not taking any hand in their [other city officials'] affairs." Hancock also testified that "some man" said, "What is all this trouble you are having with Frank Norris?" According to the barber, Chipps's reply to this question was to "slap the barber chair" and say, "Someone ought to kill the son of a bitch."

The state did not object to or cross-examine any of the Fort Worth barbershop quartet.

Bess Carroll, the reporter from San Antonio, found herself becoming bored with the litany of charges about Chipps's character. After all, how many ways and times could you talk about how a guy was mean when he was drunk? She had to file a column. Usually she did so before lunch, but this day she was blocked and couldn't come up with an angle.

She looked at J. Frank Norris, but from where she sat his face was hidden. She would love to watch his eyes react to the testimony. Then she noticed the preacher leafing through the pages of his Bible. He would read a bit, then close it and set it aside. That's it! She would write about his Bible. She had a good view of the book sitting on the table next to Norris and, pulling out her pad and pen, she began to make notes.

"A shabby Bible has at last betrayed the Rev. J. Frank Norris, national fundamentalist leader, on trial for murder," she scribbled, with a feeling of breakthrough only wordsmiths understand. The book had "been his constant companion."

During a short recess, Carroll approached Norris and courteously introduced herself to him. He recognized her name and had read the piece she had written about Mrs. Norris. The reporter told the preacher that she was working on story about his Bible. Hearing this, he reached for it on the table and "with a characteristic gesture" handed it to her. She asked if she could look at it for a bit and give it back to him at the next break. Norris told her that would be fine.

Carroll described Norris's companion as "a worn, thumbed Bible," for a "worn, thumbed man." "They have occupied a famous pulpit together; together they have gone to criminal court, where the life of J. Frank Norris hangs in the balance of Texas justice." Bess wrote, "It is just a rather used Bible, with conventional words, 'fine, Persian, silk sewed,' written on its fly-leaf."

As she leafed through its pages she read notes and examined under-lined passages. "Sermon notes line the pages of this book that has shared the gospel of fame of Dr. Norris," Carroll wrote. She noticed "one or two" newspaper clippings, but they were obviously very personal, not about him. Likely there was a story there somewhere in those clippings, but about then she started to feel a little like a snoop going through a diary. Having seen enough, she closed Norris's Bible and set it aside, eventually passing it back to Norris at the defense table. She finished her piece and sent it to the wire office. It was titled "Norris' Bible Tells What He's Thinking."

For the remainder of that Tuesday, it was more of the same. The defense had effectively painted a picture of Chipps as a man who could be very antagonistic when "in his cups," though a decent enough fellow when sober. But it seemed that he wasn't sober much of the time.

When John Woodruff, a Fort Worth city patrolman, took the stand, he told a story from five years before — one that suggested D.E. Chipps had Norris in his sights even back then. The witness described a night in January 1922 when he had the occasion to arrest D.E. Chipps for public drunkenness. While he and his charge were waiting for the patrol wagon to come and take the arrested man away, Chipps lashed out, "I am going to start me a graveyard and put you and Frank Norris in the same grave."

The patrolman said he responded to Chipps with: "I don't think I'll go into a grave with Norris. Who is he?"

"A goddamned preacher."

At times tempers flared between the lawyers, always prompting the swift clap of Hamilton's gavel. At one point, because he had been using it so much, the hammer flew off the mallet and across the room, causing a couple of jurors to duck. Everyone laughed for a few moments, and, well, since the judge had nothing to bang to stop the outburst, he joined in. Soon thereafter Hamilton announced that court would adjourn until the next morning. His Honor had no intention of taking a break, even for the inauguration of the new Texas governor a block away.

CHAPTER FORTY-THREE

"Every Wit Is Whetted to Needle Sharpness"

J. FRANK NORRIS had never really gotten over the cold he had brought with him to Austin. And though Judge Hamilton had banned smoking in his courtroom, a ruling that was rare in those days and most unwelcome among the lawyers and spectators, the smoke in the corridors and other rooms was pronounced. Cigars, pipes, and cigarettes created a cloud that hung in the air throughout the building. Every time the door to the courtroom would open and a new witness would walk in, a swirl of smoke would follow.

A stove in the room produced still more fumes. It burned nonstop in its struggle against winter's chill. Sometimes the smoky haze from these two sources would become so thick as to obscure the Star of Texas mounted high above the judge's walnut bench.

Norris, always sensitive to smoke in the first place, and subject to respiratory problems possibly connected to that gunshot wound when he was a teenager, found his lungs and throat increasingly irritated as Tuesday dragged by. Some who watched the preacher closely noticed that he was coughing heavily and pulling out his handkerchief more and more. By the time he and Lillian strolled back to the Driskill Hotel in the cold early evening air, his cough was turning painful. After having dinner delivered to their room that night, with Norris just picking at his food, the preacher's wife decided — over the objections of her husband, who never wanted to appear weak — to call the lawyers.

Norris's fever spiked that night, and the hotel doctor was called. He had bronchitis and a severely inflamed throat. And when Dayton Moses called early the next morning to check on his client, Mrs. Norris insisted that there was no way he could be in court that day, or maybe even for a few to come.

Moses contacted Judge Hamilton and told him the news. Though probably wondering about the timing of this, given the previous decision not to suspend the trial for the Tuesday inauguration, the judge knew he had no choice. He called a meeting of attorneys from both sides in his chambers. Dayton Moses told the judge that Norris had "coughed his head nearly off last night," adding that common sense suggested that the preacher should not "come out on a day like this." Simpson spoke up and told the judge that his client was anxious for the trial to move forward and would even be willing to be brought in on a stretcher if that was needed. McLean rolled his eyes at this. The judge put the attorneys on notice that he might call court into "night session" if needed to get the trial done expeditiously. They nodded, indicating they understood. The state's lawyers didn't question the legitimacy of Norris's ailments; his discomfort had been apparent to all.

Shortly before 8 AM Hamilton issued a statement that the trial would resume Wednesday morning at 9:00 due to the defendant's illness. Spectators who had already lined up were disappointed. The twelve bored jurors would have to spend the entire day in the third-floor jury room with no idea why court would not be in session.

Hearing Simpson tell more than one reporter of Norris's willingness to be brought in on a stretcher, if needed, Alex Philquist, criminal district clerk, sneered, "The judge wouldn't allow the defense to bring a man on trial for his life into the courtroom on a stretcher. It would have a bad effect on the jury."

Star-Telegram reporter N.A. Stedman speculated that the fact Norris was sick, especially if it meant that he'd be out for many days, held out the possibility of a potential mistrial. So he decided to pop a question about it to Judge Hamilton, who because of the break in the action seemed more willing than usual to chat with members of the press. Hamilton confirmed to Stedman that such a scenario was not beyond the realm of possibility, likening the protracted illness of a defendant "to the situation when a jury has retired and cannot arrive at a verdict." He explained, "that in the case of a hung jury, twenty-four hours has been held not to be an unreasonable time for holding the jury."

The very possibility that the current trial would be cut short, after its venue change a few months before, was repugnant to all.

But even Judge Hamilton welcomed the unexpected opportunity to participate in the festivities surrounding the ascension of Dan "The Man" Moody to Texas's highest office. He liked Dan Moody, though he did have some concerns about how the man drove a car, he reflected in a raised voice, hoping a reporter or two might hear. They seized on the curious remark — taking the bait. Hamilton really wanted to tell his favorite Dan Moody story on the young man's big day.

A few years before, when Moody served as a district attorney for Williamson County, he and Hamilton were due in nearby Georgetown to begin a case. It had rained for days, and the highway bridge across Brush Creek, between Austin and Georgetown, had been washed out. Hamilton told Moody that they'd have to put off the trip, adding for the reporters, "But I didn't know what an auto driver Dan Moody was then."

"Hang the bridge, Judge, we'll go over the Railroad trestle," Moody told Hamilton, and, sure enough, they did! It was one rough ride, and Hamilton prayed Moody knew the railroad schedules well enough and that no train would be coming. They arrived in court on time.

Moody's swearing-in would be extraordinary for many reasons. The outgoing governor had been the first woman to serve in that office. At thirty-three Moody would become the state's youngest governor. And the inauguration would be the first such ceremony conducted outside, instead of inside the Capitol Building.

At shortly after noon, on Tuesday, January 18, 1927, Dan Moody walked onto the platform and looked out at a sea of smiling faces, most of those smiles peering out from under umbrellas, as a steady drizzle fell from the overcast sky. More than fifty thousand people were on hand, the largest crowd to witness a Texas governor's inauguration.

Protocol said that outgoing governor Miriam "Ma" Ferguson was supposed to walk with the new governor, on his arm, but she could not bring herself to do it. Later she wrote in her diary: "It went in the newspapers all over the US, perhaps I was wrong. But I felt we owed him no courtesy, time for that to stop and justice to be done. I was commended by many and I am sure many thought me 'little,' but I felt right."

After repeating the oath of office administered by Texas Chief Justice C.M. Cureton, Dan Moody delivered his inaugural address, promising to "restore public confidence" in state government and to "exemplify the high

standards of public service" he knew the people were demanding by elect-
ing him.

The twelve men of the jury passed the time that Tuesday playing cards
or dominoes, and napping. The highlight of their day was watching the
inaugural festivities from their third-floor courthouse window. They
opened it, trading a temporary chill for the ability to hear at least some
noise. The rain didn't bother them; it was a still day and the raindrops fell
straight down.

As for J. Frank Norris, he had heard the Cowboy Band of Simmons
University march by on the street outside "interspersing its crash-bang-
boom numbers with ear-splitting whoops," and he got out of bed for the
first time that morning to look out his hotel room window onto Brazos
Street as they passed. Mrs. Moody had attended Simmons. That same band
made folks smile shortly thereafter when it broke into a rendition of "The
Old Gray Mare" as Ma Ferguson took her seat on the platform before the
new governor was sworn in. She, being a good sport, stood up and waved.

Simmons was one of Norris's favorite schools. As he watched the march-
ing musicians file by, he thought back to the day some twenty years earlier
when Dr. Oscar H. Cooper, the same man Norris had helped to get fired at
Baylor for throwing a dog out a window, presented him with his honorary
doctor of divinity degree from Simmons. Ever since, friend and foe alike
had called him "Dr." Norris, and he never tired of hearing it.

Some tried to get ahold of Norris through the hotel switchboard, but the
answer from the operator was always the same: "I have instructions not to
call room 78."

The preacher's gatekeeper, Miss Jane Hartwell, made a visit to the newsstand in the hotel lobby and told the ever-present reporters that this kind
of ailment "wasn't anything new for Dr. Norris. He's long been troubled
with his throat. It is very sensitive. Doctors for years have been telling him
he ought to have his tonsils cut out — and appendix, too, for that matter.
But the doctor just hasn't had time to stop."

Following the inaugural events of that afternoon, and while Dan
Moody's supporters danced the night away in the ballrooms of the Driskill
and Austin Hotels, the participants in the Norris case and the attendant
press had already lost interest in the political story and returned their

attention to the trial. The two hotels had become "headquarters" of sorts for the opposing sides, with Norris's people at the Driskill and the state's entourage at the Austin. They lingered in the restaurants and lobbies, relaxing and talking about the trial.

Tomorrow, the reporters hoped, would see the resumption of a murder trial that was living up to its hype. They all sensed that the event was becoming as important to the careers and reputations of the attorneys involved as to the fate of the famous defendant.

One reporter wrote, "The Norris trial probably for years to come will serve as the 'Bradstreet' of fame for the more than a score of lawyers taking part in it. Earlier victories will be dimmed. So every member of the bar cast in the big show is putting forth his best foot, playing his finest performance. Every wit is whetted to needle sharpness. Over every inch of ground the opposing sides struggle goes on behind closed doors." The writer reflected, "To their two camps in the Austin and Driskill Hotels repair the warriors, there to lay out their campaign for the ensuing day."

CHAPTER FORTY-FOUR

"The Defense Calls Dr. J. Frank Norris"

THE WEATHER HADN'T improved at all Wednesday morning, prompting some speculation that J. Frank Norris might call in sick again, but as the courtroom quickly filled up shortly before nine o'clock, the preacher was already sitting at the defense table. His back was to the spectators, and he was coughing some into his handkerchief. He had not taken off his long, black overcoat and would indeed keep it on throughout the day.

Jack Gordon noted that J. Frank Norris could have used his five-thousand-seat auditorium for his courtroom crowds as well. Clerk Alex Philquist told him that there hadn't been a crowd like this one in a Travis County courtroom since "the famous Waters-Pierce Oil Company trial back in 1907." The lawyers shuffled in, sporting red eyes and frequent yawns. It had been a short night for just about everybody. But Judge Hamilton had retired early and now had a bounce in his step as he took his place on the bench and gaveled court to order.

The first witness called that morning was Jesse M. Brown, a former assistant district attorney in Tarrant County. He was asked about Chipps's reputation, as was the next witness, Chief of Police Lee, appearing this time, somewhat reluctantly, for the defense, having already testified as a state witness. He concurred that Chipps was troublesome when under the influence of liquor, but he was insistent on adding, "He was quarrelsome, but obedient and harmless."

Marvin Simpson pressed the chief of police about conversations they had, in which Lee reportedly expressed a reluctance to testify, hinting that he was concerned about his "bosses" — Mayor Meacham and City Manager Carr. The defense attorney, over the sustained objection of Bill McLean, drew out that Lee and Carr met and talked, presumably about the case, "every day."

Fannie Greer, the telephone operator at the Westbrook Hotel who had placed D.E. Chipps's call to J. Frank Norris that July Saturday afternoon, took the stand and was asked first about a phone call she handled that day between D.E. Chipps and H.C. Meacham.

"Now, did he call Mr. Meacham, or did Mr. Meacham call him?"

"Mr. Meacham called him."

"Now, did Mr. Meacham himself personally call, or someone else call for him, if you know?"

"The best I remember, a girl called for him and asked me to put Mr. Chipps on the line, and I did so."

Simpson then tried to get Greer to describe that conversation, but McLean was quick to object. The judge invited both lawyers to approach — but instead Simpson withdrew the question and continued with the judge's nodding approval.

He then asked Fannie Greer about Chipps's phone call with Norris that day. She described the conversation between the two men — as she listened in. As she testified, Simpson tried again to reference the earlier Meacham-Chipps call, and McLean exploded, prompting the judge to call the lawyers up to him.

Several lawyers approached the bench for an intense conference. Simpson began: "The telephone conversation that we expect to prove will be substantially this — That Meacham called Chipps and said, 'Is this you Chipps?' 'Yes.' 'Can you come down here right away?' Chipps said, 'What's the trouble — ' Of course, I am not giving the words exactly."

Hamilton nodded, "The court understands that."

Simpson continued, "Then Meacham said, 'Norris is having that goddamned *Searchlight* sold here in my store, with his sermon in it about me discharging my employees. I have just had one of his newsboys put out of here for selling them.' Then Chipps said, 'Yes, I can come down there or I can go over and stop the son of a bitch now.' Meacham said, 'Well, I want you to come down here, I want to talk to you about it.'"

Hamilton looked over at Bill McLean and Sam Sayers. "Now, what is your objection?"

Sayers, who had been a behind-the-scenes participant up to this point, made the prosecution argument: "Our objection is that it is wholly irrelevant and immaterial, sheds no light on this transaction because it was never communicated to the defendant, he knew nothing about it; there is nothing in the sale of the *Searchlight* in the store that has ever entered into this, and certainly, whatever took place there had nothing to do with Norris killing Chipps. According to the state's theory or the defendant's theory, there is absolutely nothing to it, it is extraneous matter, prejudicial to the state, highly inflammatory and prejudicial, and for the jury to know whether he did or did not do that would not aid them in arriving at the guilt or innocence of this man. Norris claims self-defense and the state claims Chipps was murdered, and this testimony does not assist the issue one way or the other."

Hamilton thought for a moment and then asked Dayton Moses: "You are not going to ask him about the conversation you have detailed, but about everything connected with it?" Moses replied, "Yes, sir, because we are going to follow that up with a conversation they had after he got down there with reference to stopping him."

Hamilton paused and said, "I am going to sustain the objection at this time."

Frustrated, the defense yielded to McLean for cross and Wild Bill went aggressively after Mrs. Greer, asking her why she hadn't been available when the case was called in Fort Worth in November. He knew that Greer had virtually run away to a sanatorium in Hot Springs, Arkansas, indicating a possible reluctance to testify. She had lost her job and was distraught — eavesdropping and then testifying to it before a grand jury is not good for a telephone operator's résumé.

Mrs. Lena Chick was the next defense witness called. She had worked for Meacham's Department Store from October 1925 until she resigned on August 14, 1926. Dayton Moses conducted her examination.

"On the afternoon of July 17, 1926, did you see Meacham and Chipps there in the store?"

"Yes."

"What did Meacham have in his hand?"

"A *Searchlight,* Dr. Norris' paper, all rolled up."

Mrs. Chick then told the jury about what she overheard. Meacham said, "Goddamned Norris is going to preach about me tomorrow." She then said that Chipps said words to the effect that "there was not going to be any more trouble."

The witness specifically heard Chipps say, "I am either going to stop it or kill him." To this, according to Mrs. Chick, Meacham replied: "Be careful, if you need me, you can get me here."

As she was uttering that last sentence, Moses had his eye on the jury and noticed that some seemed to be having trouble hearing. "Just a moment," he said. "Did all of the jury hear that statement? I saw someone shake your head."

One man in the box said, "I didn't hear the last of that." So Moses asked Mrs. Chick to repeat what she had said.

"What did Meacham say?"

"He said, 'Be careful. If you need me, you can either get me here or there,' and Mr. Chipps says, 'I can take care of myself.'"

"Now, what did they do then? Did they say anything else?"

"They shook hands, and Mr. Chipps started to the elevator, got on the elevator, and Mr. Meacham turned and walked up — the last thing I heard him say when he got to the switchboard was, 'call me.' That is the last thing I heard him say."

After the lunch break, City Detective C.D. Bush testified that he had found a bullet hole in the ceiling of J. Frank Norris's study at the First Baptist Church. Then the manager of the Westbrook Hotel, Mr. T.A. Harris, testified about D.E. Chipps's general bad behavior while drinking. He was followed by W.B. "Pop" Hinkle, another city detective, who told of how he had once taken a weapon from Chipps at that downtown gas station, only to have it discharge. Hinkle was one of the officers who responded to the call to First Baptist Church on July 17.

The defense called R.B. Ridgeway, an attorney and a deputy state game commissioner. On the day of the shooting he had been sitting in his Ford sedan parked on Throckmorton Street, waiting for his wife, who was employed in Norris's office, to get off work.

Ridgeway described the scene as two men, one "large man in a suit," the other "slim and in shirtsleeves," made their way to the stairway leading up to the office area. He quoted the larger man as asking the other fellow, "How in the hell will I know him when I see him?" The witness couldn't recall exactly how the other man responded, but indicated that it sounded like he said: "Come on."

"Who were they? Now, the large man, who was that?"

"D.E. Chipps."

"And the younger man?"

"Redmond. I don't know how it is spelled. Doc Redmond?"

Hearing that name for the first time, Bill McLean interrupted, "What name?" The witness repeated his previous answer. In fact, Doc Redmond was in the witness room.

Having heard what he, as an avid hunter, knew instinctively were gunshots, and counting four of them, Ridgeway told the jury that he quickly got out of his car and went upstairs. He saw a man lying on the floor in Norris's office and he immediately made the connection in his mind between the fallen figure and the large man who had ascended the stairs shortly before.

"Mr. Ridgeway, when you went through or passed through the ante-room, as you came up, did you see anything?"

"As I came up, I never looked at the floor."

"As you passed back did you see anything?"

"Yes, sir."

"What did you see?"

"I saw a spot of blood first attracted my attention. In that spot of blood was something. I don't know what it was." Later, during cross-examination, Ridgeway suggested that the "something" might have been a "large comb case." Of course, the defense wanted to suggest that it was a gun.

Shifting gears, Simpson asked: "Did any woman pass down that stairway or out of that stairway after those shots were fired and before you started up it?"

"No, sir."

During cross-examination, Bill McLean pressed Ridgeway, "Did you see an old lady run across the street and this car came very near striking her and get into an automobile where there was another lady sitting?"

"No, sir."

As the afternoon wound down, the defense called the wife of J.M. Gilliam, business manager of the *Searchlight,* to the stand. She also told the court about hearing shots and seeing a man stoop over, as if to pick something up. With that, Simpson said to McLean, "The witness is with you." However, before McLean could begin, Judge Hamilton grabbed the familiar gavel and beat it firmly, indicating the adjournment of that day's proceedings. He was hungry, his wife had dinner waiting, and the state's cross-examination of Mrs. Gilliam could, well, wait until first thing Thursday morning.

The jurors made their way back up to the third floor for dinner and dominoes. One reporter wrote, "If the Norris trial continues much longer, the jury will have to be furnished with some new sets of dominoes."

Wednesday had been another day of unrelenting attack on the character and reputation of D.E. Chipps. Some began to wonder when McLean and company would begin to fight back — or if they even could.

The largest crowd yet appeared to be gathering in advance of the courtroom door opening Thursday morning. Likely, the increased interest had to do with the fact that Miss Jane Hartwell, J. Frank Norris's secretary, gatekeeper, and girl Friday, was due to take the stand.

Frank Baldwin, newspaper editor from Waco, Texas, found a way to connect the excitement around her court appearance to another famous case that had been in the news a while back involving the murder of a New Jersey Episcopal priest and a lady who was a member of his choir. They had been having an affair. The minister's wife and her two brothers were charged with the murder and brought to trial. During the trial, a woman named Jane Gibson gave testimony. She was a hog farmer and had been nicknamed by the press "pig woman."

With that story in mind, Baldwin mused, "The Halls-Mills case had its pig woman, but the J. Frank Norris defense to the charge of murdering Elliott Chipps has its Jane Hartwell, maiden of some 35 or 40 summers, church secretary de luxe."

But first, of course, Mrs. Gilliam — office worker and wife of the business manager of the *Searchlight* — would undergo cross-examination. Testimony from a few others also needed to be heard, creating further suspense before the secretary's appearance.

J.M. Gilliam's wife withstood Bill McLean's sometimes intense questioning without becoming flustered. He could not shake her from the testimony that she had seen "somebody in a stooping position" in the anteroom after she had noticed the man on Norris's office floor.

D.L. "Doc" Redmond was the next to testify, his name having been brought up the day before by Mr. Ridgeway, who identified him as the man in shirtsleeves who accompanied D.E. Chipps up the stairs to the office on July 17. He was twenty-four years old and single and had moved to Fort Worth about nine years earlier.

Redmond told of how he had made the trip to Fourth and Throckmorton to pick up a Bible that was being offered by the *Searchlight* as part of a subscription campaign. He parked his Ford Roadster on Throckmorton across the street from the church and walked toward the stairway door. He testified that he encountered "a large man" right there who was asking how to get to Dr. Norris's office. "How in the hell will I know him?" the man asked Redmond, who then agreed to escort him up the stairs and point the way. He observed the large man walk through the anteroom toward Norris's study and, without knocking, open the door and enter.

A short while later, while Redmond was talking to an office girl named Frances Turner about the Bible he sought, he heard gunshots. Running toward the noise, he said: "I saw a man in the anteroom. He was stooping in a position, as if to pick something up."

"Was there a woman there?"

"No, sir; there was not."

He then related how he stepped back several feet, away from the scene, then moved back into a position to see the room again.

"Who, if anyone, did you see that time?"

"I saw Dr. Norris."

"Where was he?"

"He was in his office."

"Did you see anyone else at that time?"

"Yes."

"Who did you see?"

"I saw a man falling here." Redmond walked to the scale model and pointed to a spot in the corner of Norris's office.

"Was that man you saw in that anteroom there the same man that you had talked to on the sidewalk?"

"I think so; yes, sir."

"The man you saw in the anteroom when you first ran out there was the man you saw falling over here the second time, was that the same man you had talked to on the sidewalk?"

"I think so; yes, sir."

McLean's cross-examination of Redmond probed the witness's recollection of Norris. Was he holding "a six-shooter?" the lawyer asked. Redmond replied that he didn't see Norris holding anything. At one point, McLean asked if Chipps had been stooping to pick up "a six-shooter" — the point the defense was obviously trying to suggest — but Redmond indicated that he really couldn't say.

Two more witnesses took the stand to corroborate Redmond's account, and the courtroom spectators grew impatient, anxiously awaiting the appearance of Miss Jane Hartwell. Most found themselves mildly amused, however, when Mrs. D.S. Raines took the stand. She was a stenographer in the employ of J. Frank Norris and testified that when D.E. Chipps telephoned Norris just before coming over to the church, her boss instructed her to listen in and "get this down." She recounted the conversation, describing her pastor's tone as "even," while Chipps's was "loud and angry."

She also told the court that right after this, and before Chipps made his appearance at the office, Norris called her in and inquired as to the status of the sermon she was transcribing from shorthand notes. Raines told her boss that she wasn't quite finished. This answer, she indicated, did not please Norris, who said: "Hurry up! I want to leave." She told the court that she hurriedly finished and was about to leave the office when Mr. Chipps made his entrance. She, though, was down the stairs and out the door before the shooting and never even heard the gunfire.

As the morning drew to a close, with still no Miss Jane, Norris's family doctor, O.R. Grogan, testified about the defendant's general health. According to the physician, the preacher suffered from "chronic appendicitis" and "neuritis." He told the court that "the condition of neuritis, as the term applies, is an inflammation of the nerves." He insisted that Norris's ailments kept the preacher "in somewhat of a rundown condition."

The morning session expired and gave way to the lunch break. Just as the lunch break was ending, Dayton Moses called a few reporters over to where he was standing in the corridor outside the courtroom. He paused to let the group assemble and then announced that the defendant himself, J. Frank Norris, would definitely take the stand, "probably late today."

Every wire service present frantically transmitted the bombshell news around the country. Hastily written news stories suggested, "Before the minister takes the witness chair, another motion relative to his evidence will be offered." It would have to do with "questions relative to two former trials of the pastor," when Norris had faced conviction for arson and perjury.

Following the appearance of several more minor witnesses, to lead off the afternoon session, Marvin Simpson finally announced: "Defense calls Miss Jane Hartwell to the stand." Norris's secretary walked gracefully down the center aisle of the room toward the witness box. She was wearing a "beige coat trimmed in beige fur, and wearing a red hat, red beads around her neck." One spectator leaned toward another and whispered, "She is overseer of First Baptist Church affairs." And indeed she was — so much so that one editor referred to her as Norris's "church generalissimo."

As Simpson and Hartwell settled into an early question-and-answer rhythm, all those listening would have been struck by the non-Texan formality of her speech. The word *afterward* was "ahfterward" and *chance* was "chawnce."

She appeared "neat to the last straw of a whisk broom," as one who watched her that day put it. And the lady "saturated the atmosphere with that type of efficiency you read about but never meet up with. Precise to the degree that Webster tired of before he finished his definition."

"As secretary of the First Baptist Church, what are your duties generally, Miss Hartwell? Just a general outline."

"They are many, Mr. Simpson. I have worked with the Sunday school departments, visiting in the homes, frequently visiting the sick in connection with our congregation; I have to know the members and meet them in their homes."

"What, if you know, is the membership of the First Baptist Church?"

"It is more than 8,000."

"What is the membership, if you know, of the combined Sunday school classes?"

"More than 6,000," she said with authority.

The defense lawyer led the witness slowly, deliberately through a discussion of the layout of the offices and her movements leading up to the time when shots were fired. He handled her carefully, not just because of the value of her testimony, but also because she was Miss Jane after all, and she had an almost quiet way of intimidating those around her, especially men.

"Now, Miss Jane — I believe your first name is Jane."

"Yes, sir."

"I beg your pardon for using it. Where were you at the time of the actual tragedy, if you know? When you heard the shot fired where were you?"

She described her work area.

"All right. Did you know Mr. Chipps during his lifetime?"

"I did not."

"Had you seen him on the day of the tragedy?"

"I was seated at my desk and saw someone pass through the anteroom into Mr. Norris' office." Hartwell then told how she had asked the church janitor, Balaam Shaw, to be ready to go into the pastor's office for cleaning that Saturday.

"Who, if anyone, was standing by this desk with you, or there at the desk with you?"

"Balaam Shaw, the janitor."

"A Negro?"

"A Negro."

"Now, what was Mr. Chipps doing, when you first saw him? I mean on this occasion?"

"Coming out of Dr. Norris' office, going toward the anteroom."

"Now, what did he do when you saw him there?"

"He turned there."

"Did you move?"

"I did. When I saw him coming out — I was waiting to get in Dr. Norris' office with Balaam, and when I saw him come out I said, 'Here is our chance!' and started immediately to get into the office."

"All right. Now when you got there, where was Mr. Chipps?"

"Mr. Chipps whirled and started back in — walking rapidly."

"What did you do then?"

"I saw that my chance was gone, and I threw up my hands and said, 'We will have to wait, Balaam,' and turned back."

"Did you or not hear shots fired?"

"I heard shots fired."

"How many would you say, Miss Hartwell?"

"Three or more."

At Simpson's request, Miss Jane took a pointer and rapped three times on the floor in quick succession to demonstrate the shots. She told the court that she froze for a moment, stunned by what she had heard, then she heard "some sound of something dropping," and saw a man stooping or bending.

McLean interrupted abruptly, telling the witness to speak louder. "I can barely hear you myself."

After drawing out more details about her movements in those vital moments, Simpson then asked Hartwell: "Did you see — well, I will ask you this, was there any woman or person showed up in that door from the time you walked up here until after you turned your back her, the time you said, 'We will have to wait'?"

"There was not."

She told about calling an ambulance, though the one she called curiously never responded, and of hearing Dr. Norris call his wife. Then, saving something for the final moments of direct examination, Simpson asked her what Norris said about the shooting in her hearing.

She paused and said emphatically, "I hated to do it. But I had to do it."

With that, Simpson looked over at Bill McLean and said: "The witness is with you." McLean, determined not to tiptoe with this witness, seemed to have a deliberately rude demeanor as he interrogated Hartwell. When she would pronounce a word like "ahfterward," he'd almost mimic her, "I don't mean 'ahfterward,' I mean right now." One reporter was amused, thinking it a welcome relief from a "tedious court session," but most found his manner off-putting. Certainly Miss Jane did. McLean used crude wording and provocative questions with her such as: "Miss Hartwell, isn't it a fact that you told the nigger janitor to get a mop and wipe up the blood in the anteroom?"

She said no and was visibly offended by his aggressiveness. And Wild

Bill wasn't helping himself with the jurors, either. By the time she was excused, most in the room saw her testimony as interesting theater, but not as something that shed any new light on the case, McLean's aggressiveness notwithstanding.

Would Norris be next?

No. G.E. Hubbard was called. He had built the defense's replica of the church offices for use in the trial. For some reason, the defense inserted him and his description of the already used model at this point, though his presence seemed superfluous.

Next up — again, no Norris. This time it was L.S. Grevenberg, who had been working as a clerk at the Westbrook the day of the shooting and had something very interesting to say. It had not been brought before the grand jury in Fort Worth and was being heard for the first time this day in open court.

"Did you see Mr. Chipps on the day of his death?" he was asked.

"Yes, sir."

"How many times that day do you remember to have seen him?"

"I saw him twice; that is, he went up to his room twice before he went to church."

"Now, those times you saw him, was that before or after you went on duty?"

"After I went on duty."

"Mr. Grevenberg, were you personally acquainted with Mr. Chipps?"

"Yes, sir."

"Had you ever had any conversation with him?"

"Oh, frequently, yes, sir."

"Now, did you or not have any conversation with him on the day of his death?"

"Yes, sir, I did."

Simpson had Grevenberg describe the comings and goings of Chipps that day at the Westbrook. The lumberman had entered the lobby in the afternoon.

"All right. Did he have anything, was he carrying anything in his hand?"

"Yes, sir — a package."

"What shape was the package, if you noticed?"

"Well, a rectangular package, as far as I remember."

Grevenberg then said Chipps called for ice, and a bellboy by the name of John Crabb took some to his room.

"Now, I believe you say it was about 15 minutes before he came back down that time, did you have any conversation with him?"

"Yes, sir."

"Now, in that conversation was there anything said about Dr. Norris?"

"He said that he was going over to see Dr. Norris, or go see Norris about the remarks that he had made about Meacham and Carr, that they were friends of his, and he said, 'if he doesn't retract his remarks, I am going to kill him.' I said, 'You don't mean that, do you, Mr. Chipps?' Then I asked him if he had a gun and he did not answer me."

"Now, do you know whether he was drinking or drunk?"

"He had been drinking, yes, sir."

Grevenberg further testified that Chipps had made similar remarks "three or four days" before July 17. Again talking about Norris's attacks on his friends Meacham and Carr, Grevenberg put more threatening words in Chipps's mouth: "Meacham and I are good friends, and he would do anything in the world for me and I would do that same for him. I can kill the son of a bitch and not even be brought to trial."

McLean tried to shake him on cross, asking him about comments made at a Fort Worth Panthers baseball game the day after Norris shot Chipps. He was asked if he had made comments to the effect that "Chipps had made no threats, didn't appear to be angry, and didn't talk any violence" to Mr. and Mrs. A.B. Spenser of Fort Worth. Grevenberg said he didn't know the couple and he had made no such statements.

The witness was excused. It was now just a few minutes before 5 PM. Most assumed adjournment was forthcoming. Nearly everyone in the room was, therefore, surprised when Simpson said: "The defense calls Dr. J. Frank Norris."

The preacher stood and walked toward the witness box. He raised his right hand and took the oath. Then he took his seat. But before he would be asked any questions about this case, his attorneys wanted to make very sure that his previous indictments, those from twelve years before, would not be brought up.

Judge Hamilton withdrew the jury before this discussion took place. Norris, described by one observer in the room as a "tall, athletic figure, immaculately dressed in a black business suit," sat in the box for exactly six minutes as the lawyers talked it out in front of the judge. The argument "grew hot."

As part of the process, Norris gave brief testimony, questioned by Bill McLean.

"Your name is J. Frank Norris?"

"Yes."

"Charged with the murder of D.E. Chipps?"

"Yes."

"Heretofore were you ever indicted in a felony charge?"

"Yes; two cases of arson and one for perjury."

"When was that?"

"In 1912 and 1913."

"Were those indictments pending against you some time?"

"Some three or four months."

"Since that time have you ever been indicted on a charge involving moral turpitude?"

"No."

McLean then said: "That is all."

Dayton Moses said, "Just a moment. What disposition was made of those cases?"

"I was acquitted in two cases and the third case was dismissed by an instructed verdict," Norris testified.

Within a few minutes, Hamilton ruled the prior history absolutely inadmissible. It was a victory for the defense, but there had never really been much of a chance such material would have been admitted.

Then the judge banged his gavel and announced that direct examination of the witness would be carried over until Friday morning. Court was adjourned.

CHAPTER FORTY-FIVE

"As a Man Soweth, So Shall He Reap"

AS J. FRANK NORRIS took the stand Friday morning, January 21, Marcet Haldeman-Julius observed him to be almost "ashen-faced" and "a very different man from the Frank Norris" she had interviewed six months earlier in his office in Fort Worth. Nor was he "self assured to the point of arrogance" as he had been after the change-of-venue hearing in November. Clearly, she thought, he was showing the signs of great strain.

He was still not feeling completely well and "looked as if he might have a degree or two of fever." The journalist described him that morning as "subtly withdrawn, martyred," and with an "I-am-above-all-these-things-air."

Another observer noted that Norris "betrayed no nervousness. If he felt it — but appeared alive to the graveness of his position."

Dayton Moses began his direct examination of the preacher. It was established for the record that he had been ordained when he was about twenty. His doctorate was an honorary one, received from Simmons University in Abilene, "19 or 20 years ago." He was in his eighteenth year as pastor of Fort Worth's First Baptist Church. He lived about seven miles outside Fort Worth, "reasonably near the Dallas–Fort Worth Inter-urban."

"Doctor, have you had any controversies with H.C. Meacham?"

"Yes, sir."

"When, or about what time did you have your first controversy with him?"

"It was in 1920."

"About that time did you have a conversation with Mr. Meacham or did Mr. Meacham have a conversation with you?"

"Yes, sir."

"Whereabouts was that conversation had?"

"On the Twelfth Street side of his store, the street running from Main to Houston Street."

"At that time, Dr. Norris, did you know a gentleman living in Fort Worth by the name of Mock?"

"Yes, sir."

"Did you know Mrs. Mock?"

"Yes, sir."

"What relation, if any, did she bear to the First Baptist Church?"

"She was a member and a teacher in the Sunday School."

"Do you know by whom she was employed?"

"Meacham."

"Now, the conversation that you had with Mr. Meacham, did that or not relate to Mock?"

"Yes, sir."

"State what it was."

Bill McLean objected to the line of questioning as irrelevant and immaterial. Hamilton sustained and Moses said: "It is withdrawn at this time; we will endeavor to show it is admissible later.

"Now, when was the next time you had a controversy with him, if there was another one?"

"It was in the latter part of 1922. At that time he was foreman of the grand jury."

McLean objected once again, and Moses withdrew the question.

Moses then asked some questions about Norris's tabloid, the *Searchlight*, moving toward some things the preacher had written about Meacham in 1922. As Moses got close to his point, McLean waited for the right moment and once again cried foul.

Dayton Moses was determined to continue pushing this envelope. "Dr. Norris, don't answer this until they have time to make an objection, if they so desire. Did you have a visit from H.C. Meacham shortly before the death of Chipps?"

Norris quickly responded: "Yes, sir."

This answer brought a flurry of objections from the prosecution table and provoked an angry exchange. The defense was trying to introduce something new to bolster the claim of conspiracy. J. Frank Norris was prepared to testify that a few days before Chipps came to the office,

Meacham himself had visited there and demanded that Norris not preach any more sermons about him, threatening to kill him if he did.

Hamilton called the lawyers up to him, and the attorneys began a protracted debate about what Moses was trying to introduce. Sam Sayers, one of McLean's law partners, asked the judge to withdraw the jury while the discussion went forth. He did, and they went out. And for the better part of the next two hours, the attorneys tossed volleys back and forth. Moses presented an extensive and exhaustive speech about what the defense wanted to put forward, with the prosecution opposing him at every turn. Though all of this took place outside the jury's hearing, many of the spectators, press included, heard the details.

Moses told Judge Hamilton the story of S.L. Mock and his wife, Julia, as it related to H.C. Meacham. They wanted to show that Dr. Norris had advised the husband of Meacham's mistress about his options and had therefore created conflict for Meacham, turning him into an enemy. Furthermore, in 1922, while Norris had been in battle with Fort Worth's vice interests — bootleggers, gamblers, and bordello operators — Meacham, who was foreman of a Tarrant County grand jury hearing evidence in the matters, was not supportive of the preacher's activism. Norris then wrote critically about the department store owner in the *Searchlight*.

The defense hoped to introduce testimony, via the defendant, to the effect that in early 1925, when H.C. Meacham was running for the city council, he went to see Dr. Norris to complain that there was a telephone campaign being conducted against him suggesting he was not morally fit for office. Meacham accused Norris of being behind the campaign. The preacher denied involvement, and H.C. Meacham then told Norris, according to his attorney: "I believe your statement, but I came here with murder in my heart toward you."

Next, Moses said they wanted to delve into the issue of the city deciding to tax First Baptist Church for the parts of its property used for commercial purposes. Norris's active resistance, airing the matter over the radio and in the *Searchlight,* led to Meacham's firing First Baptist members from his store.

"We expect further to show," Moses continued, "that Chipps then came to Norris and said if he preached the sermon against him [Meacham], he would kill him." Then the defense lawyer raised many eyebrows when he told the judge, "We will prove that Meacham had gone to the office of McLean, Scott, & Sayers and asked them what the fee would be if he [Meacham] had trouble with Dr. Norris and killed Dr. Norris. We will prove that McLean then said to Meacham: 'You ought to take a shotgun and kill him if the things he said about you are not true.'"

J. Frank Norris sat just a few feet away, taking it all in.

Bill McLean listened to Moses go on and on until he could stand it no longer. He erupted and "bitterly denounced" Norris as having "slandered some of the best people of Fort Worth." He denounced the idea that he had told Meacham that Norris ought to be killed as "an infamous lie." He angrily thundered, "Bill McLean has never threatened to kill anyone. And if any man or woman comes in here and swears that I have, you will find that person is a henchman of Norris and a member of the First Baptist Church. I don't carry a six-shooter," the lawyer added as he looked the Reverend Mr. Norris squarely in the eyes, "and I don't keep any in my desk. I want to make these statements before Norris is charged with my murder."

Wild Bill caught himself and took a breath to calm down. Then he explained, "What did happen, was this: Mayor Meacham came to me. He said he thought that Norris ought to be enjoined from slandering him. He said he wanted to sue him for damages. But I told him, 'No.' I told him that Norris lived off notoriety and that I thought his notoriety was about through. No one threatened to kill."

McLean added, "Every word was spoken in the presence of Gillis Johnson of Fort Worth and a more honest man I do not know. Gillis Johnson will bear me out in what I say and he is a member of the law firm that is defending Norris."

New Tarrant County district attorney Jesse Martin weighed in next: "It's child's play; it's horse play. They started off on the idea of 'apparent danger.' But now they would have us bring in other issues, which the law excludes. We might as well bring into this case every man Norris has ever slandered."

By the time the arguments before Judge Hamilton were over, the "complimentary remarks" the attorneys had been generally making for the appearance of civility had given way to raw animosity. Toward the end, Sam Sayers said something to Dayton Moses, and Moses replied, "I have stood enough from you, don't speak to me." One reporter thought the two had come close to "a fist fight."

Hamilton listened intently to all the arguments, ultimately ruling that any testimony about a "conspiracy" would be inadmissible. He then recalled the jury, and Dayton Moses continued his direct examination of J. Frank Norris.

The preacher testified about the conversation he had with Fred Holland the day before the shooting, then the call from Chipps, the threats, the cursing, and the lumberman coming into his study. He described the argument — words that had by now become very familiar to the jurors and everyone else in the room.

Then it was time for Norris to describe Chipps's provocation.

"Will you kindly stand up, Doctor, and face the jury and show the movement that you saw him make or the position of his hand?"

Norris stood and demonstrated the "hip pocket move" he said he saw D.E. Chipps make. "His right hand was at his right side, at his hip, his coat was pulled back."

"What did you do then, Doctor?"

"I jerked open the drawer of my desk and grabbed the gun."

"What did you do with the pistol?"

"And shot."

"Doctor, why did you shoot D.E. Chipps?"

Norris, by this time, had begun to sob. He looked over at his wife for a brief moment, bit his lip, and then replied, "Because I felt certain he was going to kill me." The man who faced the electric chair if convicted of murder wept even more.

"Doctor, when Chipps turned around in the anteroom and started back toward your office with his right hand to his hip, what opinion or belief did you have in your mind at that time as to what he was then about to do to you?"

"That he was about to kill me."

"Dr. Norris, would you have killed Mr. Chipps on that occasion if you had believed that your life was in no danger?"

"I certainly would not. I did not want to kill him."

Moses asked the defendant about the "relative strength" between Norris and Chipps, and the preacher testified, "He was a powerful man, much stronger and larger than I am."

"What was your belief at that time, doctor, as to whether you were physically a match for D.E. Chipps?"

"I was not."

"Dr. Norris, where was Mr. Chipps when you fired the first shot?"

"He was coming in the door, just inside of it."

As noon approached, Norris testified about his movements after the shooting, how he called his wife, then went with Chief Lee to city hall, and a little later over to the courthouse to see District Attorney Hangar.

When the defense lawyer indicated the end of his direct examination, Hamilton called for the lunch recess. Cross-examination would have to wait for a couple of hours.

Norris had done well on the stand, though one observer noted cynically, "It was a perfect dramatization of his part as he conceived it," adding, "when he entered the ministry, the theater lost a great showman." The preacher, this critic continued, told his story "with that particular blend of sincere simulation and artistic conviction that marks a John Gilbert, a Greta Garbo, or a Chaplin." Charlie Chaplin was in the news himself that week, not for his acting, but for his own legal battle over back taxes owed to the US government.

When Norris returned to his place on the stand shortly after 2 PM that Friday, Dayton Moses asked the judge if he might ask a couple of additional questions of the defendant. Hamilton agreed.

"Dr. Norris, do you know the witness, Mrs. Parker, who testified in this case for the state?"

"The first time I ever saw her was on the witness stand the other day."

"Did you ever see her or did she have any conference with you in your office?"

"No, sir."

"And you did not see her on the day of the tragedy?"

"No, sir."

"You heard the testimony of state's witness, Rains, to the effect that shortly after the killing he saw you near — somewhere near the head of the stairway, and that you said: 'I have killed me a man.' Did you make use, Dr. Norris, of that expression?"

"No, sir."

"How do you know you didn't?"

"Well, it would have been the most unnatural thing, utterly out of keeping with my feelings, and I know I did not make any such statement."

Attorney Moses then turned and looked at Bill McLean. "You can cross examine."

McLean began by pressing Norris as to how he could so well remember that he did not utter the phrase "I have killed me a man," and yet he could not remember so much else about those moments, such as to whom he handed the gun. Then he asked about the gun itself.

"Where were you when you unloaded the six-shooter with which you shot Chipps?"

"I do not know."

"What was your purpose in unloading that pistol and removing the shells there from?"

"I have never known why."

"Where were you when you did it?"

"I don't know; I was either in one of these two offices," the preacher said while pointing to two of the rooms other than his study and the anteroom in the scale model.

The preacher had apparently "discovered" the shells in a coat pocket sometime later.

"How long after the death of Chipps was it that you found those empty shells and this loaded cartridge in your pocket?"

"About three or four weeks."

"What did you do afterward with them?"

"I threw them out of my pocket."

McLean acted stunned, questioning whether he had heard right. "Did what?"

"Threw them away," the preacher clarified.

"Anyone see you threw them away?"

"Well, I think my wife was present."

The crowd in the room became instantly noisy, and Hamilton just as quickly gaveled it into silence.

"Where were you when you threw away these empty cartridges?"

"I was standing on my back porch."

McLean then took Norris through the events of the shooting, meticulously tracing every step. He had asked Chipps to leave several times, then when he finally began to leave, Norris said after him, "I repeat everything I have said." Chipps turned in the middle of the anteroom and burst back into the office, just inside the door. At that moment, J. Frank Norris, who when not yet fourteen threw himself at an armed man in defense of his drunkard father, said he reached in the drawer for the gun and shot Mr. Chipps. The lumberman staggered backward at first, and Norris left his office through a side door before the man staggered back into the study to fall in the corner. Norris handed the gun to "someone."

At one point his voice trailed off, and Marvin Simpson called out for him to speak louder. Norris coughed and said, "My throat is very sore." He gripped a handkerchief, bringing it to his mouth again and again to muffle his cough.

Elsewhere in the room another hand held tight to a handkerchief — that of Mrs. D.E. Chipps, who had worn black throughout the trial. Even her handkerchief was "black-trimmed." Having watched witness after witness savage her dead former husband, she now listened, and wept, as the man who had killed him tried to talk his way out of the electric chair.

McLean questioned the preacher about having preached the next day, morning and evening, even while Chipps was being mourned at his burial. Norris simply said when asked if he knew that his victim was being buried that day, "I so understood."

When McLean had exhausted every avenue he could think of to shake J. Frank Norris from his story, he sighed, "I think that is all." Immediately Marvin Simpson told the preacher, "Stand aside, Doctor."

Dayton Moses then indicated that the defense was just about ready to rest but asked the court if it still "adhered to its ruling" about not allowing testimony about a visit H.C. Meacham made to Norris a week or so before the shooting. They wanted to produce a "Mrs. Ellis" to back up the story.

Hamilton stood by his prior ruling that the whole "conspiracy theory" involving Meacham and company was inadmissible.

Bill McLean then asked Judge Hamilton for permission to call a rebuttal witness; it was allowed. The prosecution called a man named Clarence E. Wisecup, a dentist from Taylor, Texas, who had just happened to be changing trains in Fort Worth on Saturday, July 17, and who ventured out for a stroll, chancing upon the scene at First Baptist Church. He testified that he saw a woman almost run over by a car as she ran out of the *Searchlight* building and before the ambulance came. He had also heard someone say that, "Preacher Norris had killed a man." Wisecup knew who Norris was, having heard him over the radio.

But whatever gain the state thought had been made in reinforcing Mrs. Roxie Parker's earlier testimony was lost as Dayton Moses established the dentist's lack of familiarity with the streets of Fort Worth. The witness got confused about which street he saw the lady running on. His testimony ultimately conflicted with where Mrs. Parker said she was. When Dr. Wisecup was finished, he exited the stand, and Judge Hamilton adjourned the court until the next morning. Norris seemed pleased with how he had conducted himself on the stand, even during the pressure of McLean's cross-examination.

Mrs. Chipps left the courtroom and was observed walking down Congress Avenue with her son. With "eyes that are brown pools of sorrow," she responded to a reporter who caught up with them. He asked if her son believed "all these stories of drunken bullying of which the court has made D.E. Chipps the central figure?"

"Thank God he doesn't," she replied. "Elliott Jr. and his father were the best of pals. Why, he never even slapped the boy! And can the world believe I could have ever loved and married the kind of man they have painted D.E. Chipps in court?

"When he was just a little fellow," she sighed, "'I betcha that' became his pet expression. I remember one day Mr. Chipps overheard him 'betcha a dollar' to a boy playmate. 'Have you a dollar in your pocket?' Mr. Chipps asked him. Of course, Elliott didn't. 'Don't ever bet anything unless you have it in your pocket,' I remember his father reprimanded. He was like that." The reporter thought it a cute, if not curious, anecdote. Mrs. Chipps's eyes seemed to "brighten" at the memory.

In dramatic contrast to the widow's subdued demeanor, J. Frank Norris was relaxed and expansive. That evening the "chipper" clergyman sat in the dining room of the Driskill, "sipping an orange cooler," and told *Fort Worth Press* reporter Jack Gordon, "I am thinking maybe I'll go up to Fort Worth and preach Sunday." They chatted about the events of the day, and Norris smiled and told Gordon, "And did you notice McLean called me Doctor?" He "dumped another spoon of sugar into the tall glass" and told the reporter that if he didn't make the quick trip back to Fort Worth to speak that he had already "picked a church here, and I am going to walk right in and sit down with the congregation." Gordon tried to get him to divulge which church he had in mind, but Norris wouldn't give "him a hint." He said he didn't want to cause "the pastor any embarrassment."

As he and Norris walked through the hotel lobby, Gordon decided to try his best to be in the preacher's company if and when he made that church visit. The preacher then took the elevator to the third floor where he and his wife "rocked on the spacious Driskill veranda, lighted by romantic jap lanterns. They chatted of college days."

The next morning, as Judge Hamilton gaveled to order the second Saturday session of the trial, the state called Mrs. Fannie Greer back, seeking to shake her testimony, but was once more unsuccessful.

There had been some chatter that fourteen-year-old Carl Glaze, the "boy mystery witness," would be called by the state. He had been in town the week prior but had returned to Fort Worth, only to be summoned back to the capital on Saturday. In the end, the prosecution opted not to use him. Miss Melba Bullock testified that she had seen Glaze running from the building, and also that she saw no woman running away.

The state then called C.B. Rogers, who had been employed by Moore Rubber Company, the tire shop occupying the space directly below Norris's office. He testified that he heard fellow tire shop employee H.H. Rains quote the preacher as saying, "I have killed me a man."

After a brief recess, the word from the prosecution table was "The state rests." Simpson, though, was not quite finished. He called George Eagle, a Fort Worth undertaker, to the stand. Eagle testified that he had received a call on July 17, about a shooting at First Baptist — the call came "from a lady" — and that he dispatched an ambulance. The witness recognized the voice as that of church secretary Hartwell. It had been a cause for some question and confusion as to why it took so long for an ambulance to arrive, the inference being that maybe Miss Jane had not called one. This speculation fed the image of the general indifference in and around the church offices as a man lay dying on the floor. But Eagle's testimony was accepted and not challenged by the prosecution.

The defense then called Mr. H.B. Green, who worked for radio station KFQB. He testified about the gun, having seen it on many occasions in the pastor's desk drawer. At 11:35 AM, Hamilton announced that court would be adjourned to wait for two final defense witnesses who were en route from Fort Worth. The judge indicated that a night session was possible, but in the end the witnesses did not arrive in time and everything was held over until Monday morning. Cold and rain had slowed the two men on their journey.

As people made their way out of the courtroom, one of the main topics of conversation, even among the lawyers, was speculation about what kind of charge Judge Hamilton would make to the jury. Specifically, the greatest question had to do with the concept of "provoking the difficulty." The prosecution had, throughout the trial, tried to argue that Norris's antics and behavior had provoked things. If the judge allowed this to be a jury consideration, the preacher's chances for acquittal diminished.

J. Frank Norris and his wife stayed in that Sunday morning and tuned in to the church service back in Fort Worth. But that evening, Norris invited Jack Gordon to go back with him to Austin's First Methodist Church to hear Pastor W.F. Bryan once again. Gordon was elated, knowing that this experience would make a great item for Monday morning's paper.

The preacher and the reporter entered the building shortly after the service had started, while the capacity crowd was loudly singing the first hymn of the night. It was a popular song called "Saved by Grace," and while Gordon grabbed a hymnal and looked around at others near him to see the page number, Norris was singing at the top of his voice, despite his "ailment." As Gordon looked at him, the preacher said, "I know 100 hymns by memory and 'Saved by Grace' is my favorite."

Following the hymn, the audience was seated and Norris "in a stage whisper" started talking about his daughter Lillian, who had married a man from Harvard and was now in "a famous trio that tours with the Boston Symphony Orchestra every year." Gordon didn't want to be so obvious as to take notes, so he hoped to remember all these colorful details for his column.

Then they were back to their feet, the church singing "When the Roll Is Called Up Yonder." The reporter observed that the preacher's face "bore a look of peace." Soon seated again, it was time for the offering. Jack Gordon reached into his pocket, and all he had was a dime and some dollar bills. He decided to part with the coin and "felt sheepish when Dr. Norris laid in it a crisp dollar bill." Organ music was playing, and it hit Gordon that during the times he had sat in First Baptist Church services back in Fort Worth, he had never heard — or seen, for that matter — a church organ. He asked Norris, "Didn't Baptists believe in organs?"

"Oh yes, but a piano is best in a church. The organs aren't fast enough. And we have a big choir." Norris always relished his role as a church efficiency and organizational expert.

By this time a few had noticed the famous visitor, then a few more, and finally pretty much all those in the place were at least aware that J. Frank Norris was in the room. Certainly Dr. Bryan knew it. The preacher announced his text, "As a man soweth, so shall he reap." The reporter didn't listen much to the message, trying instead to keep an eye on the preacher seated next to him, but doing so unobtrusively. Norris "squirmed in his chair nervously" and often "sighed." As the message droned on, he "seemed a little tired and ready to go. Twice he pulled out his watch."

They left the building during the singing of the doxology, and as they parted company on the sidewalk, the preacher told the reporter, "That was a good sermon." Gordon raced back to his hotel room and pounded out his piece for the next morning's edition of the *Fort Worth Press*. It was titled "Norris Squirms in Pew as He Listens to Sermon."

But whatever discomfort Norris had felt in church the night before was long gone by the time he took his seat at the defense table shortly before nine o'clock on Monday morning. The first hour was given over to completing the testimony phase of the trial, now nothing more than a mundane restating of facts and countercharges.

Then came time for the all-important summations. Six hours would be allowed for each side to make final appeals, and it was assumed that several lawyers from the prosecution and defense would have their say before the jury. But before the judge could call for this segment of the trial to begin, McLean made a motion requesting that the judge charge the jury that the issue of "whether or not the pastor provoked the difficulty" would be allowed as a factor in their ultimate deliberation. Both sides waited nervously for a moment as Hamilton paused, seemingly for dramatic effect, before rapping the gavel with the accompanying utterance, "State's motion is denied."

It was a clear victory for the defense.

After a short recess, Special Prosecutor John Shelton was the first to speak. Hired by H.C. Meacham when the trial was moved to Austin to assist McLean, Scott, and Sayers navigate the legal waters in the state capital, he began in a "comparatively low tone, his droll voice rising when he asked that the pastor be put to death." He had no doubt that J. Frank Norris had shot Dexter Elliott Chipps to death in cold blood and that he did so for "publicity." He also charged that perjury was rampant on the defense side.

He told the jury that he would not "hesitate to call a murderer a murderer and a liar a liar." Attacking the essence of the defense's case — that Chipps was a drunk — Shelton said, "Gentlemen of the jury, for more than four days here you listened alone to testimony that the dead man was a man who drank. I don't care if he was a man who drank. I don't care if he bought half the liquor that was brought to the town of Fort Worth. That did not give Frank Norris the right to take his life, because as yet the Legislature has never said that there is an 'open season' on men who drank."

He described Norris as someone who "claims to be a minister of the gospel," but who really just saw the murder of Chipps as "his hope of future publicity, of getting his name in the newspaper headlines."

As the prosecutor addressed the jury, fourteen-year-old Dexter Jr. sat with the prosecutors "with the hopes that the slayer of his dad will be punished." Across the room sat Norris's boys, George in knickers and Frank Jr. in military-school-issued khaki.

After Shelton finished, Hamilton announced an adjournment for lunch. When court resumed around half past two that afternoon, Marvin Simpson stood and made his way toward the jury box to begin his part of the defense's summation. During his hour before the jury, he did his best to counter Shelton's argument and tone. "I agree with Mr. Shelton that Dr. Norris had no right to kill Chipps because Chipps was drunk. But the law didn't give Chipps the right to get drunk and go there to try and kill Dr. Norris," Simpson argued.

The defense lawyer, "with collar open, tie hanging, and sweat dripping," alluded to H.C. Meacham as the "man who employed 10 special prosecutors at a fabulous price." He also cited the Bible, saying the gospels differ from each other in some details yet draw the same big picture — the way, he insisted, that defense witnesses differed on some details, though telling the same story. It was an interesting argument to make on behalf of a defendant who promoted the concept of biblical inerrancy in his ministry. Yet it was also an effective argument that sought to explain some of the vast differences between prosecution and defense testimony.

The high point of Simpson's summation, as he energetically spoke, his red hair tousled, was when he used the biblical story of David and Goliath to describe and defend his client. And by the time he was done, his voice becoming husky, the dividing line had been drawn — one that would be reinforced throughout that day and into the next.

To the prosecution, J. Frank Norris killed D.E. Chipps because he was a publicity-seeking egomaniac.

To the defense, J. Frank Norris was the shepherd boy David, with his trusty and primitive sling, and D.E. Chipps was the ugly and taunting giant, Goliath.

No middle ground. One journalist wrote that as the prosecutors spoke, it was almost as if one could hear "the state paging bony old death all day here today. Early in criminal court the call was begun softly at first, then in melancholy overtures — death, and nothing less for the Rev. J. Frank Norris. Round and about sometimes like awesome cheer leaders urging on a grisly, fleshless specter, went the prosecutors with their death cry 'Come On Death.'"

Later that afternoon, as the prosecution and defense alternated speakers, it fell to young Jesse Martin, the brand-new Tarrant County district attorney, to speak for the state. He gave what was described as "a clear, concise, even brilliant resume of the State's case." But some in the room already began to see it as "harvesting all one could of its scantily sown crop." He defended Mayor Meacham, calling him "one of the finest men in Fort Worth."

With the five o' clock hour approaching, and his punctual dinner waiting for him at home, Judge Hamilton suspended the proceedings, setting the stage for a showdown sometime on Tuesday between Dayton Moses and "Wild Bill" McLean.

On the way out of the courthouse, Gene Fowler, correspondent for Universal News Service, caught up with Norris. The preacher told Fowler that he was "confident of acquittal" and hinted that there was already a "mass meeting" — a victory service of sorts — being planned in Fort Worth.

CHAPTER FORTY-SIX

"I Hold in My Hand a Verdict"

TUESDAY'S PROCEEDINGS OPENED with defense attorney "Judge" Ike White speaking for almost an hour on the topic of D.E. Chipps's character and behavior when "in his cups." Described by one observer as a dead ringer for the late William Jennings Bryan, White mocked the dead man as a braggart who boasted of the success of his lumber business and as someone who was always "just drunk enough to think that he was big, smart, and brave."

Prosecutor J.D. Moore followed White and tried his best to punch holes in various aspects of the defense's case, but most in the room just watched the clock and waited for the main event — Moses versus McLean.

Dayton Moses had been preparing his final summation for days. During the trial for the most part he had left direct questioning and cross-examining duties largely to defense colleague Marvin Simpson. Simpson was "given to bullying and pettifogging," which served him well with the witnesses for the prosecution. Moses, though, the better-known lawyer — and by most accounts the star of the defense team — would serve as the relay team's anchor. He was "tireless" and "watchful," a "drudger" where Simpson was "mercurial."

Moses was a master of his emotions. Even when shouted at he "contrived to keep his own voice low, his manner controlled. By his very composure, he dominated." When it was finally time for him to address the jury for his allotted time, Moses began: "May it please the court, and the gentlemen of the jury: The time has come when the last word will be said on behalf of this defendant, who is on trial for his life and his liberty."

Moses took exception with the sarcasm of some on the prosecution side for mocking the idea of Norris's two sons being in the courtroom, as if their presence were staged for sympathy. "Their father is on trial for his life. Would you deny your son the right to sit beside you in the darkest hour of your night?" he asked the men of the jury.

The attorney traced Chipps's steps, as well as those of his client that fateful day, and the story he told was designed to say "self-defense" at every turn. "Never before in the history of Texas has there been a relentless, a more cruel prosecution than there has been in this case," Moses said. Referring to the new district attorney from Fort Worth, he told the jurors, "I wonder if Martin's zeal for prosecution and hatred for my client did not make him discourteous to the defendant by referring to him as 'Norris.'" This was a point Moses drove home, indicating that the prosecution's refusal to call J. Frank "Doctor" or "Reverend" throughout the trial, usually just saying "Norris," was itself a deliberately designed attempt to denigrate his client.

He hinted at something more: "It was in the power of counsel for the state to have lifted the curtain to see whether there was not in that closet a skeleton and a sinister hand." In other words: "deep, laid conspiracy."

Dayton Moses then spent a great deal of time describing the success of J. Frank Norris as a pastor and preacher — the size of his congregation, the number of his followers. He compared Norris to Martin Luther, John Wesley, and Roger Williams, all religious leaders who had been persecuted.

He took issue with the reckless way in which prosecutors had thrown around the charge of perjury with reference to defense witnesses. Then he suggested that several of the state's witnesses were, in fact, guilty of lying under oath, including Mrs. Roxie Parker and Mr. H.H. Rains. He called Mrs. Parker's testimony untruthful and begged the jurors, "Gentlemen, she was not there. She was not there!" He reminded the twelve attentive men, "If you have a reasonable doubt as to her presence, you must under your oaths and under the law, resolve that doubt in favor of the defendant."

At this moment, Moses pulled his watch from his pocket and noted that it was past noon. He turned to Judge Hamilton, saying, "Your honor, may I suspend now?" Hamilton replied with his gavel and left the bench. A few others left the courtroom, but on this day, more people had brought a lunch than any day before, not wanting to lose their spot for the Moses-McLean show, not to mention the end of the famous trial.

After lunch, when court resumed at 2 PM, Moses continued his attack on Roxie Parker's testimony, careful to diplomatically acknowledge his misgivings about speaking ill of an elderly lady, even referencing his own mother. Moses was in a groove, and for the next hour the jury's attention was on his every word. Waxing eloquent, he approached the climax of his speech:

> Gentlemen, as Elijah said when he made the journey to Mount Horeb, and at the entrance of that cave saw the wind and the earth quake and fire, God wasn't in it. Listen gentlemen, to that still small voice; listen to what that still small voice says to you — your conscience — and obey that conscience in this case, gentlemen; we don't ask for mercy, we ask for justice, under the law. Render a decision that is in accordance with the law and the evidence, a decision that, when you go home to your loved ones, you can look at the wife of your bosom and say, "Sweetheart, I rendered a verdict in that preacher's case that my intelligence and my conscience told me was right." Gentlemen, I have every confidence in you; I ought to have the right to have confidence in your good faith, and trusting in the sincerity of the answers you gave upon your examination. I am going to commit to your hands the future, the welfare of this man, and the future and the welfare and the happiness of his family.

"Wild Bill" McLean found himself in uncharted territory. He was a defense lawyer, not a prosecutor, and unaccustomed to losing. As he walked toward the jury box, nodding to Moses in gracious recognition of his fine performance, he had to have known, to use an analogy from the world of boxing, that he was behind on points and needed a knockout. And you don't achieve that back on your heels. McLean needed to go on the attack.

He began: "Moses' and Simpson's speeches are just Norris mouthpieces. They never would have abused Jesse Martin as they did, but they are listening to Norris. That is what he lives on. The evidence shows what kind of man he is.

"They say we call him Norris. The most pitiful tale on earth, a case of murder. Right then, that Mr. Moore and Mr. Shelton and Mr. Martin say, he shall be deprived of that doctor of divinity in our reference to him!"

For the next two hours, a mix of contempt and passion in his voice, he sought to demonize J. Frank Norris as the defense had done to D.E. Chipps. He painted Norris a cold-blooded murderer and hypocritical charlatan. "Talk about your actors, gentlemen of the jury. Oh, these movie picture stars never equaled Norris. Perfect control; then he commences crying and sobbing before the jury, the sign of hypocrisy, begging men to acquit him," he said. Then, almost with a sense of resignation he continued, "and when you shall have done it, and when he goes back to his infamous slandering of good people, and when you pick up the paper and see this time he didn't kill a poor unfortunate drunk, but that he snuffed the life out of a better man, he is your criminal not mine."

And with that, Bill McLean made his way back to the prosecution table, where not one colleague reached out a hand to congratulate him on his effort. The legendary lawyer seemed to have given up at the end, virtually conceding the case. Consumed by anger and frustration, he'd even disparaged the dead man, whose widow sat just a few rows behind him, stunned by McLean's depiction of D.E. Chipps as a "poor unfortunate drunk."

Hamilton then instructed the jury, and the lawyers listened for anything that might favor one side or the other:

> Now, if the jury believes from the evidence in this case, beyond a reasonable doubt, that the defendant, J. Frank Norris, did, with a gun, shoot and kill the said D.E. Chipps, as charged in the indictment, but you believe from the evidence, or have a reasonable doubt thereof, that at such time the said D.E. Chipps was making, or about to make, what appeared to the defendant, as viewed from his standpoint at the time, taking into consideration the relative strength of the parties and the defendant's knowledge of the character and disposition of the deceased, to be an unlawful attack upon the defendant, producing a reasonable belief in the defendant's mind from the words, acts or which had been uttered, done or manifested at any time prior thereto by the said D.E. Chipps, that the defendant was in immediate danger of loss of life or of serious bodily injury, then the defendant had the right to shoot and kill the said D.E. Chipps, whether, in fact, the

said D.E. Chipps was armed or not, or whether he, the defendant, was in any real danger of either loss of life or serious bodily injury being inflicted upon him by the said D.E. Chipps, or whether the said D.E. Chipps at such time was in fact making any attack upon the defendant, if the defendant, as viewed from his standpoint at the time, and from his standpoint alone, reasonably believed that the said attack upon him and that, therefore, he, the defendant was in immediate danger of either loss of life or of serious bodily injury. And if you so believe, or have a reasonable doubt thereof, you will find the defendant not guilty.

The defense lawyers fought off smiles, while at the prosecution table, McLean and company knew that the case they had all once thought a sure thing, one that would shut the mouth of J. Frank Norris for good, had turned against them. At 4:42 PM Judge Hamilton dismissed the jury to their third-floor room, where they were to begin deliberation, and court was adjourned.

Now came the waiting. J. Frank Norris somehow slipped away from the room and went for a walk — a long walk with his fourteen-year-old son — around the neighborhood, and nobody knew where he was. Most of the crowd wandered to nearby restaurants, with the thought that maybe a verdict would be returned that evening. The judge had indicated that if the jurors deliberated past 9 PM, he'd hold things over until the next day. Encouraging as the judge's instructions might have been for Norris, the wait for a verdict had to be excruciating. Meacham, Carr, and other city leaders were fighting for their pride and justice for their friend Chipps. The attorneys had at stake their reputations and future fortunes. Norris, however, would be executed, fried in the electric chair, if found guilty of murder.

However, the wait would not be that long. At 5:56 PM, just an hour and fourteen minutes after they had left the courtroom, the jury sent word that they were returning to court and had reached a verdict. The news raced through town like a wildfire. Judge Hamilton, accustomed to murder trials with long jury deliberations, had just sat down at home for dinner when the phone rang. Lawyers left behind meals that had just been served at the

Austin and Driskill Hotels. Everyone hightailed it back to the courthouse.

Everyone, that is, except J. Frank Norris. No one knew where he was, and several went out to look for him. Finally, Norris and his son walked back into the courthouse at about 6:45 PM, greeted by the news that there was a verdict. They made their way to the courtroom, which according to one newspaper account was packed with "more than a thousand persons."

"Have you reached a verdict?" Judge Hamilton asked. The foreman handed an envelope to the clerk, who passed it to the judge. Hamilton looked over the room and said, "I hold in my hand a verdict. I do not know what it is, but anyone who makes a demonstration will be fined 100 dollars and spend three days in jail." Law enforcement officers stood and made their presence obvious.

Hamilton read the words: "We find the defendant Not Guilty."

One observer described the scene: "A smothered clapping started, 'I'll arrest the next man or woman who does that,' shouted Sheriff Bargesly, and it subsided. People thronged around Norris and Mrs. Norris, kissing them, and as Norris made his way over to Simpson, he fell on his shoulder, tears on his face, and hugged him."

Standing near the courtroom door in the back of the room when the verdict was read, Chipps's son cried. "I can stand it all right," he said to one reporter, "but I am worrying about my mother." For her part, Mae Chipps said: "If Fort Worth and the state want Frank Norris they can have him. I am thankful I have my life and my son. My faith in God has not weakened."

Back in Fort Worth, within two hours of the verdict, it was reported that "thousands of Fort Worth citizens joined the First Baptist Church in prayer services." Ultimately, the church was "packed to capacity and automobiles blocked traffic for two blocks around the church."

The next night, back home in Fort Worth, the Reverend Dr. J. Frank Norris spoke to a capacity crowd at First Baptist Church. The chairman of the church's deacon board, Harry Keaton, described the event: "This will not be a celebration, but a time of thanksgiving to Almighty God for His marvelous deliverance."

The next Sunday, January 30, 1927, Norris delivered his first Sunday sermons after the trial. In the morning his subject was prayer. His evening sermon was titled: "Hate Doesn't Pay." Had the trial changed J. Frank in any way? Would he abandon his political activism and civic provocations for concerns of the spiritual realm?

Within a few weeks it would be clear not much had changed. The *Searchlight* featured the bold headline: "Romanism Dominates the Press." Fundamentalist and populist firebrand J. Frank Norris was back in business.

EPILOGUE

MAE CHIPPS SETTLED back into her life in Fort Worth and her comfortable home on Lipscomb Street after the trial, devoting herself to her son. The civil suit she had filed against J. Frank Norris went forward, but absent a guilty verdict in the criminal matter it quickly lost its steam. She seemed to lose interest as well. Lawyers McLean, Scott, and Sayers gave it their best effort, largely out of the guilt of having failed in a prosecution that had once seemed destined for conviction. Within a few years, as Norris and his attorneys, including Simpson and Moses, fought and delayed, the suit went away with hardly a whimper from the widow, being dismissed in the autumn of 1930.

H.C. Meacham never recovered from the stress of the trial. His health deteriorated dramatically. He resigned as mayor of Fort Worth, leaving his city council seat as well, in April 1927, because of his physical decline. J. Frank Norris proclaimed Meacham's withdrawal from city politics a personal vindication.

Not long after he left office, the city council voted to name the Fort Worth airfield, which had opened in 1925, for the retired mayor. The airport bears the Meacham name to this day.

Meacham died suddenly at his home on Elizabeth Boulevard in December 1929, not living to see his business empire decimated by the Great Depression. He was sixty. His obituary mentioned the death of his friend Chipps at the hand of Norris. Many felt that the preacher had really killed Mr. Meacham as well.

One of Meacham's daughters, Minnie, married Chipps's pallbearer Amon G. Carter a few years later, the newspaperman's unresolved feud with her daddy notwithstanding. The Carters would remain a preeminent Fort Worth family for decades. Amon built a media empire around the *Fort Worth Star-Telegram* and WBAP radio that later included television. He was a tireless promoter of all things Fort Worth, and when it came time for Texas, founded as a republic in 1836, to celebrate its one hundredth birthday, Carter made sure that his town did it up right. He hired the legendary Broadway producer Billy Rose to create a "show of shows" to be presented on a cow pasture converted into a venue called Casa Mañana.

Amon was concerned that J. Frank Norris, who had avoided community quarrels for many years leading up to 1936, might give the show trouble. After all, the ads for it featured "bare-breasted girls." So he called the preacher on the telephone.

"Are you going out of town this summer?"

"I might. Why?"

"We've got this centennial show and some nude girls, and we're going to sell liquor."

"I see. I've been intending to hold some revivals. I guess I could start them early."

Norris kept away from Fort Worth most of that centennial summer, traveling "2,700 miles delivering the word of God, while Sally Ann Rand hid her naked body behind fans and balloons as she danced away the troubles of Fort Worth."

The drive overseen by Meacham and with legwork done by Chipps to place a large portrait of Carter in the lobby of the Fort Worth Club got scrubbed in the wake of Chipps's death and Norris's murder trial. The idea was ultimately resurrected and a painting hung in 1939. Amon Carter died in June 1955.

J. Frank Norris, though largely shying away from local civic battles the rest of his life, found a way to leverage the celebrity of his murder trial into greater ministry success. He would never become the national fundamentalist leader he'd aspired to be, but he did remain a significant presence with noteworthy achievements. His continued battle with the Texas and Southern Baptist denominations led eventually to the founding of his own makeshift denomination, with several hundred churches eventually directly or indirectly connected to his enterprises.

He changed the name of his tabloid toward the middle of 1927 from the *Searchlight* to the *Fundamentalist of Texas*. After a few years, it became simply the *Fundamentalist*. He also started a sort of seminary. Ironically, it was eventually located on the former property of an infamous casino in

Arlington, Texas, called Top O' Hill Terrace that Norris had helped shut down.

During the 1930s and 1940s J. Frank Norris inspired a steady succession of rugged individualists who felt "the call" to be like him. A young man named John Birch studied under Norris for a while before going to China, sponsored by First Baptist Church, as a missionary in 1940. Birch eventually became embroiled in the war that swept the region and served as an intelligence aide to Claire Lee Chennault of Flying Tigers fame. When Jimmy Doolittle and his men bombed Tokyo in April 1942, John Birch helped several of the crewmen avoid capture by the Japanese after they ran out of fuel and crashed in China.

Norris was heartbroken to learn of his protégé Birch's murder by Chinese communists a few days after the surrender of Japan in August 1945. Part of the building at Fourth and Throckmorton Streets in Fort Worth was quickly renamed John Birch Hall. And though the preacher never lived to see it, the name of his young missionary would be used by a man named Robert Welch for the anti-communist organization he founded in 1958, the John Birch Society. The "Birchers," as they were often called, saw conspiracies everywhere — very much as J. Frank Norris had.

Norris participated in politics for the rest of his life, fancying himself something of a kingmaker. He campaigned across Texas in 1928 for Herbert Hoover and against the anti-Prohibition Catholic Democrat Al Smith. When Mr. Hoover carried Texas, he acknowledged Norris's role in the victory by inviting him to sit on the platform at the Washington inaugural.

Shortly after the 1927 trial, Norris announced plans to build the bigger church in Fort Worth that he had talked about during his time in Austin. He told his followers: "A contract has been signed for a plot of ground 250 feet wide and 300 feet long, making a total of 75,000 square feet of floor space. This is the most mammoth task ever undertaken by the First Baptist Church."

He also told them, "It will be fire-proof."

However, before plans for the project could move forward, and just weeks before his big trip to Herbert Hoover's inauguration, the main buildings of First Baptist at Fourth and Throckmorton burned to the ground in January 1929. Arson was suspected. Norris was in Austin the day it happened. The blaze was thoroughly investigated, but no one was ever charged. While the church was negotiating with insurance companies and contractors in an effort to rebuild, the stock market crash and the subsequent Great Depression swallowed up any plans.

The church would eventually rebuild, but the new auditorium, though seating five thousand, began as little more than a gigantic, ugly shell with crude wooden benches. It remained in use for years but never progressed much beyond that. The remnants of that building exist today in the walls of Fort Worth's Third Street Parking Garage.

At the other corner, Fourth and Throckmorton, the church built an office–Sunday school complex in the 1930s. All these properties were eventually sold. The Chase Bank Building, complete with a popular P.F. Chang's restaurant on the spot where D.E. Chipps was killed, now stands on that downtown block.

In 1934 Norris conducted a religious campaign in Detroit, and that city's Temple Baptist Church asked him to be its pastor. He worked out an arrangement where he would pastor First Baptist in Fort Worth and the Detroit church, commuting every other week between the two and installing an expert administrator to oversee the Motor City ministry. By the late 1940s it was reported that the combined membership of the churches totaled twenty-five thousand.

In his final years Norris expressed regrets about having used sensationalism in his ministry to such a degree. And he abandoned his rabid anti-Catholicism. In the aftermath of World War II, he came to see his former religious adversaries as important allies in the war against his new enemy: communism. He even had an audience with Pope Pius XII in the late 1940s. One of the earliest fundamentalist clergymen to jump on the Zionist bandwagon, having done so shortly after the end of World War I, Norris was asked by President Harry Truman for a written opinion on the "Palestinian question" in the weeks prior to our recognition of the modern state of Israel in 1948.

Fundamentalism itself drifted in two directions after the 1920s. The die-hard devotees retreated to their churches and homes, emphasizing their separatist inclinations and moving from counterculture to subculture. This camp would reemerge, however, as a potent political force in the late 1970s as part of the new religious right. Others moved more into the Protestant Christian mainstream and became evangelicals, then new evangelicals, and were viewed with suspicion, even contempt, by adherents of the fundamentalist-separatist strain.

J. Frank Norris died in August 1952 at the age of seventy-four while speaking at a Florida youth camp. He always enjoyed working with young people and looking for the next preacher with star potential. Norris had no way of knowing it, but the very month he died a skinny young man named Jerry Falwell from Lynchburg, Virginia, enrolled in a Missouri Bible College, one that traced its roots to Norris's career.

The preacher's Fort Worth funeral at First Baptist Church was a massive affair attended by thousands, after which a lengthy procession made its way out to Greenwood Memorial Cemetery, where J. Frank Norris was buried. He was laid to rest near the graves of H.C. Meacham and D.E. Chipps. Amon Carter would be buried nearby a few years later.

Mrs. Mae Chipps, the widow of the man J. Frank Norris killed on that fateful hot summer Saturday afternoon in July 1926, would join them all at Greenwood in 1966.

ACKNOWLEDGMENTS

SINCE TAKING UP this project in earnest in late 2007, I have been blessed by the help and encouragement of family members, friends, coworkers, editors, publishers, and some who labor day after day seeing to it that books, newspapers, and other such perishable records have a prolonged and organized existence.

I count it a distinct privilege and honor to have worked with Mr. Bill Thompson, someone who has a sterling reputation in publishing circles. Among his many claims to fame is the fact that he worked closely with several prominent authors at the beginning of their careers, most notably Stephen King and John Grisham. Both of these now highly successful writers have often acknowledged Bill's influence and support. The fact that he took an interest in this work and this author is something I will never forget.

Bill Thompson suggested that I contact Chip Fleischer at Steerforth Press, one of the best pieces of advice I have ever received. Chip took a cultivating and passionate interest in my book from the moment he began reading the manuscript, and his editorial work and counsel have been invaluable. That such a gifted wordsmith worked so closely with me to create the finished project is truly one of the great blessings of my life. I am immeasurably indebted to Chip and everyone associated with Steerforth.

My wife, Karen, and daughters, Jennifer, Deborah, and Brenda, have been passionately supportive and devotedly patient with my preoccupation with this book. I am also very grateful to my three sons-in-law, Tom, David, and Mike, for their cultivating interest. And then there are my seven grandchildren, David, Karen, Ashton, Vintage, Grayson, Tiernan, and Sawyer. I have pictures.

My father, Dr. Gerald Stokes, instilled a passion for the past in me when I was very young, purchasing my first set of history books at the local A&P store as part of some promotion connected to dishwashing soap, as I recall. I remember that they included a foreword by then-president John F.

Kennedy, who wrote about his love for history. He was sadly gone a couple of years later, but I have had a lifetime of conversations about great events of long ago with my dad over golf, meals, long phone calls, and even through cyberspace.

Laura Bailey, a valued staff member who has inexplicably forsaken the lush eastern seaboard for the dusty plains of Oklahoma, but who remains in our hearts, was so very helpful with this project at a crucial time. She spent countless and no doubt frustrating hours transferring page after page of J. Frank Norris's *Searchlight* tabloid from microfilm to paper, working evenings in the Virginia Room of the Fairfax Public Library.

Vickie Bryant oversees the wonderful collection of J. Frank Norris memorabilia at Arlington (Texas) Baptist College, and I am indebted to her for the use of that microfilm bearing the images of Norris's *Searchlight* spanning the crucial years of 1924 through 1927. In connection with this, another special thank-you goes to the previously mentioned Laura Bailey, who while copying this material for me made sure to create a full and indexed record for the benefit of the Texas school. It is my hope that these materials will now be more easily accessible to future students and scholars who desire to delve into the story of J. Frank Norris and American fundamentalism. I am also grateful to Cesilee Ferrell for her work in the archives of newspapers in Austin, Texas.

Brenda McClurkin and all of the wonderful staff members at the Special Collections Division of the University of Texas at Arlington Libraries were so very cooperative when it came to my research into the Meacham/Carter Family Papers in their competent custodial care. They helped to make a tedious and occasionally frustrating search for detail an exceedingly manageable task.

Special thanks also goes to Sharon Carvalho, who created the excellent index for this book. And finally, I am grateful to Dr. Bradley Chipps and Dr. Kenneth Chipps, grandsons of the man shot to death in the story. They helped with little bits of vital color, as well as some of the photographs.
— DRS

A NOTE ON SOURCES

THE STORY OF THE Reverend J. Frank Norris killing Fort Worth, Texas, businessman Dexter Elliott Chipps in July 1926 has interested me for a long time. I first heard about it via a passing comment someone made to me in the early 1970s, and the idea to write about it lodged in my head many years ago. Along the way I picked up items here and there and filed them away. Then occasionally I'd pull the file out — first a swollen folder, then a small box, then several more — and review the ever-accumulating material. Sometimes, though, the boxes would go undisturbed for months at a time.

Over time, the files bulged, and one day I noticed that I had gathered a substantial amount of poorly organized stuff. My wife "encouraged" me to clean the mess up and do something with the material I had collected. Eventually indexing more than six thousand pages of newspaper articles, court records, and notes from other published works, this story began to take shape in my mind — then on paper.

In 2007 I finally decided to commit serious time and energy to this project. I made several trips to the fascinating city of Fort Worth, Texas. I likely wore out my welcome at its wonderful public library's Central Branch on West Third Street, located just a block away from where the central element of this story took place. Walking the city's downtown streets, I tried to imagine what it must have been like when the electric interurban competed with Model Ts for control of its thoroughfares. I tried to envision a long-ago time when the oil boom was peaking and everything still felt at least a little like the old Wild West. And I traced the path D.E. Chipps took eight decades ago as he briskly walked toward his rendezvous with gunfire, trying to picture the curious crowd filling the street at the scene.

As part of my research, I read countless Fort Worth newspapers from back then — particularly the periods of 1924 through 1927, as well as those from 1911 through 1914. I stretched the limits of those sometimes high-maintenance microfilm reading contraptions, and I am pretty sure I was more than a little bit of a nuisance to attendants on duty in the library's downstairs periodical section. Every visit would end the same way — with my pockets empty of quarters. I would then gather up the fruit of that particular session, usually more than a hundred pages of photocopies, and make my way back to my hotel to sort through, organize, and thoroughly review my harvest for the day.

I always stayed at the Hilton hotel at Main and Eighth Streets, largely because of its history and connection to the story. The old Westbrook Hotel — considered by many to be the premier Fort Worth hotel in the 1920s — would have been my first such choice, but it had had an appointment with the wrecking ball many years before.

The Hilton, also known for years and still remembered by many as the Hotel Texas, was where President John F. Kennedy spent his last night on November 21, 1963, before his Dallas appointment with dark destiny the next day. Every floor on the property bears a large portrait of a scene from that famous day-before hanging on the wall to greet your eyes as you get off the elevator. And every room has a plaque mentioning the Kennedy connection. Across the street from the Hilton is a fine steak place called Del Frisco's, which thrives on the former site of what was once the beautiful Wheat Building, where D.E. Chipps had his wholesale lumber business office.

In researching this book I have relied on newspaper and periodical reports, published trial transcripts, court records, archived material, and other published works to construct and color the story. Many of the details in this book come from J. Frank Norris's own words — as preserved in the *Searchlight,* as well as other works he authored or authorized. Norris also had a habit of reprinting press accounts about him — the good and the bad — verbatim in his newspaper. This practice provided important corroboration of his own version of "the truth." I have done my best to check his view of reality with other available documents and publications wherever possible. I believe the manner in which Norris is characterized throughout this book is consistent with the facts and that I have written fairly and accurately about his personal demeanor and behavior.

The papers of Mayor H.C. Meacham, which are archived at the University of Texas at Arlington Library, turned out to be a rich source of color and detail. I enjoyed spending several days going through them, getting a full sense of his life, as well as that of the city he loved.

For materials used with greater frequency, I will use the following abbreviations in the bibliographical notes:

New York Times: NYT
Fort Worth Star-Telegram: FWST
Fort Worth Press: FWP
Fort Worth Record: FWR
Searchlight: SL
Meacham/Carter Family Papers: MCFP
Austin Statesman: AS
Austin American: AA
Haldeman-Julius Monthly (Little Blue Books): HJM

For books quoted from more than once, the author's last name will be used after the first mention.

PROLOGUE
The details of the courtroom scene at the beginning of the actual Norris trial in Austin, Texas, are drawn from coverage in AS, FWP, HJM, and FWST.

CHAPTER ONE
The description of William Jennings Bryan's funeral train is drawn from coverage in NYT. Information about fundamentalism and the Scopes trial is drawn from *In the Beginning: Fundamentalism, The Scopes Trial, and the Making of the Antievolution Movement* by Michael Lienesh, University of North Carolina Press, Chapel Hill, 2007; *Summer for the Gods: The Scopes Trial and America's Continuing Debate Over Science and Religion* by Edward J. Larson, Basic Books, New York, 1997. Information about the decade of the 1920s is drawn from *Anxious Decades: America in Prosperity and Depression* by Michael E. Parrish, W.W. Norton, New York, 1992; *The Unexplored Twenties: These United States and the Quest for Diversity,* edited by Daniel H. Borus, Cornell University, Ithaca, NY, 1992; *Sinclair*

Lewis: Rebel from Main Street by Richard Lingeman, Minnesota Historical Society Press, St. Paul, 2002. The portrait of J. Frank Norris is drawn from *Voices of American Fundamentalism: Seven Biographical Studies* by C. Allyn Russell, Westminster Press, Philadelphia, 1975; HJM; June 1999 article in *Fort Worth, Texas — The City's Magazine* by Will J. McDonald; *God's Rascal: J. Frank Norris and the Beginnings of Southern Fundamentalism,* by Barry Hankins, University Press of Kentucky, Lexington, 1996; the novel *Fort Worth* by Leonard Sanders, Texas Christian University Press, Fort Worth, 2005.

CHAPTER TWO

The *Searchlight* (SL) was J. Frank Norris's tabloid newspaper. It was filled with his transcripts of his sermons, writings, and other material related to his apparently obsessive preoccupation with self-promotion. I have a complete set of copies of the *Searchlight* — every issue — for the crucial years covered in this book, particularly 1924–1927. Throughout this work these are relied on for certain details, quotes, and color — though I always sought corroboration from other contemporary sources where clearly necessary, and when possible. For attorney Clarence Darrow's opinion about his potential fundamentalist adversaries, I have relied on his account in *The Story of My Life* by Clarence Darrow, Da Capo Press, New York, 1996. Details about the memorial service for William Jennings Bryan at First Baptist Church in Fort Worth are drawn from FWR. Other details about the passing of Bryan, the state of fundamentalism as a movement in the mid-1920s, and Norris's pulpit style are drawn from *William Jennings Bryan: Orator of Small Town America* by Donald K. Springer, Greenwood Press, Santa Barbara, 1991; NYT; *Time* magazine; *A History of American Fundamentalism* by George Dollar, Bob Jones University Press, Greenville, SC, 1973.

CHAPTER THREE

The narrative dealing with the early family life of Norris is drawn from *The J. Frank Norris I Have Known for 34 Years* by Louis Entzminger, Fort Worth, 1946 (though it was alleged at the time that Norris himself was actually the author); The Handbook of Texas On Line; *Conquest or Failure* by E. Ray Tatum, Baptist Historical Foundation, Dallas, 1966; Hankins. The description of summer revivalism drawn from *Religion in Our Times* by Gauis Glen Atkins, Round Table Press, New York, 1932.

CHAPTER FOUR

Details of this period of Norris's life are drawn from Tatum; Hankins; Russell; Entzminger; *The Beginnings: A Pictorial History of the Baptist Bible Fellowship* by Billy Vick Bartlett, Baptist Bible College, Springfield, MO, 1975; *Memphis Commercial Appeal.*

CHAPTER FIVE

Fort Worth: Outpost on the Trinity by Oliver Knight, Texas Christian University Press, Fort Worth, 1990; *Hell's Half-Acre* by Richard F. Selcer, Texas Christian University Press, 1991; *Fort Worth: The Civilized West* by Caleb Pirtle III, Continental Heritage Press, Fort Worth, 1980; Hankins; SL; *How Fort Worth Became the Texasmost City* by Leonard Sanders, Amon Carter Museum, Fort Worth,1973; Tatum; FWR.

CHAPTER SIX

FWR; SL; Hankins; *Fort Worth Characters* by Richard F. Selcer, University of North Texas Press, 2009; Tatum; "J. Frank Norris: Salvation Specialist" by Don H. Biggers, in *Notorious Trials* by M.H. Julius, EJP Publications, Cornwall, England, 1973; Entzminger.

CHAPTER SEVEN

Pirtle; *The Big Rich: The Rise and Fall of the Greatest Texas Oil Fortunes,* by Bryan Burroughs, Penguin Press, New York, 2009; Petroleum Club of Fort Worth website; FWST; *1920: The Year of Six Presidents* by David Pietruzsa, Carroll and Graf Publishers, New York, 2007; *The Fiery Cross: The Ku Klux Klan in America* by Wyn Craig Wade, Oxford University Press, New York, 1987; *The Party of Fear: From Nativist Movements to the New Right in American History* by David H. Bennet, Vintage, New York, 1990; *The Ku Klux Klan in the Southwest* by Charles C. Alexander, University of Kentucky Press, Lexington, 1965.

CHAPTER EIGHT

SL; FWP; *Hood, Bonnet, and Little Brown Jug: Texas Politics, 1921–1928* by Norman D. Brown, Texas A&M University Press, 1984; Springer; *The Ku Klux Klan in American Politics* by Arnold S. Rice, Public Affairs Press, Washington, DC, 1962.

CHAPTER NINE

My Reminiscences by Roy E. Kemp, self-published in Fort Worth, no date; *World's Work,* January 1924; *Main Street* by Sinclair Lewis, Signet Classics, New York, 1961; *Amon: The Texan Who Played Cowboy for America* by Jerry Flemmons, Texas Tech University Press, 1998; Pirtle; *Time* magazine, October 30, 1933.

CHAPTER TEN

Isaac's Storm: A Man, a Time, and the Deadliest Hurricane in History, by Erik Larson, Vintage Books, New York, 1999; Knight; SL; MCFP; Deposition No. 74489, *Mrs. D. E. Chipps v. J. Frank Norris,* Tarrant County, Texas; *The Story of the Progress of Fort Worth, 1925–1927,* pamphlet in MCFP; Julius.

CHAPTER ELEVEN

FWR; MCFP; FWP; SL; Biggers; *Will Rogers: A Biography* by Ben Yagoda, Knopf, New York, 1993; FWST; HJM; *Annual Report: City of Fort Worth for the Year Ending September 30, 1926.*

CHAPTER TWELVE

Descriptions of the Fort Worth Club and the dedication of its new building in 1926 are drawn from *The Fort Worth Club: A Centennial History* by Irvin Farman, Fort Worth Club, 1985. Details about Jack Dempsey's 1926 visit to Fort Worth to sign for the fight with Gene Tunney drawn from Flemmons.

CHAPTER THIRTEEN

HJM; MCFP; Deposition No. 74489; SL.

CHAPTER FOURTEEN

FWP; HJM; Flemmons; Deposition No. 74489; Hotel Texas website.

CHAPTER FIFTEEN
FWP; SL; Kemp; MCFP.

CHAPTER SIXTEEN
HJM; FWP; *When Panthers Roared: The Fort Worth Cats and Minor League Baseball* by Jeff Guinn, Texas Christian University Press, Fort Worth, 1999; FWST.

CHAPTER SEVENTEEN
HJM; SL; AS; FWST; FWP; *The Dynamo,* an in-house periodical published by the J.C. Penney Company in the 1920s.

CHAPTER EIGHTEEN
HJM; FWST; FWP; Flemmons. The description of "newsboys" is drawn from *The Sun and the Moon: The Remarkable True Account of Hoaxers, Showmen, Dueling Journalists, and Lunar Man-Bats in Nineteenth Century New York* by Matthew Goodman, Basic Books, New York, 2008.

CHAPTER NINETEEN
FWST; Tatum; HJM; FWP; *AP: The Story of News* by Oliver Gramling, Farrar and Rinehart, New York, 1940; *1927: High Tide of the 1920s* by Gerald Leinwald, *Four Walls Eight Windows,* New York, 2001; NYT; *Time* magazine.

CHAPTER TWENTY
FWP; HJM; FWST.

CHAPTER TWENTY-ONE
FWP; FWST; MCFP; HJM; NYT; *Houston Chronicle*. Information about the Clara Hamon murder trial is drawn from *The Teapot Dome Scandal: How Big Oil Bought the Harding White House and Tried to Steal the Country* by Laton McCartney, Random House, New York, 2008.

CHAPTER TWENTY-TWO
Leinwald; HJM; SL; FWP; *These United States: Portraits of America from*

the 1920s, a series of essays originally published in *The Nation,* specifically the article "Texas: The Big Southwestern Specimen" by George Clifton Edwards, March 21, 1923; FWST.

CHAPTER TWENTY-THREE
Brown; FWP; Kemp; SL.

CHAPTER TWENTY-FOUR
FWST; NYT; FWP; *Ada (Oklahoma) Evening News.*

CHAPTER TWENTY-FIVE
HJM; FWP; *Last Call: The Rise and Fall of Prohibition* by Daniel Okrent, Scribner, New York, 2010; SL.

CHAPTER TWENTY-SIX
FWST; FWP; *Time* magazine.

CHAPTER TWENTY-SEVEN
SL; FWP; *Time* magazine.

CHAPTER TWENTY-EIGHT
SL; Brown.

CHAPTER TWENTY-NINE
San Antonio Light; Tatum; SL; *Tunney: Boxing's Brainiest Champ and His Upset of the Great Jack Dempsey* by Jack Cavanaugh, Ballantine Books, New York, 2007; MCFP.

CHAPTER THIRTY
Bridgeport (Connecticut) Telegram; SL; NYT; AS; *San Antonio Express;* MCFP; *San Antonio Light;* AA.

CHAPTER THIRTY-ONE
AA; *San Antonio Light;* HJM.

CHAPTER THIRTY-TWO
HJM; MCFP.

CHAPTER THIRTY-THREE
SL; Deposition No. 74489; *Mexia (Texas) Daily News;* MCFP.

CHAPTER THIRTY-FOUR
SL; *San Antonio Light; Port Arthur (Texas) News.*

CHAPTER THIRTY-FIVE
History of the Fort Worth Legal Community by Ann Arnold, Eakin Press, Austin, 2000; *Mexia (Texas) Daily News;* FWST.

CHAPTER THIRTY-SIX
FWST; *San Antonio Light;* FWP; AA.

CHAPTERS THIRTY-SEVEN THROUGH FORTY-SIX
By the time of the start of the Norris trial in Austin, Texas, in January 1927, the story was being widely noted on a daily basis in virtually every newspaper in the country. In fact, several papers published a word-for-word trial transcript. For this final section of the book, which deals in depth with the detailed description of the trial itself, I have relied primarily on the following sources. You can assume that anything in quotes comes from one or more of these publications:

> *Fort Worth Star-Telegram*
> *Fort Worth Press*
> *Austin Statesman*
> *Austin American*
> *New York Times*
> *Time* magazine
> *Haldeman-Julius Monthly*
> *Searchlight*

EPILOGUE
Minutes of the District Court 96th Judicial District of Texas; Pirtle; SL.

INDEX

Note: Page numbers with the prefix "A" indicate picture plates